seven
summits

seven summits

General Editor
Steve Bell

Mitchell Beazley

SEVEN SUMMITS
General Editor: Steve Bell

First published in 2000 by Mitchell Beazley,
an imprint of Octopus Publishing Group Ltd
2–4 Heron Quays, London EI4 4JP
Copyright © Octopus Publishing
Group Ltd 2000

Executive Editor	Rachael Stock
Executive Art Editor	Emma Boys
Project Editor	Mary Loebig Giles
Diary Editor	Claire Musters
Design	Kenny Grant
Production	Rachel Staveley
	Karen Farquhar
Picture Research	Jenny Faithfull

ISBN 1 84000 2085

A CIP catalogue record for this book is
available from the British Library.

Typeset in Helvetica Neue, Melior,
Univers and Impact

Printed in China
by Toppan Printing Company Ltd

Captions

page 1 Carstenz Pyramid, enshrouded in cloud.

pages 2–3 The seracs of the Khumbu Icefall experience
two-way traffic.

right Sherpas carry their loads in the shade of the
Khumbu Icefall, while Nuptse catches the sun.

pages 10–11 A breathtaking sunset gilds Everest,
Nuptse, and, to the right, Makalu, from Gokyo Ri.

pages 38–9 Four Seven Summiteers savour their
moments on the summit of Earth's highest peak (Rob Hall
on the radio, Ekke Gundelach in yellow, Hall Wendel at
the head, and David Keaton, behind the camera).

contents

dick bass

foreword

I never planned to climb anything except out of bed each morning – and that was tough enough! I was a low-lander from Texas, used to all the modern-day creature comforts; as an adult I'd never done any physical exercise regimen for endurance or strengthening. I definitely didn't want to cook on my own, had never been exposed to really cold weather, and thought I needed a relaxed, warm "think tank" bath to start each day.

But in November 1980, when I was 50, all that suddenly changed when Marty Hoey, the head of the safety patrol at Snowbird Ski and Summer Resort of which I was the owner, told me my "hot air" (meaning my non-stop verbosity) wouldn't get me up that mountain (McKinley). In effect, Marty, the only female guide on McKinley and Rainier, threw down the gauntlet that instantly gave me the compulsion to show her that I could do anything she could do, including climbing mountains. Such a reaction stemmed from my youth. Having been small for my age and young for my school grade, I resented anyone telling me I couldn't, or shouldn't, attempt things because of my size or age. She triggered that long held, passionate predilection to prove I could do anything that anyone else could, if it caught my fancy.

In the spring of 1981, Marty led me and my four grown children, two boys and twin girls, all in their early 20s, along with four other Snowbird men in their 30s, on McKinley. The first day, while trudging up the Kahiltna Glacier on skis with a 70lb backpack and pulling a 35lb plastic sled, I discovered, in spite of no physical conditioning whatsoever, I was not only able to keep up, but even felt continuously energized by reciting uplifting poems and aphorisms. I had learned and loved these ever since being inspired by a remarkable grade school teacher. They kept me pumped up and efficient by not wasting any of my energy on the usual draining negatives of physical discomfort and mental anxiety. They gave me tremendous endurance.

Eleven days later I summited, feeling gangbusters all the way, and seeming to grow stronger as I went higher. By nature I have a slow resting pulse, low blood pressure, and exceptional lung capacity from never having smoked; but as Marty and other climbers maintained, it's mostly in the mind, and there my poetry was a secret weapon.

On the return to high camp at 17,200ft I thought of how I'd enjoyed climbing the highest mountain in North America and how it had given me a renewed sense of self-confidence and self-respect, both of which had been hammered down by governmental regulatory barriers and the huge debt of Snowbird. That gave me the idea of climbing the other six continental highs as a way to mentally condition for my pressure-filled life, as well as to have an epic, captivating adventure.

I would probably be only talking of climbing those mountains even today, 18 years later, were it not for an apparent coincidence that I really believe was ordained from on High. Soon after McKinley, in July

1981, I met Frank Wells, the President of Warner Brothers, and learned he'd been dreaming of doing all the continental highs, since summiting Kilimanjaro in 1955. In an unhesitating, cavalier way we shook hands and agreed we'd do it together.

Frank and I undertook the Seven Summits as an exciting adventure, and defined the goal as climbing the highest mountain on each of what we learned in school were the seven continents. It was an imaginative undertaking and we never dreamed that someone would question our criteria, much less rationalize a better way to define the continents.

There have been grumblings over the years by some die-hard climbers that Frank and I "bought" the summits. The fact is we did not pay any guide fees, but we did invite some world-class climbers to join us, which was only prudent considering our relative inexperience. For what was involved though, we faced the same physical and technical obstacles as anyone else. When David Breashears and I summited Everest in April 1985, it was a free climb. We weren't roped together and didn't have the security of fixed ropes on summit day (except for the 30ft Hillary step, which didn't help much because we had no jumars and our bulky down mittens didn't grip well on an icy rope). Today, fixed ropes and jumars along the exposed summit ridge have become standard on professionally guided South Col Everest attempts.

During my climbs I had a hopeless, helpless debt of $45 million dollars because of Snowbird. (I am no kin of the billionaire Bass family of Fort Worth.) I was barely able to borrow additional money for the climbs, but thank goodness Frank and I did not have to spend a lot of time and effort securing piecemeal sponsorships and donations. We were the first group to climb Vinson with our own private funding and organization of transportation and supplies. No small feat considering the logistical arrangements and expenses involved.

Contrary to what some maintain, Frank and I did not commercialize the climbing of remote high mountains, particularly Everest. Our book popularized what had generally been considered to be a virtually unattainable feat, reserved for only the highly experienced and committed. We showed that it could be achieved by those with basic strength and training, sufficient material means, and a great adventurous spirit. Anyone should have the right to do so, but I fervently advocate that regulations be enforced to keep everyone environmentally sensitive and protective.

No matter what anyone accomplishes first, there will always be those who want to change the rules in order to claim the title for themselves. One has to accept that as a part of human competition, but you can make your own choice. All I can say is, we did it our way and learned in the process that if you never stop, you can't get stuck!

pat morrow
foreword

After all these years, what does completing the Seven Summits project mean to me? As a young photojournalist trying to get a "foothold" in the adventure bizz, the project provided hearty fodder for my stories. And, in turn, the resulting coverage attracted sponsors and climbing partners who helped me find ways around the astronomical costs involved in getting to the peaks.

I first came across the whimsical notion of climbing the continental high points in 1981, while hunkered down in a storm midway up Aconcagua's Polish Glacier Route. My tent mate, Gordon "Speedy" Smith, an ex-pat Brit, and I were training for an attempt by a Canadian expedition on Everest the following year.

With plenty of time to dream in our soggy sleeping bags, we marvelled at the fact that no one had yet stood atop the highest peak on each continent. And what better way to see our world than to follow the paths that lead to all these peaks? We naively mused that if we could make it up South America's highest mountain that year, and Asia's highest the year following, the rest would fall easily into place. As it turned out, the climbs themselves were a dream, but reaching them was often a nightmare.

Texas businessman, Dick Bass, entered the Seven Summits arena at around the same time as me. What started out as a lark evolved into a media race, with me pitted against him. Dick completed his own version of the Seven Summits 15 months before I completed mine; but he ignored the difficult and problematic Carstensz Pyramid, in favour of a stroll up Kosciuszko.

Being a climber first, and a collector second, I felt strongly that Carstensz Pyramid, the highest mountain in Australasia (the geopolitical region encompassing Australia, New Zealand, and New Guinea), was a true mountaineer's objective. Little did I know that it would take two attempts, over a period of two years, just to reach the base of Carstensz.

As it turned out, Dick and I weren't the only ones smitten with the Seven Summits idea. Reinhold Messner, the visionary climber from the South Tyrol, was one of several who had been working quietly on the logistics involved in the challenge. Long before we set out, Reinhold had already climbed six of the seven summits, usually by a difficult route. The only reason Reinhold wasn't the first person to complete the seven was that he was too busy gambolling up the 14 tallest mountains in the world.

Then there was Naomi Uemera, the renowned Japanese solo explorer. By the early 1980s, Uemera had climbed five of the seven continental peaks, including Everest. With his sights set determinedly on Antarctica, his plan was to sail to the coast and attempt the 1000km approach to Vinson by dog sled. Before leaving for Antarctica, he launched a solo winter "training" climb to McKinley in February 1984. After making radio contact from the summit, the Samurai adventurer was never heard from or seen again.

Apart from the bureaucratic obstacles surrounding Carstensz, it was Vinson that proved to be the most difficult for me to reach, both politically and monetarily. Lacking the dog-handling skills of Uemera, I relied entirely on the British flying ace Giles Kershaw to win the full cooperation of the Chilean government and to pilot an expensive ski-equipped plane to the mountain's base.

I have often been asked which of the Seven Summits was the most difficult to climb. This has to be the new route that Bernhard Ehmann and I climbed up on the South West Flank of McKinley. It was technically and physically demanding and was also my first high-altitude climb. Back in 1977, I had yet to learn how to pace myself in an oxygen-deprived atmosphere.

People are usually surprised to hear that one of my favourite climbs in 22 years of mountaineering is Africa's Kilimanjaro. By far the easiest of the Seven Summits, with a meandering trail that lures the uninitiated to a great height too quickly, it was also the most fascinating. Beginning with the tropical game parks at its base, the ascent takes you through all the major climatic zones of the world.

Everest, in 1982, still retained some of its mystery, even though its resident god, Chomolungma, had been admitting summit guests for the previous 29 years. Fellow Canadian Laurie Skreslet and I were visitors number 123 and 125. Currently the tally is over 800 climbers.

In the end, it's gratifying for me to know that through my own selfish efforts to reach and climb these mountains, the Seven Summits project has opened the doors to both Antarctica and Irian Jaya. My wife Baiba and I, along with Giles Kershaw and Martyn Williams, set up Adventure Network International, which to this day delivers climbers and other glacial voyeurs to the heart of the icy continent. Our recommendations to the Indonesian government to set up a permit system for the hitherto forbidden Carstensz has allowed a steady stream of Western climbers to immerse themselves in the natural and cultural wonders of Irian Jaya.

With these logistical hurdles surmounted, the challenges posed by the Seven Summits climbing project now lie very much in the domain of the weekend warrior. The goal is well within reach of anyone with moderate climbing skills and a disposable income.

This is not to say that it can't be a highly rewarding way of seeing our world. After all, the dawn view from a soggy sleeping bag even halfway up any one of these seven mountains is guaranteed to be inspirational.

Pat Morrow

mapping the seven

McKinley
North America
6194m/20,320ft
Alaska, USA
Alaska Range

First ascent:

Harry Karstens, Walter
Harper, Robert Tatum,
and Hudson Stuck, 1913

McKinley's massive proportions present one of the greatest vertical gains in the world, measuring 6000m/20,000ft from foot to summit. Just south of the Arctic Circle, the summit rises above the wild and untamed Alaskan plain, 240km (150 miles) north of Anchorage.

Aconcagua
South America
6960m/22,834ft
Argentina
Andes

First ascent:

Matthias Zurbriggen, 1897

With claims to fame as the highest mountain in the western and southern hemispheres and second highest of the Seven Summits, the wedge-shaped "Stone Sentinel" lies to the east of the main Andean chain just inside Argentina's border with Chile.

Vinson
Antarctica
4897m/16,023ft
Sentinel Range

First ascent:

Barry Corbet, John Evans, Bill
Long, and Pete Schoening, 1966

Deep within the frozen Antarctic, at 80°S, Vinson was the last continental summit discovered (1957) and climbed. Extremely dry and cold, the unforgiving environment is devoid of all flora and fauna. The mountain poses a straightforward climb in the most hostile yet beautiful of environments.

Kilimanjaro
Africa
5895m/19,340ft
Tanzania

First ascent:

Hans Meyer and
L Purtscheller, 1889

One of the best known mountains in the world, Kilimanjaro is one of the easiest of the continental summits to climb. Surrounded by the hot, dry plains of the Massai steppe and capped by snow, the mountain is known for its spectacular vegetation and wildlife. It is is located just inside Tanzania's border with Kenya.

Everest

Asia
8848m/29,028ft
Tibet/Nepal
Himalayas

First ascent:

Sherpa Tenzing Norgay and
Edmund Hillary, 1953

Straddling the border of Tibet and Nepal and known as "Goddess Mother of the Earth," Everest is the unrivalled apex of the Himalayas and the highest mountain in the world. Everest's extreme height and difficulty stretch even the finest climbers to their limits.

Carstensz Pyramid

Australasia
4884m/16,024ft
Irian Jaya
Sudirman Range

First ascent:

Heinrich Harrer, Philip Temple,
Russell Kippax, and Albert
Huizenga, 1962

Surrounded by dense jungle that is inhabited by a tribal people, the limestone crest of Carstensz Pyramid is the highest mountain on the island of New Guinea and on the Australasian continent. Carstensz vies with Kosciuszko for its Seven Summit title.

Elbrus

Europe
5642m/18,510ft
Kabardino-Balkaria
Caucasus

First ascent:

F Crauford Grove, F Gardiner,
H Walker, A Sottajev, and
P Knubel, 1874

The highest point of the Caucasus, between the Black and Caspian Seas, this extinct two-headed volcano is plastered in 70 glaciers' worth of ice. Located at the southern edge of Russia, in what was formerly the USSR, Elbrus was off limits to most until the mid 1980s, but is now accessible from Russia.

Kosciuszko

Australia
2228m/7310ft
New South Wales
Snowy Mountains

First known ascent:

Sir Paul Edmond
de Strzelecki, 1840

Kosciuszko, the high moorland summit that crowns Australia, is a popular tourist attraction in the Snowy Mountains. It is the easiest of the continental summits to climb, though many climbers consider Carstensz, which lies outside Australia, to be a more worthy continental high point.

introduction
steve bell

The quest to climb to the highest point of each continent has inspired a generation of climbers from all over the world. The so-called "Seven Summits" offer a tremendous challenge, demanding great determination from the strongest of mountaineers, yet remaining attainable by dedicated novices. Climbers of all levels of ability can aspire to climb the continental summits, and the number of those who have completed all seven has risen dramatically in recent years. The fact that the Seven Summits is a realistic and relatively attainable goal makes them attractive; the collection of summits is a global objective, not restricted to one mountain range, country, or continent, and completing them requires travel to some of the most wondrous corners of the world. It is hardly surprising that the idea has caught on.

Of the many popular collections of mountains that climbers try to complete, the Seven Summits offers the widest variety of experiences. Each of the seven continents is unique and so are their highest points.

The wind-beaten and barren "Stone Sentinel" of Aconcagua commands the South American Andes; Kilimanjaro's snow-capped volcano is the backdrop to African game parks; the double-headed crown of Elbrus reigns as the surprising king of Europe; the recently discovered Vinson Massif hides within the ice wilderness of Antarctica; McKinley, the "High One" of North America, spills its glaciers onto the untamed Alaskan plain; Australasia gives us a choice of a pleasant hike up Kosciuszko or a journey back in time to the pyramid of Carstensz; and the highest of them all, Everest, offers the most prized of all summits to the determined and the lucky.

The people who are drawn to climb the Seven Summits, and their motives for doing so, are no less varied. For some it is an excuse to travel around the world; others may have climbed several of the mountains already, then simply decide to finish them off for fun; a few may never have climbed before, become captivated by the Seven Summits, and then sell their climbing boots after completing them. For everyone it is a huge challenge which demands determination, commitment, fitness, and risk. Whatever the motivation, the reward is

great. For most people, completing the Seven Summits is a major milestone in their lives, representing a challenge undertaken, adversities faced, and experiences shared.

Many of these experiences are vividly described in this book. Intensely personal accounts by those who have climbed the Seven Summits provide a unique insight into what the challenge means, and what it takes to achieve success. Gerry Roach takes us on a mountaineering roller-coaster spanning nearly 32 years; Junko Tabei describes her first female ascent of Everest; Ronald Naar discovers that mysterious forces are at work on Carstensz; Viki Groselj finds time to absorb the beauty of Antarctica during his rapid ascent of a new route on Vinson; and Gerhard Schmatz plunges from elation to despair when he loses his wife, Hannelore, on Everest. These are just a selection of some 17 outstanding accounts by climbers from ten different countries. They are guaranteed to move and inspire anyone who has an interest in mountains and anyone who climbs them.

By virtue of their continental summit status, the burden of visitor impact on each of these mountains is far greater than for other peaks. Every year this burden increases, and there is little doubt that this is partly due to the ever growing number of people taking up the Seven Summits challenge. In an effort to draw attention to this important environmental concern, a conservation section is included with each mountain description. This section provides a brief summary of the significant environmental issues affecting each peak as well as advice on how each individual visitor can contribute to the preservation of the natural environment.

This book is a celebration of the Seven Summits and the quest to climb them. It provides a record of the climbers who have completed them, detailing their feats and ascents, and includes personal accounts and insights gained along the way. It also attempts to address some of the more controversial considerations of "collecting" mountains and considers the important environmental issues facing popular mountain regions. *Seven Summits* aims to inform, entertain, and provoke through this unusual combination of information, experience, and comment about a modern mountaineering phenomenon which has captivated climbers and climbing enthusiasts throughout the world.

A Brief History of the Quest for the Seven Summits

The idea of climbing to the highest point on each continent cannot be attributed to any one single person. Any number of imaginative mountaineers could have independently pondered some version of it. Perhaps Mallory, with his visionary attraction to challenge, would have considered climbing other continental summits if he had survived his famous attempt on Everest in 1924. But until the 1950s, any such musings would have been a pipe-dream, with Everest's summit untrodden and Antarctica's pinnacle undiscovered.

The concept of the Seven Summits has evolved with the improvement in accessibility and knowledge. This evolution has been steered by the activities of a handful of ambitious climbers, who

together can claim to be the architects of the Seven Summits challenge.

In September 1956 William D Hackett, a soldier from Oregon, USA, reached the top of Mont Blanc to become probably the first person to reach the top of five continents. This of course assumes that Mont Blanc, the

above A particularly long ladder in Everest's Khumbu Icefall spans a yawning crevasse and unstable ice, making this part of the climb harrowing.

left A climber crosses the dry steppe as the massive cone of Kibo, Kilimanjaro's main summit, dominates the Saddle en route to the Kibo Hut.

highest mountain in Western Europe, is the overall European summit. For most people, the now accepted European summit of Elbrus was out of reach behind the Iron Curtain of the Soviet Union, together with the rest of the Caucasus mountains, until the mid 1980s. Bill Hackett's other summits were McKinley (1947 – the fourth ascent of the mountain), Aconcagua (1949), Kilimanjaro (1950), and Kosciuszko (February 1956).

There is no doubt that Hackett did have aspirations to complete the rest. After an attempt on K2 in 1960, he obtained a permit for Everest the following year, but unfortunately, a lack of funds forced him to abandon the trip. In 1985, at the age of 67, he finally had the opportunity to climb Vinson Massif in Antarctica. While his teammates,

introduction

who included Pat Morrow, Giles Kershaw, and Martyn Williams (who later founded Adventure Network International) successfully reached the summit, Hackett's own efforts to summit the mountain were thwarted by frostbite.

The solitary Japanese adventurer, Naomi Uemera, broke from his habit of climbing alone and reached the summit of Everest in 1970 with fellow countryman Teruo Matsuura. They were members of a large team attempting the then unclimbed South West Face, but switched to the South Col Route to claim the first Japanese ascent of the world's highest mountain. Uemera had already climbed Mont Blanc, Kilimanjaro, and Aconcagua, so when he made the first solo ascent of McKinley three months after Everest, he became the first person to climb five continental summits including Everest.

Long before Uemera entered the arena, a Swiss climber called Dolf Reist had intentions on the five continental summits including Everest. In 1956, he had the advantage of being one of only six people to have climbed Everest, so there was no rush to climb the others. Believing that he had plenty of time, Reist, who had climbed Mont Blanc in 1955, left it for another five years before climbing his next continental summit, finally completing the five summits in 1971, six months after Uemera.

But Uemera was by no means finished. After making the first solo journey to the North Pole he decided to go to Antarctica, where he would travel by dog sled from the coast and climb Vinson, again alone. His training climb for this daring objective was a solo winter ascent of McKinley in February 1984. He achieved this remarkable goal, but on

his return from the summit he disappeared in one of McKinley's terrible storms and was never seen again. A popular hero in Japan, Uemera's loss was deeply felt.

Also forcing the boundaries of adventure throughout this period was the South Tyrolean mountaineer, Reinhold Messner. Perhaps the greatest mountaineer of his time, his achievements and opinions were dominant forces in the development of current mountaineering ethics and style. Messner's fitness and skill, honed to the highest level on the Dolomite cliffs of northern Italy, were applied to mountains all over the world. It was therefore inevitable that the idea of climbing the continental summits would appeal to him, particularly as no one had climbed more than five of them.

In 1978, when Messner and the Austrian high-altitude athlete Peter Habeler reached the summit of Everest without using bottled oxygen, the mountaineering world was stunned. After breaking this major psychological barrier, Messner announced that he was the first person to climb six of the continental summits. He had climbed the same peaks as Uemera and Reist, but he had also climbed Carstensz Pyramid in 1971. So it was Messner who first included Australasia in the list of continental summits and, notably, it was Carstensz that he considered to be its highest point. So in 1978, Messner only had Antarctica's highest peak to scale, to become the first person to complete the Seven Summits. Over the years he made strenuous efforts to get to the elusive Mount Vinson, but by the time he did, in late 1986, the chalice had already been taken. Not that Messner, who said, "The Seven Summits

above Canadian climber Pat Morrow, the first person to complete the Seven Summits with Carstensz, relaxes at Vinson Base Camp in 1985.

left Reinhold Messner, the greatest and most influential mountaineer of his day, was instrumental in defining the Seven Summits challenge.

Reinhold Messner's influence on the definition of the Seven Summits did not end there. In 1983, he climbed Elbrus in the Caucasus Mountains, declaring that Mont Blanc should not be considered the highest point of the European continent. Elbrus, which is more than 800m (2700ft) higher than Mont Blanc, is geographically within Europe, though at that time it was also in the Soviet Union and was far less accessible to climbers than the giant of the French and Italian Alps. Messner's perspective was quickly adopted by others and, as a result, Mont Blanc, the highest mountain in Western Europe, was henceforth deleted from the list of continental summits in favor of the higher and now accessible Elbrus.

was just a bit of fun," would have been too concerned about this, as his other climbing achievements make the Seven Summits look like a walk in the park. Even so, in 1983, the world's greatest mountaineer made the hike up Kosciuszko, just to be sure he got the right Antipodean summit.

Meanwhile, two Americans had their own idea of climbing the continental summits. Dick Bass and Frank Wells were not hard core adventurers like Messner and Uemera, but they had the determination and the resources to make it happen. They also set their own definition of the summits, sticking strictly to continental land masses and ignoring islands. So Kosciuszko in the Snowy Mountains was their Australian summit rather than Carstensz on the island of New Guinea. They also added Antarctica to the list, to make seven continental summits. Through 1983 the duo, climbing with invited expert mountaineers, climbed six of their Seven Summits. Only Everest eluded them. They attempted the North Ridge in 1982 when one of Bass's close friends, Marty Hoey, was killed in a fall. The following year they were members of a very successful expedition on the South Col Route when six Americans, including Gerry Roach, and two Sherpas reached the summit. Bass and Wells got high on the mountain but were forced, for various reasons, to turn back. Wells made no further attempts on Everest and his quest for the continental summits progressed no further. However, in 1985, Bass joined a Norwegian expedition led by the shipping tycoon Arne Naess. This was a model expedition that was

history of the quest

well funded, well led, and resulted in a record 17 people reaching the summit. Dick Bass was one of them and became not only the first person to climb the Seven Summits with Kosciuszko, but also, at 55 years old, the oldest person to climb Everest, a record he would hold for the next eight years. Other notable summit members of this expedition were Ralph Höibakk and Arne Naess (who later completed the Seven Summits with Carstensz Pyramid) and Britain's best-known mountaineer, Chris Bonington.

After being foiled twice on Everest, Dick Bass was lucky not to be beaten at his own game. A strong Canadian mountaineer called Pat Morrow had the advantage of having climbed McKinley in 1977 and Everest in 1982, so he set out to finish off the rest. Not having the financial resources of Bass, he only managed two more peaks, Aconcagua and Kilimanjaro, before Bass completed his Seven Summits. But the race between these two unlikely opponents was already well publicized and became fuelled by controversy when Morrow adopted Messner's definition of the Seven, that is, with Carstensz rather than Kosciuszko. After a series of setbacks, Morrow proved his tenacity and resourcefulness by finally reaching Vinson Massif in 1985, completing his Seven Summits the following year with Carstensz and Elbrus. Because he had already climbed Kosciuszko, Morrow was also the first person to climb both versions of the Seven Summits.

So now the Seven Summits had been climbed, the Kosciuszko version by Dick Bass and the Carstensz version by Pat Morrow. The debate over which version is the more worthy still rages, occasionally with some acrimony. Meanwhile, most climbers don't seem to care one way or the other, and choose to climb both versions simply for the excuse of extending the quest and travelling to another country. During the times that Carstensz is off-limits to climbers, Kosciuszko enjoys a resurgence of interest from those seeking to climb all of the seven continental high points.

Up until the 1990s, only a handful of people had climbed either version of the Seven Summits. By the middle of 1999 they had been completed by more than 60 people, and interest in them from both expert and novice climbers is rapidly growing.

Self-expression: Defining the Challenge

Each one of the Seven Summits gives climbers the opportunity to express themselves through the route and style of their climb. There is no fixed way of climbing these mountains. There is the easiest way, by the standard routes at the best time of year, or climbers can push up the odds by taking a harder route, an unclimbed route, or attempting the climb out of season, such as in the winter, or even using skis. It is this opportunity to define the challenge and tailor it to fit one's ability and ambition, that has made the Seven Summits a serious objective for a number of leading mountaineers. Few climbers would complete the Seven Summits by the same routes and in the same style as Reinhold Messner or Doug

right Dougal Haston battles his way up the Hillary Step during his and Doug Scott's ascent of Everest's South West Face in 1975.

above Doug Scott and Dougal Haston's 1976 ascent of McKinley's South Face was the first time the mountain had been climbed alpine style.

right High-altitude litter at 8000m on the South Col of Everest includes oxygen bottles, abandoned tents, and several dead bodies.

with oxygen. But whether oxygen users breathe copious amounts from low on the mountain or merely sleep on it for a couple of hours in the top camp, they have still used oxygen. No difference is recorded in the style of their ascent despite the achievement of the latter being considerably greater than the former.

There are also important safety implications. A climber who needs a lot of oxygen is more dependent on it for survival. The ability to descend from high on the mountain without the aid of supplementary oxygen greatly reduces the risk of tragedy. Even with thorough preparation, oxygen supplies can become exhausted, equipment may fail to operate, or a bottle could be dropped. Some of the recent fatalities on the mountain could have been avoided if climbers were less dependent on oxygen. The amount of oxygen used is therefore an important safety and ethical issue that needs to be considered by anyone attempting Everest.

As the quest to climb the Seven Summits grows in popularity, it likely that more mountaineers will use them as a stage for their particular style of climbing. However, while there will be those who may try to climb the Seven Summits solo, or in winter, or by their hardest routes, they will always be few in comparison to the vast majority of climbers who will maximize their chances of success by taking the easiest options available.

Scott. If they had to, the Seven Summits would not be the universally sought after collection of climbs that it is. The attainability of these summits gives them widespread appeal, but the extreme possibilities that exist on them can also draw attention from the world's most talented climbers.

Of course, self-expression in mountaineering extends far beyond the Seven Summits. Climbers have the freedom to determine how they climb any mountain, whether they wish to be led up the most straightforward route by mountain guide, or make a solo ascent in winter by the most difficult route. All mountains, if they are to be climbed, have a base level of difficulty which is absolute. It is easy to make a climb more difficult, but aside from thorough preparation, it is perhaps impossible to make a climb easier. This base level of difficulty determines each mountain's status in the Seven Summits' hierarchy – Kosciuszko is a walk, while Everest is journey to the edge of extinction. But even Everest, by its standard route, is not as impressive an achievement as Scott's first ascent on the South Face of McKinley or Messner's solo of his direct finish to the South Face of Aconcagua.

However, as far as the Seven Summits are concerned, there is one wild card. The otherwise absolute baseline of difficulty can be varied on Everest by increasing the amount of supplementary oxygen used. Although it has been proved that the mountain can be climbed without oxygen, the vast majority of climbers still use it. Without oxygen, Everest would be beyond the ability of most people, and the Seven Summits would be relegated to the domain of the elite. But how much oxygen should be used? It stands to reason that if oxygen makes the climb easier, the more oxygen used the easier the mountain becomes. But how easy should we make it? Records have been kept of those who have climbed Everest without oxygen and those who have climbed it

The Seven Summits : In ascending order of difficulty (Assuming ideal climbing conditions)

Summit	Grade of Easiest Route		Grade of Hardest Route*	
Kosciuszko	1	N/A	–	N/A
Kilimanjaro	2	Tourist Route (Marangu)	15	Breach Wall Direct (Messner)
Elbrus	3	Normal Route	–	N/A
Carstensz	5	Normal Route	6	Tabin or Scott Route
Aconcagua	5	Normal Route	15	South Face Direct (Messner)
Vinson	5	Normal Route	8	Slovenian Route (Groselj)
McKinley	7	West Buttress	15	South Face (Scott)
Everest	10	South Col/South East Ridge	20	South West Face (Scott)

This graded list of the continental summits will certainly provoke debate, but two things are certain: the first is that Everest is the hardest of the Seven Summits to climb, the second is that Kosciuszko is the easiest. The relative difficulty of the remaining peaks is far more fluid, based on each climber's personal experience, ability, and perspective. The grades given here are not a recognized system. They are only intended to reflect the comparative difficulty of reaching each summit. They encompass technical difficulty, strenuousness, physical hardship, and altitude. For many climbers, the biggest challenge is finding the money to get there, but cost is not reflected in these grades! *The hardest routes are restricted to those that have been climbed by Seven Summiteers. They exclude any harder routes that may have been completed by other climbers.

The Mountain Environment

The almost explosive development of the tourism industry from the 1960s to the present has noticeably made an impact on the mountains. Although many less frequented mountain areas remain pristine, the Seven Summits are irresistible magnets for today's mountaineers and have drawn an onslaught of visitors, putting overwhelming pressure on fragile ecosystems. Everyone who visits these mountain areas – and none more so than those who climb on the continental summits – should be aware of the effect they have on the environment and whenever possible minimize such impact.

Information dissemination and education on environmental issues are therefore very important. The national parks and other bodies responsible for environmental matters on the continental summits play a vital role in this, some with more diligence than others. Additionally, expedition leaders responsible for taking climbers and visitors to these areas need to be environmentally proactive, ensuring that all members of their group cooperate with current accepted practice. A brief environmental overview of each of the Seven Summits is included in the mountain sections of this book. What follows is a general description of the sometimes complex environmental issues that face the mountain traveller and those responsible for the preservation and protection of the mountains.

Main Environmental Impacts

Trails, when properly and regularly maintained, can be a positive feature of the mountain environment. They provide ease of access to remote areas and enhance communication and trade between people; they are actually a sign of culture. But trails become a problem in areas of fragile land when they are overused or when they start eroding surrounding slopes. Trails going through wet areas have a tendency to degrade the immediate surroundings. Rainwater run-off can cause serious trail erosion, particularly on steep hillsides. Campsites can also become heavily overused, with trampled vegetation exposing bare soil.

It is possible to minimize trail erosion and trampling of fragile areas. The most important contribution is to follow the existing trail rather than increase its size by walking on the edge or to one side of it. Those responsible for the maintenance of paths may consider stepping stones in wet areas, stone-laid paths at regularly used campsites, drainage channels on inclines, wooden boardwalks over wetlands, and bridges over rivers. Any such measures need care to ensure they are not more ugly than the impact they are supposed to counteract.

Deforestation along trails and campsites can be caused when trekking and climbing expeditions rely on firewood for cooking. The best countermeasure is for all personnel, including porters, to use kerosene and gas stoves for cooking. A ban on camp fires while making cooking

above Garbage bags like these are issued to climbers by Aconcagua National Park to help protect this popular mountain environment.

right The renowned NZ mountain guide, Rob Hall, celebrates his successful ascent of Vinson, from the summit.

stoves a requirement to enter a mountain area is a nice ideal, but unfortunately it is often unreasonable to expect local porters to forego their age-old wood-fire traditions. Hotels and teahouses in Nepal use considerable amounts of firewood to cater for trekkers. However, certain areas in Nepal, including the Everest trekking area, have started using kerosene stoves and electricity, thus saving precious forests.

Litter and garbage is one of the most obvious ways in which visitors make an impact on mountain areas. This eyesore is not only damaging to the environment, but is also an aesthetic problem. It can be surprising and sad to see how much litter can be left by ignorant or careless hikers and climbers. This highly visual negative effect of mountain tourism is often addressed through high profile clean-up campaigns. But, it is far better to tackle this problem by prevention.

All hikers and climbers should separate their garbage into biodegradable, burnable, and non-burnable items. All garbage must be carried out from higher areas as the decomposition of organic material is hindered by high altitude. Burning is usually only effective below 4000m (13,000ft) due to the low oxygen levels, unless an incinerator is used. At lower altitudes biodegradable waste can be buried and burnable waste properly burned. Of course, it is always best to carry out what you have carried in, for disposal at an appropriate place.

Human waste and sanitation can also jeopardize the environment. Since it is rarely practical for human waste to be carried out, it must be dealt with on location. The altitude and cold temperatures keep many micro-organisms from existing in the soil, thus inhibiting the breakdown of faeces. It is important to designate special areas, away from the camp and water sources, for toilets. At least 50m (150ft) away from any open water is advised. A pit latrine should be dug and should

be filled in afterwards. Quicklime will assist decomposition. Dish washing and other hygienic facilities, such as showers, should also be situated some distance from open water, and soaps and detergents should be biodegradable.

Mountaineering equipment that has been used and left behind in the high mountains, such as oxygen bottles and fixed ropes, also constitutes litter. Popular climbs can become festooned with fixed ropes and old tents and, in the case of Everest, oxygen bottles. Climbers must therefore make provision to remove all equipment and waste before leaving the mountain.

Other considerations include not disturbing wildlife and having respect for the cultural beliefs and customs of the local people who spend their lives in the mountains.

Climbing permits, which are required for most of the Seven Summits, help to monitor visitors and their impact on the mountains. Most of the authorities concerned brief expeditions on environmental protection and often restrict the number of visitors. The complete closure of mountain areas can be a final resort to preserve fragile environments and this has been used as a solution in both the Himalayas and North America.

Most people who seek recreation in wild and untouched places have a special care for the environment, and therefore wish to reduce the impact they have on the surroundings. This wish can be realized with a little time, effort, and consideration, and by following the simple maxim, "Take nothing but photographs and leave nothing but footprints." So when visiting any of the world's mountains, support the existing environmental management programmes, make your contribution, and encourage others to follow suit. If we all do this, the mountains will always be there for us to visit, climb, and enjoy.

The Seven Summits and Other Collections

Climbers are incurable collectors. The appeal of climbing the highest mountain – in the world, in a continent, in a country or state – is obvious and inevitably such mountains will attract more attention than lower peaks nearby. But many climbers are drawn by collections of such mountains, giving them a greater long-term objective that might take years to complete. This phenomenon exists at nearly every level of mountaineering, ranging from climbing all of the Scottish Munros to the ultimate high-altitude challenge of climbing all 14 of the 8000m peaks.

Collectable climbs are not only defined by height. They may be a group of difficult classics, such as the six great Alpine North Faces, or a variety of climbs with nothing in common apart from being selected for a well-known book, such as the *Hard Rock* genre, Gaston Rebuffat's *One Hundred Best Routes of the Mont Blanc Massif*, *Fifty Classic Climbs of North America*, *Himalaya Alpine Style*, or the recent *World Mountaineering*. Such collections give many climbers direction and focus. They provide a means of measuring progress and additional satisfaction is derived from the "ticking off" process. They also ensure that when a big climb has been achieved, there is always another objective to fill the vacuum of ambition.

Climbers drawn to the Seven Summits are likely to be susceptible to other collections of climbs. To demonstrate the almost limitless possibilities, here is a selection of mountaineering collections:

- The 14 8000m peaks
- The Russian Snow Leopard –
  the five 7000m peaks in the CIS
- The 18 Trekking Peaks of Nepal*
- The Second Seven (the second highest
  mountain on each continent)*
- The Seven Island Summits
  (the highest point of the largest islands)
- The Munros (Scottish peaks over 3000ft)
- The Alpine 4000m peaks
- The six great North Faces of the Alps
  (Eiger, Matterhorn, Grandes Jorasses,
  Petit Dru, Piz Badile, and Cima Ovest)
- The Equatorial Snowcaps
- The 50 USA state high points
- The South American 6000m peaks*
- The Colorado 14,000ft peaks
- The Three Poles (South and North Poles,
  plus Everest)

*At the time of writing, these are not known to have been completed by a single person.

It could be argued that the Seven Summits is the most elegant and logical collection of climbs. It is a worldwide challenge, not restricted to a single range of mountains, nor to one country or continent, that offers the climber an array of mountaineering experiences in some of the exotic and beautiful corners of the world. This alone makes the continental summits an incredible quest, but what makes the Seven Summits particularly special is that the summits are within reach of the average climber. While the world's elite mountaineers extend the boundaries of the possible on mountains like Everest and McKinley, these same mountains can be climbed via their standard routes by determined novices, assuming that expert guidance is provided. And the remaining continental summits are considerably easier. The Seven Summits is therefore a less demanding objective than many of the other collections of climbs listed above, though for

most it offers the greatest reward, not least because success and survival are far from certain.

During the 21st century, more exciting adventures of this kind will be contrived to test our strength and spirit, in an age when such challenges are no longer forced upon us, but are sought out by choice. If just one of these new adventures can match the variety, attainability, and sheer wonder of the Seven Summits, then we will be very fortunate indeed.

glenn porzak
the case for kosciuszko

On 30 April 1985, American businessman Dick Bass reached the summit of Mount Everest and became the first person to climb the highest peak on the world's traditional seven continents. Controversy erupted, however, in August of 1986 when Canadian Patrick Morrow reached the summit of Elbrus and proclaimed to the world that he, not Bass, was the first to climb the Seven Summits. Morrow had already climbed 4884m Carstensz Pyramid in the western half of New Guinea known as Irian Jaya, and asserted that this was the summit of the true seventh continent known as Australasia. Also known as Oceania, this alleged continent includes New Zealand, New Guinea, and certain other Pacific Islands, along with Australia. If true, Carstensz Pyramid would replace the lowly 2228m Kosciuszko as a continental summit.

Following Pat Morrow's completion of his Seven Summits with Carstensz in 1986 and his assertion that he, not Dick Bass, was the true champion, the debate was kindled. The debate began in earnest when Reinhold Messner sided with Morrow, and various adventure travel companies saw the potential for profit in guiding clients up the technically difficult and remote Carstensz Pyramid. As there was no demand for a guided hike up Kosciuszko, the mountain guides quickly adopted Morrow's seventh summit.

below The gentle slopes of Kosciuszko can be ascended by ski, bike, or on foot.

Having climbed Kilimanjaro, Aconcagua, and McKinley in the mid 1970s and then Vinson Massif in 1985, I had already completed the five hardest of the traditional Seven Summits when I reached the summit of Everest in 1990. As there were only a handful of people who had climbed all of the continental summits, I completed the circuit by ascending Elbrus in the summer of 1991 and then Mount Kosciuszko with my ten-year-old son the following spring. While personally rejecting the notion that Australia is not a continent, I also reached the summit of Carstenz Pyramid in May of 1994. Having now climbed both disputed peaks, with the opportunity to reflect on the Seven Summits debate, I would offer a few observations.

The first is a technical argument based on plate tectonics. Morrow's argument rests on the premise that New Guinea is part of the Australian continental shelf and plate. However, New Guinea does not entirely perch atop the Australian continental shelf. The island is a jigsaw of three plates geologically linking Southeast Asia, the Southern Pacific, and Australia. Only the island's low southern plains are geologically part of the Australian plate. The Java Trench, which cuts through the heart of New Guinea, is the geological border that separates Asia from Australia. Carstensz Pyramid lies to the north of the mountain chain that marks the Java Trench, on the Philippine plate of Asia. Thus it is not on the same tectonic plate as Australia.

My second observation looks at political classifications. Carstensz is located in the western half of New Guinea known as Irian Jaya, which belongs to Indonesia. Politically, that country is classified as part of Asia, not Australia. Only eastern New Guinea, or the independent country of Papua New Guinea, has any political ties to Australia.

Philosophically, Bass's claim also appears to be superior. Dick Bass defined the challenge to climb the continental summits. Then, as an inexperienced climber and middle-aged business executive in his mid 50s, he went out and did it. Perhaps that irritates some hard-core mountaineers, but it shows what can be done with a bit of persistence and, yes, enough money. The story ranks up there with the likes of Woodrow Wilson Sayre's *Four Against Everest*, except that Bass actually pulled off his audacious scheme. For that alone, no one should ever deprive him of being the first.

But technicalities, politics, and philosophy aside, two simple facts stand out. By any definition, New Guinea is an island and Carstensz Pyramid is the highest mountain in the world on an island. Therefore, I assert that Kosciuszko is the Seventh Summit. But, as the highest summit in the world not located on a continent, Carstensz is surely the Eighth!

pat morrow

in defence of carstensz

The game of climbing constantly changes its rules. One day it's de rigueur to chip holds or spray a ladder of bolts into the rock, the next these are being denounced by the climbing community as a destructive cop-out akin to clearcut logging or strip mining. Climbing etiquette has changed so often that a colourful jargon has evolved to delineate the technique du jour, ranging from hangdogging, red point, and pink point to on sight, protection placed from the ground up, and protection placed from the top down.

And in the alpine climbing world, the argument that the first ascent of a route can be claimed even if the climbing team doesn't reach the summit has been hotly contested. What about those 14 8000m peaks? Don't several of them have subsidiary summits that haven't been climbed yet? So, it begs the question, whose rules do we play by in the Seven Summits game? On the surface, the project seems straight forward enough. However, geographical semantics get in the way of a good "clean kill." If one defines the geographic region that encompasses Australia, and the islands of New Zealand and New Guinea with the accepted term "Oceania," or "Australasia," then without question Carstensz Pyramid is the highest peak in that region.

Imagine the geographical area of North America, which harbours an archipelago of Arctic Islands similar to Oceania. What if a higher mountain than Denali sat in the middle of Baffin Island? Which one would climbers tend to gravitate toward, despite the fact that Denali was the highest on the "continent"?

And if you settle on the textbook definition that the country of Australia is a continent, there is another curve ball. The highest peak in Australian territory is not Kosciuszko, but rather, a 2745m mountain called Big Ben on storm-tossed Heard Island, deep in the Southern Ocean. In order to reach the island, one needs a dedicated boat since it is far from the shipping routes. Do we have any takers? Imagine the regatta that could be assembled to reach the island. May the fastest boat win!

below The rocky, extremely abrasive face of Carstensz offers a number of technically challenging climbs.

gerry roach eight summits

Gerry Roach's lifelong passion for the mountains spans more than a generation. A true odyssey, his quest for the Seven Summits is rooted in this passion, illustrating the ecstasy and the extreme danger, the frustration and the sheer emotion of climbing some of the world's greatest mountains. It bears witness to how the mountaineering game has changed over time, and how tenacity and determination can motivate us to achieve the improbable.

McKinley: Touching Greatness

Don Sheldon paused with one foot on the step of the tiny Cub aeroplane and said, "Remember boys! When she clobbers up, hunker down! When she clears up, go like a jackrabbit!" Then he pulled himself up into the cockpit, fired the engine, roared down the glacier in a cloud of snow, and lifted off. The Cub's roar quickly dropped to a distant drone. Sheldon turned the Cub south down the Kahiltna, waggled his wings once, and was gone. At last we were alone with our peaks. The silence was deafening.

I was on the South East Fork of the Kahiltna Glacier with three school chums, Geoff Wheeler, Mike McCoy, and Dick Springgate. We had come to climb the "High One," Denali. Lean and fit, we were the youngest team ever to tackle the peak. The year was 1963 and, at 19, I was a mere morsel of a man. That was good and bad. It was good because I didn't know much. That left me effused with enthusiasm,

curiosity, and a willingness to learn. It was bad because I didn't know much. That left me vulnerable to Denali's vicious whims. However, Sheldon's reverence for this place had infected me and I approached the High One with extreme caution.

I gawked up at Mount Hunter and shrank in fear. "Impossible," I thought. I gazed across the Kahiltna at Foraker and thought, "maybe someday." Then we started the climb up the Kahiltna towards Denali. For a week we ploughed a trough up the glacier and relayed our meagre supplies to a camp just below the Kahiltna Pass. Here we met two parties on their way down, nursing their frostbite and speaking in hushed tones of what was above. We were learning. Then they passed and we were left alone on the mountain, destined not to see another person until the end of our trip. All the talk and pompous bragging was over. There was only one thing left for us to do – climb the High One.

above McKinley is enshrouded in cloud though the weather is perfect lower down on the Kahiltna.

left The steep southern side of McKinley towers high above the surrounding peaks.

right Gerry Roach poses like a hero atop the triangle that can be found on Kosciuszko's summit.

We hunkered down through a long storm. Three jackrabbit days later we were in the Basin at 14,000ft, below the West Buttress. The next day we ploughed a trough to the headwall and stomped up it. That night the wind filled our trough. The next day we ploughed a new one. Snow conditions were good, we had hit our stride and we were going for it. Higher, on the crest of the West Buttress, we climbed through an encompassing alpenglow. Then disaster struck.

At an impromptu rest stop, Mike set his pack down on the rope just as Dick dashed to the edge to take a picture. Flip! Mike's pack was gone. We watched in horror as the pack tumbled toward the Peters Glacier 2000ft below. Then our horror deepened as the pack opened. A dozen dots scattered and rolled to stopping points spread over half a mile. Mike lost it and danced about like a madman bellowing, "Both stoves! Both stoves!"

I nervously replied, "Whaddaya mean both stoves? Dick has one."

Mike did not break stride in his twisted dance and bellowed on, "I swapped out. Both stoves are down there! It's all my fault!" Geoff and I shot each other our secret Summit Club glance. We were into it now. Geoff calmed Mike while I huddled with Dick trying to make sense of the mess. Finally, we sank to the snow. The alpenglow was gone.

We rose to the task. Geoff and Dick descended into the Arctic night to get the gear while Mike and I explored ahead for a campsite. We went all the way to the traditional campsite at 17,200ft and realized it was too high. We returned to the wide spot on the ridge at 16,800ft, just below Washburn's Thumb, pitched our tent and waited. Geoff and Dick

returned, crawled into the tent and crashed. Geoff thrust a bag at me and said, "We only found one stove." The flame spreader on our one stove was gone, but we got a cup of water each before succumbing to sleep. The next morning I pondered prudence: a retreat to 14,000ft and our spare stove. Then Mike roared, "I've been thinking about it all night! We've gotta go for it!" The weather was good. We left for the summit at 1pm. It was 4 July.

On the long, ascending traverse to Denali Pass we grew impatient and cut straight up the slope. Sucking ice and hard candies, we were on stride again. We hit the summit slopes well above Denali Pass, took a brief rest, and continued up into the evening. The alpenglow found us in the Football Field. Geoff and I finally reached the summit at 10.30pm, just as the sun set. Dick and

> "All the talk and pompous bragging was over. Now we had to climb the High One."

Mike joined us minutes later. North America was at our feet. I scanned the day's remaining glow beyond the North Peak far below. The Muldrow sank into the shadows. Foraker gleamed and beckoned. I vowed to climb it someday. Hunter still looked impossible. It didn't sink in until I was back in Sheldon's Cub flying out. Sheldon bellowed over the engine, "So, she was a HOWL-ing success eh?"

Thoughts swirling, I hollered back, "You bet!"

Kosciuszko: Journey

Life rocketed ahead. I finished my undergraduate degree, married Barb Adair, finished graduate school, climbed in the Yukon, took a job at the Denver Research Institute, and tried to settle down. Ha!

In December 1968 I went on a round-the-world business trip to launch a balloon-borne experiment in the Antarctic. Barb went with me as far as she could.

We stopped in Hawaii and hiked up Mauna Kea, one of the earth's highest island summits. We climbed in New Zealand and travelled across Australia. En route, we hiked up Kosciuszko. To be sporting, we parked 10 miles from the summit and walked up the road, swiping at flies like windshield wipers. Near the top, we left the road and enjoyed the largest fly-free snow slope we could find. To our amazement we had the summit all to ourselves.

This was my second continental summit and the only one I was likely to climb in shorts. Even though I considered man-made objects completely optional, I felt compelled to climb the tripod that had been built on the summit by Australian authorities. I slithered up the slippery pipe and posed like a hero on top of the silly thing. It was the highest point in Australia.

I left Barb in Perth and sailed for the Antarctic on the icebreaker Fuji. At the Japanese base of Syowa on East Ongul Island I launched balloons, collected data, and dreamed about getting to Vinson some day. Vinson was over 2000 miles away from Syowa and there was no chance of getting there on this trip, but I gazed across the ice cap and pondered the task. In my secret dreams, I vowed that if I ever climbed either Everest or Vinson, I would devote the rest of my life to climbing the other peak. Barb rejoined me in Cape Town and we flew home, but this journey planted many seeds.

Kilimanjaro: The Siren's Song

More years leaped by. All attempts at settling down failed. Barb and I travelled to Peru and climbed the South Face of Chacraraju and Huascarán in 1971. Then, after years of careful planning, we left our jobs and home in March 1973 to climb around the world for a year. After climbing Mount Logan in June, we climbed across Norway and the Alps to land in Nairobi in September.

Africa conjures magical images for all but the most heartless soul. The colourful history of the search for the headwaters of the Nile is punctuated with commentary about early beliefs that equatorial Africa contained snow-covered mountains. While Western map-makers wondered, the African tribes knew. For them, East Africa's snow-covered peaks were "Spirit Mountains." Could Barb and I swoop into this fabled land and claim the Spirit Mountains?

After Mount Kenya, we bounced south from the Kenya–Tanzania border in a rattletrap bus and had our first view of Kilimanjaro. I could not believe my eyes. I had no idea Kilimanjaro was so huge, since most pictures only show Kibo, the mountain's upper reaches. The lower mountain receded into the African haze and covered half the horizon.

Kilimanjaro was a pilgrimage not a climb. We left the Marangu Hotel with our five-man "rough it" staff and strolled up through the forest as descending porters passed us, singing, "Jambo! Poli, Poli!" In the Kibo spirit, we sang the upward miles away. At high camp, Barb and I sat outside during the short equatorial twilight, watching a cloud band hover around neighbouring Mawenzi. The air was calm and strangely quiet. I felt suspended in Kilimanjaro's cradle. As night rapidly rose from the moorland and engulfed us, a porter's song floated across the cradle. His brief haunting hymn gently sedated the camp.

Night starts always carry an air of expectancy. A midnight start is over-kill for Kibo but early starts had evolved as part of the ritual. Under still, silent stars, our summit climb felt like an exotic rite of passage through darkness. Our guide, Erco set a slow, *poli*, pace and we padded up the pumice. He repeatedly offered, "Rest?" In turn we always replied, "No. Good pace!" Finally, Erco demanded, "Rest!"

below Barbara Roach catches her breath and enjoys the sunrise from the roof of Africa after the final sprint to the summit of Kilimanjaro.

Our steady pace had violated some unspoken rule. We hunkered down under a large lava boulder and looked for dawn but the sky was still pitch black. After five minutes, Erco motioned up and ordered, "Poli!" Alternating rest and *poli* sessions, we climbed up into the night.

My fantasies of night music and bellowing lions faded when we reached Gillman's Point. A cold breeze blew across the crater and we felt the fabled snows. We perched in the lee of a rock and watched for dawn over Mawenzi. The sky was still black. With sign language, Erco offered us the opportunity to proclaim Gillman's Point the summit and head down. I motioned up and said, "Enough poli poli! Let's go Uhuru!"

Dawn flecked the eastern horizon as we crept around the crater rim. An unusual urgency mingled with my usual summit fever and I hurried forward as dawn silhouetted a strangely distant Mawenzi. We were close to both sunrise and the summit as increasing light urged me on. I rushed up the final slope, turned, and watched the sun break the horizon. I saluted Africa's nascent sun.

Barb and Erco rushed up behind me. We all felt it. Barb and I danced on the summit as songs of Kilimanjaro resonated in our minds. Our long shadows frolicked in the alpenglow. It was a magic moment. As sunlight filled the summit crater, we saw that our night rite had delivered us to the snows of Kilimanjaro. A sea of strange snow formations rose directly from dry pumice and our eyes roamed over a kaleidoscope of shape and colour. Standing on top of Kilimanjaro at sunrise reminded me of why I started climbing.

above During a brief moment of respite from the wind, Gerry Roach reaches Aconcagua's summit and celebrates the fourth of his continental summits.

left Climbers face the toughest part of their ascent as they climb the long loose Canaleta near the top of Aconcagua.

Aconcagua: Assassin

My wanderlust was firmly entrenched. In January 1975, Barb, Bob Cormack, who was with us on Logan, and Roger Kirkpatrick sat cross-legged on our living room floor pouring over a pile of maps, trying to get an understanding of our new adversary. Barb asked, "Why is Aconcagua such a deadly mountain if it's easy to climb?"

While Bob and I discussed latitude skew, Roger sat in a corner reading a *National Geographic* article about Argentina. The "Assassin" had already defeated Roger twice and he piped up, "Woah! Listen to this! The photographer for this article chartered a powerful twin-engine plane to fly over the mountain. Wind bucked the plane so hard the pilot could hardly approach the mountain. The pilot gained altitude away from the peak and signalled they would only be able to make one pass over the summit. As they flew swiftly over the summit, the photographer fired away until he realized they were going backwards! He checked the plane's air speed. It was 160mph!"

Bob stammered, "That means the wind on the summit was over 200mph!" We fell silent. Barb hugged her knees and rocked. She knew what was coming. This would be a climb not a pilgrimage.

After conquering a mountain of bureaucracy in Mendoza and in the army base at Puenta del Inca we had to, among other things, pass a physical. Mine turned into a harrowing run through a minefield.

A week later, after several hair-raising river crossings in the Horcones Valley, we were at Plaza del Mulas Base Camp wondering where our mules were. We had the hut to ourselves but for once wanted company. The missing mules had our gear. We descended to find the army rebuilding the trail across a washout. Wet dynamite exploded with a pitiful, "Poof!" so we resorted to picks and shovels as the soldiers tipped whisky bottles. As darkness approached, we finally got the mules across the washout. But the whisky had taken its toll.

At 11pm, the procession reached Plaza del Mulas and Barb detoxified the tired crew with soup and hot chocolate. All that remained was climbing the Assassin.

Six days later we crammed into the tiny, 6 x 8ft Antarctica Hut, which was in an improbable place at 18,200ft in the middle of the vast Gran Acarreo on Assassin's northern slopes. As darkness held me, I listened to the signature of the wind outside. The blasting gale prevented sleep and I reflected on Denali. I had felt Denali's greatness from a distance in 1963. Now, 12 years later, I prepared to climb the highest peak in South America. So far, Assassin was a photograph, a vision, and an entertaining show. As I listened to the wind tear at the hut, I felt poised for the first time on this mountain. We were just under the jet stream. Now, we had to climb up into it. I knew our test waited on Assassin's highest 3000ft.

Three days later we started for the summit from the Berlin Huts. We pushed up into the tempest and took an hour to gain the first 900ft. It was clear and −45°C but the 100mph wind made it feel much colder. The higher we went, the worse it got. We staggered up the slope above the ruined Independencia Refuge as gusts made a mockery of our climb. Crawling on to Hurricane Ridge, I tried to stand but could only crouch.

After more than 19 years of mountaineering, I discovered a new dimension to mother earth's ability to express outrage. The wind blasted far harder here than anywhere below. Or in Colorado. Or in our collective experience. Any speech was impossible. We blinked a tear-blurred vision through our goggles. I held up two parallel mittens to Bob to indicate 200mph. He nodded and crossed his mittens in a plus sign to suggest more than 200mph. I looked up at the peak only 1000ft above us. The sky and summit were perfectly clear. The wind was not daring all comers on this day, it was commanding them.

> "The wind blasted far harder here than anywhere below. Or in Colorado. Or in our collective experience. Speech was impossible."

The possibility of failure tugged at my mind. The thought scared me and I lurched forward toward the summit. The others followed in a rag-tag formation. Imperceptibly, we battled upward against an outraged nature. A gust of Jovian proportions blew Barb 30ft up the slope. She was unable to come back down and staggered along on a higher line. We four were high, alone, and very vulnerable on Assassin. We huddled in the lee of a small pillar in the middle of the scree slope leading to the Canaleta. The wind guarded Assassin's summit with an impenetrable shield. I stood and pointed down. No one argued.

We weren't finished. Two mornings later we were back on Hurricane Ridge. I shouted, "We can do it! This wind can't be more than 60!" We bent to our task. At our high-point pillar, we stopped and nibbled some chocolate. I pointed up and said, "Today, we will not turn back!"

As we started into the Canaleta, Roger quoted Edmund Spenser, "But let this day, let this one day be mine." We engaged the Canaleta's much-discussed test in full stride and found it easier than expected. A snow slope on the right side helped. The view opened with a rush when we reached the summit ridge. We forgot about the dying wind. Assassin's South Face fell sheer below us for 9000ft. The great void startled me. My mind – trapped by huts, wind, failure, and the Canaleta – was swiftly set free. We were very close.

As I quickly resumed the final slope, I grasped why the summit is so important. Only here could I be free. Freedom is power. Freedom is love. In spite of earth's Assassins, freedom lives. It was not clear whether I was going to the summit, or the summit was coming to me. Suddenly, we were one.

It was my fourth continental summit and the third that Barb and I had reached together. Fantastic snow sculptures left by the wind graced the ragged summit rocks. We scanned the sky and realized the wind had not died, just travelled elsewhere. We were free but we were tiny. For a tiny, tremendous half hour, we played free in the sky.

Everest: Earth Summit

In June and July of 1975, I did my dream climb. Barb and I, with four others, climbed Mount Foraker's North Ridge, which we called the Archangel. From Foraker's summit I gazed across at Denali and made good on the promise I made to myself in 1963. I also looked across the Kahiltna at Hunter. It still looked impossible.

In December 1975, I travelled to Seattle to show slides of the Archangel at the American Alpine Club's annual dinner. There I met Arlene Blum and we chatted amiably about earth's peaks. That night she invited me to climb Everest. She also invited Chris Chandler. The 1976 American Bicentennial Everest Expedition was launched.

The organizers were the "three lawyers" Dan Emmett, Phil Trimble, and Frank Morgan. For three of the eight months we had to put the trip together, we had no permit. Then, for another three months, we had no money. At the last moment, CBS Sports agreed to film the expedition and we were on our way in August 1976.

Barb was on the team along with Bob Cormack and Chandler's friend Rick Ridgeway. Arlene also invited her friend Hans Bruyntjes. Dee Crouch and Joe Reinhardt completed the 12-person team. Because of the monsoon we could not fly to Lukla and so trekked in from Lomasangu with all our stuff on porter's backs. Our 180-mile approach had a life of its own. Rain, mud, leeches, prayer flags, Sherpas, porters, days, dances, nights, and more rain punctuated our ever more spiritual journey. At Tengboche, we froze while the monks blessed us. Many thought we had no chance to climb the Big E but we knew we could give it a good try. I said, "This mountain is made of rock, ice, and snow just like the others. We can do it!"

We had the mountain completely to ourselves. Our first forays into the Icefall were terrifying. Tension mounted and tempers flared. Fear of death tugged at everyone's heels. On my days off, I lay in my tent near the altar with its smoking juniper as my companions trudged by to the Sherpa's chants. I wondered if I would ever see them again. I couldn't admit it at the time but I had never seen any mountains like the high Himalayas. Simply stated, they were higher, steeper, tougher, and more dangerous than any I had ever seen before. Fear of failure tugged

right Two climbers, enshrouded in shadow, approach the top of the Khumbu Icefall just as morning sunlight illuminates the beautiful peak of Pumori (7145m/23,443ft), which lies just to the west of Everest.

gerry roach

at me right along with fear of death. I knew we could get high, but could we manage to reach the tippy top? And, could we actually make it back in one piece?

As September marched by, we marched up. Storms slowed us and wrecked our best tents. Illness left a third of the team on its back much of the time. Still we inched up. I have never been with a team that wanted the summit more than this one. As October approached, summit fever, stomach fever, altitude, fear, and passion converged. It was time to try for the summit.

An untimely stomach upset caused me to switch from the first to the second summit team. I took solace in the fact that Hillary and Tenzing were the second team. Bob and Chris headed up with the Sherpas and Rick, Hans, and I followed two days later. On 7 October our best Sherpas established a high camp with Bob, Chris, and Sherpa Sidar Ang Phurba, on the South East Ridge at 27,200ft. On 8 October, summit day, Ang Phurba's oxygen equipment malfunctioned. He went down while Bob and Chris started up with two bottles of oxygen each. Rick, Hans, and I waited in Camp 4 halfway up the Lhotse Face. One by one, the Sherpas came down. They wouldn't stop to talk. Something was wrong.

At 1pm Barb's excited voice crackled over the radio, "I can see them approaching the summit!" Barb and the lawyers had a good vantage point across from Base Camp. But, to our surprise, Ang Phurba, who had been the last Sherpa high on the mountain, crawled into our tent, hung his head, and said, "Me and my team finished." He descended and left us to worry about Bob and Chris near the summit. The hours dragged by. At 4.15pm Barb announced that Bob and Chris were on the summit! They had done it! At 4.45pm they started down. Late! Could they survive? At 6pm Bob and Chris reached the South Summit on their descent. Then darkness overtook them. Was the Big E the real Assassin?

Early on 9 October, Rick, Hans, and I started up. We didn't know if we were on a summit climb or a rescue mission. We met Bob and Chris just below the South Col. They were okay! I hugged Bob for a long moment. He cracked a joke then said, "Hardest thing I've ever done. Now, it's like escaping through a closing door. We gotta keep moving down. Oh, the Col camp's a shambles. No O₂." Then they were gone.

Logic and passion collided. Rick, Hans, and I teetered on our crampons for several minutes gazing at the vertiginous heights. Everest's famous plume screamed its warning. As Rick and Hans dropped their eyes and prepared to descend, I took three more steps up somehow desperately hoping they might be the last three. To this day, after more than 40 years of mountaineering, the moment I turned my back on Everest in 1976 remains the most intense single moment of my life. I had failed.

Back in Colorado, I raced up mountains in record time and routinely kicked summit cairns to smithereens. I felt as though I had blown the chance of a lifetime.

Now life got complicated. In 1978 I went on an expedition to Manaslu with Glenn Porzak as leader. I reasoned that, if I couldn't climb Everest, at least I should climb one of the earth's highest peaks.

> "To this day, after more than 40 years of mountaineering, the moment I turned my back on Everest in 1976 stands as the most intense single moment of my life. I had failed."

above Campsites like these are a common sight along the approach to Everest where the signs of Tibetan Buddhism are as much a part of the landscape as the mountains.

left Members of the 1976 American Bicentennial Expedition make their way through the crevasses of Everest's Western Cwm, threatened by avalanches from the mile-high peaks of the North Face of Nuptse.

Manaslu served us 50ft of snow in 50 days and 80 per cent of the route was avalanched. We beat a retreat from 24,000ft and barely escaped with our lives through another closing door.

This time I returned to Colorado and quit climbing. When a climber announces they are quitting, ask for their gear. If they are serious, they will hand it over. I hung on to mine.

In 1981, I travelled to Tibet to try Xixabangma. Third try's the charm? Oh rot! A series of events kept us far below the summit. Worse, on the drive out I endured a grand view of Everest floating on the horizon.

Confused, I let go. I made another attempt at settling down, got a job and bought a house. Then one evening in late 1982, Glenn Porzak called and asked, "Gerry, do you have any interest in going back to Everest?" My heart zipped up. Another extraordinary series of events transpired, and in March 1983 I found myself back in Namche Bazar. I was on the Dick Bass and Frank Wells Seven Summits extravaganza. By mid April, we were halfway up the peak.

This time I made sure I was on the first summit team. On 7 May, Larry Nielson, Peter Jamieson, Ang Rita, ABC cameraman Dave Breashears, and I started for the summit at 5am from the South Col with three bottles of oxygen for the five of us. Times had changed. Larry and Ang Rita chose to climb without oxygen. We started from one camp lower than Bob and Chris in 1976 and had less oxygen than they did.

I was so drawn to the summit that I took a shortcut similar to the one we used to skirt Denali Pass in 1963. My choice nearly cost us the summit. We floundered in bad snow for many hours then finally climbed a steep pitch to reach the South East Ridge at 28,000ft. We paused there to collect our wits. It was socked in but there was no wind. Dave decided to descend with all the camera gear. Larry and I leaned on our axes and sniffed the thin air. After seven years of cairn-kicking meditation I was not so easily deterred. We nodded and pointed up.

Half an hour later our weather sniff proved accurate when it suddenly cleared. Dave, still on the ridge, hollered up, "Wait for me!" There is no waiting above 28,000ft and I hollered back, "Use your O_2!" We reached the South Summit at 3pm and the summit at 4pm just as our oxygen ran out. Dave and I set up the camera gear and transmitted images of Larry summiting without oxygen, the first American to achieve this feat. I stood on top for 35 minutes and didn't want to leave.

I had a strong sense that I had climbed Everest for many people, not just for myself. This was beyond personal achievement. As I descended, a flood of emotion grew. I still carry it with me today.

Elbrus: Soviet Snows

In my fever and focus on Everest, I had largely ignored Frank and Dick's Seven Summit quest swirling around me. Of course, I was working on the Seven but I knew I could not do it without Everest. When that peak was done, I remembered my vow to climb Vinson. The race for the Seven Summits crossed my mind, but I was never really in the race. I just continued doing what I had done for decades. One peak at a time.

In 1984, I landed some lucrative contract work that pulled me out of a financial hole. Then, in 1985, I had a big year. In July, I was off to Russia to climb Mount Elbrus. It was a refreshing trip after the difficulties of the Himalayas. We climbed Elbrus in the first few days there and enjoyed a sunny summit stay on the West Peak. On the way down I ditched the guide and zoomed up the lower East Peak by myself. I was already chuckling at the thought of climbing the highest falsie on every continent.

Vinson: Coming Home

In November 1985 I left for Vinson with Dan Emmett, Phil Trimble, Frank Morgan, Glenn Porzak, Dan Bass, Yvon Chouinard, and Doug Tompkins. We had a special Twin Otter aeroplane waiting for us in Punta Arenas. Two other groups were ahead of us, including Pat Morrow's Canadian team. Our pilot was Giles Kershaw and our co-pilot was Rick Mason.

It took us four days to fly from Puenta Arenas to the mountain. First, we stalled out in Puerto Williams. The next day we flew across the Drake Passage, refuelled at the Chilean's Marsh Base, then stalled out again, this time at Palmer Station where we were not scheduled to land.

right Members of Gerry Roach's 1985 team descend to the Branscomb Glacier from the saddle that had to be crossed from the original Base Camp. Later teams set their Base Camp on the Branscomb Glacier itself, thus avoiding this tricky section.

The following day we refuelled in Rothera Base, then took off for the mountain once more only to be forced to land in the middle of nowhere due to rough weather. On the next day we avoided such problems and finally reached Vinson.

Yvon and Doug had no interest in Vinson and took off in a different direction to do new routes on Shinn and Epperly. The rest of us started for Vinson. We had stove problems from the outset. We had to envelop the stove in a bonfire to get it going and could not cook in the tents. We crossed the pass and, sniffing the frigid air, entered the basin between Shinn and Vinson. This time I smelled a storm coming.

We pitched our three tents in the lee of some large avalanche debris blocks and secured them with ice screws. There was no possibility of digging a shelter and there were no crevasses. We knew that the little bit of drift snow here could easily blow away and the underlying ice was granite hard. We did build a one-man igloo by rolling debris blocks from far above. This rude shelter, which we used for cooking, saved us from a more desperate fate. The storm arrived right on cue.

The pressure fell, the temperature plunged, the wind rose to Assassin standards and flying ice chips threatened to rip the tents. Once a day, one of us sprinted to the igloo and got the stoves going.

With this effort, we had two cups of water and one cup of warm food per day. Conversation ran out at the end of day two. This was a serious storm. Fear of failure plagued me on day three. This was a dangerous storm. Fear of death took over on day four. This was a desperate storm. On day five I feared for my soul. This was an evil storm; the worst I had ever endured. I desperately wanted to be done with the Seven Summits.

The tents held. When the wind relented from 100 to 40mph and the temperature rose from −147° to −129°C, we crept from the tents in sad shape. I still longed for the summit. We abandoned thoughts of the traditional Camp 3 and knew that we had one last-gasp attempt at making it to the summit. Jaded, we feared this lull would be short and our worst fate would be to miss it. In a questionable choice, we left to make our summit attempt at 4pm.

The three lawyers and Dan Bass turned back below the Shinn–Vinson saddle. Glenn and I doubled our short rope and climbed on into the Antarctic night. It was frigid, and despite our best efforts, chilled from the five-day storm, we could not manage to get warm. Together we stumped toward the distant mountain summit on autopilot. I mused, "So, this is what experience allows you to do!"

> **"This was an evil storm, the worst I have endured. I desperately wanted to be done with the Seven Summits."**

Approaching the summit pyramid we climbed across acres of clear ice that seemed more enduring than granite. Our crampons barely gave purchase as we gazed into the soul of a continent.

On the summit ridge, a glancing ray of sun lured us on. I felt like I was coming home. It was time to enjoy the ride. At 1.30am on Friday, 13 December, I pulled up into the sunlight. I had done it.

The wind had gone elsewhere and, warming in the sun, we lounged on the summit for over an hour. I snapped photographs of mountains and more mountains, all of which were lower. Beyond them, frozen ice horizons were visible as far as the eye could see. Antarctica was at our feet. When I was on top of Everest, I looked beyond the mountains and saw life and warmth embracing them. Here, there was only the cold-fingered grasp of ice. Except for our companions far below, there was not another living thing within our sight – not a lichen, a piece of moss, a bird, or even a speck of dust. We were as isolated as two people could be and still be attached to earth. We were on top of Vinson Massif. And I was home.

Carstensz: Beyond the Seven

Finishing the Seven Summits was just one more step in my life-long continuum of climbing. I joked that I was the first non-millionaire to have completed the Seven Summits but I did feel good that I had done it my way. Over time, I moved on to other peaks and new projects. The 90s were good to me. In 1990, I started at Wonder Lake, traversed over Denali's summit and came out at Talkeetna. But times had changed. A guided party stole our snowshoes near Denali Pass and we had to descend without them. In 1991, I climbed Denali's West Buttress Route in a two-week round trip from my home in Boulder, Colorado. On these trips I looked beyond Denali and gave Mount Hunter a closer inspection. It no longer looked impossible to me.

In 1994, my friends Glenn Porzak and Mike Browning organized a trip to Carstensz Pyramid in New Guinea. The peak had drifted in and out of political accessibility and it seemed like a good time to tackle it. Our flight to Ilaga finished our two-day journey from Boulder to the land of penis gourds. Our stay in central Irian Jaya was as out there culturally as Vinson was out there physically. Our six-day trek to the mountain took us through highlands unspoiled by the West and past limestone caves. The unpretentious Dani tribesmen, who acted as porters for us, fiercely defended their culture.

We tackled Carstensz the day after reaching Base Camp. We started up the

left Below the headwall of the Branscomb Glacier, Roach's campsite shelters in the lee of avalanche debris from Vinson.

rock a little after dawn. In teams of two, we moved steadily up the easy 5th-, 3rd-, and 4th-class terrain to the ridge, which we reached as the rains started. At the crux notch, we took one look at the wet 5.10 pitch that climbs directly out of it and hiked around to the 5.8 pitch. This pitch would be fun in the sun but it was a grunt in the rain. We belayed over two more exposed notches on the ridge beyond before the scramble to the summit opened up for us. Glenn, Chris Kopsinski, and I all touched the summit together, finishing the eight summits for all three of us. It was socked in and raining hard. We beat a soggy retreat.

In our remaining days, we climbed two snow peaks east of Carstensz. Equatorial snows are disappearing and I wanted to touch them one more time. Back at Ilaga, there was a shoot out at the airstrip the day before our flight home and we were stuck for a few days

A week after leaving Ilaga, I was at Base Camp on Mount Hunter. It was, at long last, my time. I climbed Hunter's West Ridge with my good friend Chris Haaland in a six-day push. As near as we could figure, we were the seventh and eighth people to have summited Denali, Foraker, and Hunter. Though this is a much smaller number than the list of those who have conquered the Seven Summits, I hold this trilogy on a par with the Seven. Of course, I'm not the first person to have climbed both Hunter and Carstensz. Heinrich Harrer made the first ascents of both these peaks.

In 1996, I had a permit to climb Everest as part of Dave Breashears film crew. But I was appalled at what had happened to the Everest experience and just said no to the opportunity. When I returned home I was shocked to hear news of the disaster. A friend asked,

"Gerry, how did you know?"

I replied, "I just sniff the wind."

In 1997, I looked beyond Everest for adventure. In February, I climbed Aconcagua with Chris Haaland. I took a laconic solo stroll up the Canaleta and lounged on the summit for over an hour waiting for Chris to arrive from the other side. It was a sharp contrast to our struggle in 1975, but the Aconcagua experience has undergone far less change than the Everest experience. In July 1997, I summited Gasherbrum II in the Karakoram and got a good look at K2. It did not look impossible...

right Dani tribesmen, their lives unsullied by the industrialized world, act as climbers' porters.

below The limestone slab of the North Face of Carstensz offers the best rock climbing of the Seven Summits.

everest

The Nepalese Sherpas to the south have always called it Sagamartha; their Tibetan cousins on the northern plateau revere it as Chomolungma, "Goddess Mother of the Earth"; but ever since surveyors discovered that it was the world's highest summit in 1852, it has borne the name of a former British Surveyor General – Everest.

Seen most dramatically from the north and west, Everest's massive pyramid towers unequivocally above its neighbouring giants – Cho Oyu, Lhotse, and Makalu. Even K2, in Pakistan, is nearly 250m (800ft) lower. Everest is the unrivalled apex of the greatest mountain range on earth – the Himalayas, which means "Abode of Snow" and is the source of the great rivers sustaining the teeming population of the Indo–Gangetic plain. As well as being a fount of life, the Himalayas are also home to the many deities sacred to Hindus and Buddhists, and anyone seeing those glittering, ethereal summits for the first time cannot help feeling a little awed.

Only in the last 80 years have the Sherpas who live immediately beneath Everest set foot on its slopes. For most of them, climbing Everest is a high-risk job, not a hobby, and without their support few of the foreigners who have now reached the summit would have made it. Even by its easiest routes, Everest presents harder, more complex problems than any of the other Seven Summits; but it is the altitude – nearly 2000m (6600ft) higher than Aconcagua – that is the real test. Experts are still refining the measurements. But we know that, give or take a few metres, the summit is 8848m (29,028ft) above sea level, which happens to be at the very limit of human capability. Without oxygen it is marginal; even with the help of supplementary oxygen and Sherpa staff preparing the route and stocking camps, anyone attempting the highest summit should do so with respect and caution.

Climbing Seasons

For those who seek the ultimate masochistic challenge, it is possible to climb Everest in winter. Summit temperatures as low as to –50°C, combined with winds over 200kph (120mph), blasting away much of the snow to leave bare rock and iron-hard ice, make it an extreme undertaking, rarely repeated since the first winter ascent of 1980.

The vast majority of ascents are made in the spring, usually reaching Base Camp in early April, with a view to summiting around the second week of May. During this finite window of opportunity, before the arrival of the monsoon, temperatures are comparatively warm and the winds are generally less vicious than in the autumn. However, the weather is variable and can be very unsettled, and afternoon snow squalls are common. Success really depends on having a fine spell lasting four or five days once the team is ready for a summit attempt.

The extraordinary solo ascent of the North Face by Reinhold Messner in 1980 was made during the summer monsoon – the warmest, wettest time of the year, traditionally considered too dangerous for climbing. He was canny, slotting his lightning ascent into a temporary lull in the weather. The advantages of this unorthodox approach were thick snow covering normally awkward sloping rocks; warmer, damper air putting less strain on the throat; and more protection from ultra-violet radiation. Few have repeated Messner's monsoon success.

Crystal clear skies are the reward for climbing in the autumn – if you are lucky – for they cannot be assured. By banking up awkward rocks, heavy snow cover left by the monsoon can make some routes such as the South West Face easier than in spring. However, cold temperatures mean that the snow is

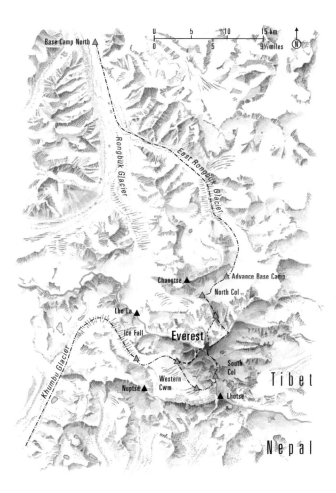

"Those seeking the ultimate masochistic challenge climb Everest in the winter."

often powdery and unstable. Post-monsoon attempts are usually a race against the coming winter winds, which hardly affect lower peaks but are devastating above 7000m (23,000ft). Frostbite is a much bigger risk than in spring and success rates are much lower.

Topography of the Mountain

Everest is a three-sided pyramid with the South West Face in Nepal, and the East and North Faces in Tibet. The frontier follows the West and South East Ridges, while the North East Ridge lies entirely in Tibet. From the south, the mountain is almost obscured by the wall of Nuptse (West Peak) and Lhotse (South Peak). Hidden behind this wall is the extraordinary enclosed valley of the Western Cwm – the approach to the South West Face and the high saddle called the South Col, from where the Normal Route continues up the South East Ridge. The Western Cwm's glacier is squeezed out through a steep narrow corridor, tumbling in a chaos of jumbled blocks known as the Khumbu Icefall – an unavoidable danger on the southern routes.

The East Face is the biggest and possibly the most dangerous on Everest. Like many east faces in the Himalayas, it is draped with spectacular snow

North Side

West Side

flutings and hanging glaciers, poised above formidably steep rock buttresses. Its avalanches feed the Kangshung Glacier, which drains east into the deep gorge of the Arun River. Although this Kangshung side lies in Tibet, the climate and landscape with lush forests and glorious alpine meadows are similar to those in Nepal.

To the north everything changes dramatically. The light is more intense, the air is parched dry, and the vegetation is sparse. After the winter winds much of the North Face is often bare rock, particularly the famous Yellow Band, which glows orange at sunset. These layers of sedimentary rock are a reminder that Everest originated in the bed of the ancient Tethys Sea, long before India collided with Tibet to thrust up the greatest mountain barrier on earth. The North Face is framed on the right by the very hard West Ridge, rising from the saddle of the Lho La, and on the left by the even longer North East Ridge. Dropping down from a shoulder on the North East Ridge towards Changtse (North Peak) is the North Ridge. As you look at the mountain, two glaciers flow down either side of Changtse – the Rongbuk on the right and on the left the East Rongbuk, which is the approach to the North Col and North Ridge. The most prominent features on the North Face are two gullies cutting through the horizontal bands – the Great Couloir and the Hornbein Couloir.

Climbing History

When Charles Howard-Bury set out to lead the first expedition in 1921 virtually nothing was known of Everest and the team had to walk all the way from Darjeeling, through Sikkim, and across the Tibetan plateau – a pattern repeated on seven subsequent British pre-war attempts on the North Side. In 1924 Edward Norton, equipped with nailed boots, an ice axe, and a few layers of wool clothing, made a solo traverse into the top of the Great Couloir and got to within about 250m (800ft) of the summit. He did this without oxygen – a record unsurpassed for 54 years. Four days later George Mallory and Sandy Irvine disappeared attempting the crest of the North East Ridge. They took oxygen and it is conceivable that they actually climbed the formidable Second Step, the difficult rock barrier high on the ridge, to reach the summit but, in the absence of any evidence, the mountain was assumed to be still unclimbed.

Climbing Routes

① South Col/South East Ridge

Derided by the ignorant as the "yak route," the most popular way up Everest should never be underestimated. It is extremely long with a variety of difficulties (mainly on snow and ice) over four main sections: the dangerous Khumbu Icefall, the steady plod up the Western Cwm, the steeper 1500m (5000ft) high Lhotse Face, and the long, long summit day from the South Col, first up a broad couloir, then along the South East Ridge, with a final sting-in-the-tail at the Hillary Step, just below the top.

② South West Face Central Couloir

The first ascent in 1975 was a landmark in Himalayan climbing and the route has only twice been repeated (once in winter). From the Western Cwm, the route climbs the huge Y-shaped couloir, taking the left fork through the rockband then traversing back right across the face and up a gully to the South Summit and the final section of the East Ridge.

③ North Face – Messner Variant

During his 1980 solo jaunt, Reinhold Messner climbed about halfway up the North Ridge, then traversed to the right to the Great Couloir, which he followed, bearing right to the summit.

④ North Ridge/North East Ridge

The climbing proper starts from Advance Base at 6400m (21,000ft) on the East Rongbuk Glacier, making this line shorter than the normal South Col Route. Above the North Col, the route becomes increasingly rocky, with some awkward terrain and frequent vicious winds between 7000m (23,000ft) and 8000m (26,000ft). Although the top camp is higher than on the South Col Route, the actual terrain on the summit day is definitely harder. The legendary Second Step feels very precarious, even with the ladder placed by the Chinese. On the final section there are some delicate areas poised over an awesome drop down the North Face.

Soon after World War II Tibet was closed to foreigners, but Nepal opened its doors, allowing Eric Shipton's 1951 team to reconnoitre the Khumbu Icefall and reach the Western Cwm. The next year Sherpa Tenzing Norgay and Swiss companion Raymond Lambert, almost reached the summit by the South East Ridge. Tenzing Norgay returned in 1953 with John Hunt's British and Commonwealth expedition to make the historic first ascent and reach the summit with Edmund Hillary.

Nearly a thousand people have summited since the first ascent, most of them in the 1990s. Highlights since 1953 include the American traverse of 1963, when Tom Hornbein and Willi Unsoeld climbed an indirect line up the West Ridge, then descended to the South Col. The South West Face was snared by Chris Bonington's meticulously organized expedition in 1975, while the Russians climbed a harder, still unrepeated line to the left in 1982. The direct ascent of the very hard West Ridge "Integrale" was achieved by a large Yugoslav team in 1979. However the climb that really opened up the future was the first oxygen-free ascent of the mountain in 1978 by Reinhold Messner and Austrian climbing partner Peter Habeler, fulfilling predictions of the British pioneers who had been so close 50 years earlier. Messner and Habeler proved

that it was possible to climb Everest without supplementary oxygen, reaching the summit in just over 10 hours from the South Col. Even more remarkable was Habeler's astonishing one-hour descent back to the South Col. Two years later, Messner took another giant step into the unknown with his solo oxygen-free ascent of the North Ridge and North Face, made possible when Tibet was reopened to foreigners. He was the only person on the mountain at the time, marking an historic first – the only true solo ascent of the mountain.

Following Messner's lead, a small Australian team led by Tim Macartney-Snape climbed a direct line up the Great Couloir in 1984, summiting without oxygen. Then in 1986 the Swiss experts Jean Troillet and Erhard Loretan astounded the world by climbing the Japanese Direct/Hornbein Couloir in just 42 hours up and down.

The Kangshung Face, deemed "unclimbable" by Mallory, was first climbed in 1983 by a large American expedition, with George Lowe leading most of the spectacularly difficult lower buttress. In 1988 a four-man Anglo–American team, climbing without any Sherpa support or oxygen, made a new route further left, emerging at the South Col.

Leszek Cichy

Leszek Cichy and Krzysztof Wielicki defied the elements to make the first ascent of Everest in winter. The Polish climbers reached the summit on 17 February 1980, enduring temperatures below – 40°C. From the the South Col they climbed light, with only one oxygen bottle each, both of which ran out on the South Summit. Despite this, and the cold, they reached the top and returned safely. Since then, Everest has only seen two more winter ascents, by the Koreans and the Japanese. Cichy went on to become the first Pole to complete the Seven Summits. In 1996, Wielicki became the fifth person to climb all 14 8000m peaks.

left As the early morning sun catches distant peaks, climbers using oxygen approach the balcony on the South East Ridge, less than 500m from Everest's summit.

below Balanced precariously across a crevasse, a Sherpa prepares the route through the notorious Khumbu Icefall.

Scott on the South West Face

Unless Mallory and Irvine did so in 1924, no Briton stood on Everest's summit until 1975, when Dougal Haston and Doug Scott completed the much-tried ascent of the South West Face. Reaching the top at sunset, they spent the night on the South Summit, surviving the highest bivouac in history. For Doug Scott (shown above), Everest launched a remarkable sequence of Himalayan ascents and his eventual completion of the Seven Summits.

On the other side of the mountain, guided ascents of Everest have become a reality. Dick Bass, who completed his Seven Summits in 1985, showed what could be done with lots of grit, determination, and cash. Commercial expeditions have become the norm on Everest, with guiding companies such as Adventure Consultants and Himalayan Kingdoms taking comparatively inexperienced climbers to the top.

Over the years there have been startling disasters, starting with seven Sherpas who died in an avalanche below the North Col in 1922. In 1988 four Czechs disappeared in a storm, having made the second ascent of the South West Face. Their deaths were barely acknowledged in the West, but by 1996 new satellite communications ensured that, when eight people died in a storm, it attracted great media attention worldwide.

Incredibly, many have added further challenges to the already dangerous climb. In 1988 Jean-Marc Boivin descended by parapente, Pierre Tardivel skied down from the South Summit in 1992, and

two speed records were set – by Hans Kammerlander in his 1996 ascent of the North Col route in 16 hours 45 minutes and by Kaji Sherpa in his 1998 race up the longer South Col route in 20 hours 20 minutes.

Approach Routes

Most parties fly from Kathmandu to Lukla, then spend about one week walking up through the spectacular mountain scenery of Sola Khumbu, the Sherpas' homeland, passing Namche Bazaar and the famous Thyangboche monastery on the way to Base Camp, sited on the glacier at the foot of the Khumbu Icefall at 5364m (17,600ft). Sherpa staff normally organize porters and yaks to deliver baggage to Base Camp ready for the climbing team's arrival. With 10 extra days to spare, the full walk-in from the road-head at Jiri is a delightful way to slowly acclimatize.

Trucks can drive all the way to the Northern Base Camp at the tongue of the Rongbuk Glacier at 5200m (17,060ft), a few miles beyond Rongbuk monastery. It is possible to do the journey in just two days from Kathmandu. However, this sudden height gain could be very dangerous and an acclimatizing stopover, for instance at Nyalam, 3750m (12,300ft), just inside the border of Tibet, is frequently

below The "Magic Highway" of morraine, leads through the ice pinnacles of the East Rongbuk Glacier to Everest's North Side.

recommended. Even better is to spend a few days trekking in Nepal before driving up to the plateau. Yaks are normally hired to take supplies from Base Camp up the East Rongbuk Glacier to Advance Base beneath the North Col.

The northern approach road crosses the 5150m (16,900ft) Pang La with stunning views of Everest and the surrounding peaks. After crossing the pass to the village of Phadhruchi, the right branch leads to Rongbuk, while the left heads east then south into the Arun Valley to the village of Kharta, start of the delightful walk-in to the Kangshung Base Camp. Baggage is normally carried by yaks for five days over the Langma La, 5500m (18,045ft), or by a longer route crossing the lower Shao La. Base Camp is usually at 5200m (17,060ft) on the north bank of the Kangshung Glacier.

Climbing Everest Today

As if the sheer enormity of the undertaking itself wasn't enough, one of the biggest hurdles to climbing Everest is the cost. Each expedition is required to pay a royalty to the host country which, in the case of Nepal, starts at $70,000. The Tibetan (Chinese) royalty is considerably less, but it is tied to heavily inflated service costs which make the Tibetan side of the mountain almost as expensive to get to. While national teams still attempt the mountain, the majority of climbers are members of professionally led expeditions and pay a fee to the organizer for their place on the team. It is not unusual to have 15 or so expeditions on the standard routes at the same time, and in recent years as many as 30 people have reached the summit on the same day. But this familiarity with the mountain has brought dangers and, even with modern equipment and knowledge, Everest continues to provide a tremendous and risk-laden challenge for climbers.

Conservation

At 7900m (25,920ft) the South Col is often referred to as the highest garbage dump in the world. Empty oxygen bottles, old tents, other equipment, litter, and even dead bodies are found here. In an attempt to address this growing problem the Nepalese government now charges a several thousand dollar environmental deposit to each expedition. This deposit is paid back after the liaison officer has confirmed that the expedition has removed its

garbage and equipment from the mountain. Compostable, burnable, and some other rubbish can be deposited with an organization in Namche Bazaar. However, used oxygen bottles, gas canisters, and batteries have to be taken back to Kathmandu and exported out of the country. That, at any rate, is the theory.

A similar system operates on the Tibetan side, however the deposit is probably too small to have much of an effect. In practice, on both sides of the mountain, market forces apply: visiting Western climbers rarely have the strength to carry down their own used oxygen bottles and other debris and prefer instead to pay their Sherpas special bonuses to do the work for them.

Litter on the mountain has become an upsetting aesthetic problem, but of far more significance and complexity, certainly on the Nepalese side, are the potential problems of erosion and deforestation, which have arisen partly from the local population pressures and partly from the explosion of tourism in recent years. Visiting trekkers and climbers have an important role to play in preserving the mountain environment and can make a significant impact simply by ensuring that all of their cooking is done on either gas or kerosene stoves, rather than by using wood fires.

Rob Hall's Sacrifice

In the early 90s Rob Hall was admired as the master operator of guided Everest expeditions. Hall climbed Everest five times, but on his final ascent on 10 May 1996 found himself descending from the summit very late in the day, with a severely exhausted client, just as a ferocious gale hit the mountain. Rather than leave his client, Hall insisted heroically on remaining with Doug Hansen, who disappeared during the night. By morning, Hall was himself too weak to move. Vicious winds thwarted rescue attempts and Rob Hall is presumed to have died during the night, some time after his final radio call at 6.00pm on 11 May. Eight people died during that storm, including Yasuko Namba, who perished on the South Col after reaching her seventh summit. Just three years earlier, Hall's friend and regular climbing partner, Gary Ball (shown to the right of Rob Hall, above) with whom Hall climbed the Seven Summits in seven months, died of altitude sickness on Dhaulagiri in Nepal in 1993.

gerhard schmatz

success and tragedy on everest

Entwined in Everest's history of achievement there is immense tragedy. Gerhard Schmatz and his wife had already climbed four of the Seven Summits together when Hannelore failed to return from the summit of Everest. Had she survived, there is little doubt that she would have been the first woman to complete them all. Schmatz has since completed the Seven Summits as well as the highest peak on the seven largest islands.

In May 1973, after returning to Kathmandu from a successful Manaslu expedition, I wrote to the Nepalese Foreign Ministry for permission to climb Everest. I did not seriously expect it to be granted as there were too many other influential, interested parties and, quite apart from that, we did not have the financial support of an alpine organization or government office in our own country.

Over the next four years, my wife Hannelore and I climbed many mountains in many different countries. In June 1977 we returned from a successful expedition to Lhotse to find that permission had been granted for us to climb Mount Everest in the autumn of 1979.

We immediately began the extensive task of preparation. At that time, everything that we and the Sherpas would need for a three-month expedition had to be found in Europe and transported to Nepal, since it was still impossible to obtain the food and equipment necessary for

"Hannelore and I had been inseparable for 20 years, not only in our daily life together, but also in dangerous situations in the mountains of almost every continent."

such an expedition out there. Hannelore had an incredible talent when it came to obtaining and transporting the expedition gear. She wrote hundreds of letters to acquire what we needed and then collected everything together with a sponsored truck. With the help of friends, she spent months in a warehouse packing several tons of material into 30kg loads, which could be carried by the porters. The work was incredibly hard and monotonous.

Apart from Hannelore and me, there were six other experienced and successful climbers in the team: the New Zealander, Nick Banks; the Swiss, Hans von Känel; Germans Tilman Fischback, Günter Kämpfe, and Hermann Warth; and last but not least the American, Ray Genet, whom Hannelore and I had met while climbing McKinley in 1978. He had been living in Talkeetna at the foot of McKinley, often regarded as the world's coldest mountain, and had led and accompanied expeditions. He had climbed McKinley 35 times.

Although post-monsoon expeditions of earlier years did not often begin their approaches before September, we intended to follow the example of the 1975 British expedition and make our start during the rainy season. Our hope was to reach Base Camp right at the beginning of the climbing season, avoiding the very cold weather of October and jet stream winds.

After arriving in Kathmandu, however, the Ministry told us that the earliest we could leave for the mountain would be 10 August and that were not permitted to reach Base Camp before 1 September. After some tough negotiating, we were given permission to begin the 250km walk-in on 31 July, giving us a whole month for the approach to Base Camp. This was very useful for our acclimatization, but it could not make up for lost time.

After setting up Base Camp, we explored the Khumbu Icefall and tried to make it as safe as possible for the team with ladders and fixed ropes. The snow and ice conditions were terrible. Nevertheless, on 4 September, we set up our first camp at around 5900m, above the Icefall. The Western Cwm caused us some difficulties, although it is relatively flat. We had to overcome giant crevasses and a large number of vertical ice walls before we could begin to set up Camp 2 at a height of around 6300m.

The Lhotse Face was covered in deep snow. It had changed so much since our 1977 climb that we had to take a completely different route. At about 7200m on the face, we set up Camp 3, which was protected by a vertical wall of ice.

Higher up the Lhotse Face, at about 7500m, we had to pass the so-called Yellow Band. Then we crossed the Geneva Spur to reach the South Col (7986m), the lowest point between Lhotse and Everest. Here we set up our top camp on 24 September.

Right at the beginning of the expedition, Hannelore had indicated several times that her goal was the South Col. But when she found that she was in top physical condition and going as well as the other team members, Hannelore felt she should attempt to reach the summit. Even so, she was still cautious and decided to proceed with two experienced Sherpas as an independent party.

Glad to have reached the South Col and ready for the final stage, we were forced by a snowstorm to return to Base Camp. Here, we decided we would proceed in two groups rather than three. The first group consisted of Hermann and Hans, two Sherpas, and myself. We wanted to spare Hannelore the work of breaking the track. The second group consisted of the remaining five team members and three Sherpas.

On 28 September, the weather improved again and we began the final ascent. After three days the first group reached the South Col once more. At 3am on 1 October, after a reasonable night, we began to prepare for our summit climb. Everything took longer at this altitude, especially making tea. At 6am we were at last ready to set off. On one rope were Hermann, Hans, and the Sherpa Lhakpa, on the other myself followed by Sherpa Pertemba. The weather was middling. Below and high above us were layers of cloud. But it was relatively warm and unusually calm. The snow and ice conditions were very bad. We would never have expected such soft snow in a region so exposed to the wind.

We sometimes sank in up to our knees, which considerably hampered our progress. Just before noon, we reached the southern summit of Everest (8760m). We could see the route of ascent we now had to follow. First there was a razor-sharp ridge of ice, then the steep exposed Hillary Step that had proved so troublesome on the first ascent.

We also had trouble with the Hillary Step. Due to the steepness and the snow conditions, we could not climb it. The snow was too soft to kick reliable steps and too deep to find ice for the crampons. From our narrow perch on the ridge there was a 4000m drop to the east and an almost 2500m drop to the west. But at last, we found some firm rock to climb up and we knew that our goal could not be far off.

At around 2pm, overjoyed, we reached the summit. We hugged and congratulated each other on our success. The pennants were taken out of our rucksacks and triumphant photos taken. Although it was now starting to snow, time seemed to fly past.

After about an hour, we began our descent. Again the Hillary Step proved difficult, but the rest of the descent passed without a problem, and we reached the South Col just before 7pm, after night had fallen.

above Two climbers make their way along the corniced South East Ridge as they approach the Hillary Step on their way to the summit.

left Hannelore Schmatz enjoys the sunshine while leading a rope through the Khumbu Icefall, on her way to the summit of Everest.

success and tragedy on everest

47

The second party had already arrived there at noon. They congratulated us on our success and shared our delight. After Hannelore hugged me, Pertemba and I described the bad snow and ice conditions. We asked her to give up her decision to climb to the summit. Somewhat indignantly, Hannelore told us that we shouldn't try to dampen her enthusiasm. Günter, who was listening, pointed out Hannelore's excellent physical condition and said that she had climbed to South Col from Camp 3 that day without any problems and in good time. After our talk we crawled back into our tents to find sleep.

The members of the second group started their preparations very early. At around 5am, they left camp. Tilman and Sherpa Ang Phurba made up the first rope party, Nick, Günter, and Ray the second, and Hannelore and the two Sherpas, Ang Jangbu and Sundare, the third.

Those of us who had been to the summit the day before descended as quickly as possible to Camp 2, almost 2000m below. We kept casting worried looks at the sky, as the weather was visibly deteriorating. We did not think that our friends would continue with their ascent and expected them to turn around and come back. That evening, our assumption was proven wrong. At 6pm the first roped party arrived back at the South Col, and the news reached us by radio that everyone, including Hannelore, had made it to the summit. We were overjoyed.

We went to the mess tent and in high spirits celebrated our success. We established that our Everest expedition was: the smallest to reach the summit; the quickest to date (32 days); and the first where all members had reached the summit. Moreover, I was the first person over 50 to summit. As if this weren't enough, Hannelore and I were the first married couple to have conquered Everest.

Our joy was somewhat dampened however, when our friends told us via walkie-talkie that on his arrival at the South Col, Sherpa Ang Jangbu had told them that Ray, Hannelore, and Sherpa Sundare had decided to bivouac on the South East Ridge. We immediately radioed the Sherpas in Camp 3 and told them to leave for the South Col first thing in the morning to provide whatever help they could. But, despite the news, our fears were not too great, as we knew that Ray was with the party on the South East Ridge. On McKinley he was regarded as the complete expert in all aspects of survival and snow-cave construction.

We later learned that the climb had proceeded as planned, except for the fact that Ray decided to climb alone. Apparently, the walking pace of the others did not suit him. The weather conditions were better than we, further down, had thought. Günter spoke to Hannelore shortly before she reached the summit. She seemed in good physical condition. Due to worsening weather, they didn't stay on the summit long.

The descent via the South Summit also passed without mishap. Ray, who had gone up by himself, had joined Hannelore's rope on the way back. Later, when his oxygen ran out at a height of around 8500m, he refused to go on. He wanted to bivouac. Hannelore and Sherpa Sundare stayed with Ray while Sherpa Ang Jangbu descended to the South Col. Ray tried to dig a snow cave that, due to the softness of the snow, he was only half able to complete.

above Hannelore and Gerhard Schmatz, and Herman Warth make their way through the Khumbu Icefall.

left Climbers trek across the 1500m high Lhotse Face as the sun illuminates spectacular high cloud formations over the summit of Lhotse.

With the onset of darkness, a high-altitude storm set in that lasted throughout the night. The following morning Ray died. Hannelore and Sherpa Sundare had to continue the descent without him in a state of shock and immense depression. Finally, at a height of about 8300m, Hannelore sat down and, with the words "water, water…" she too died. Sundare was devastated.

At this point, Sherpa Ang Nawang and Tilman Fischbach had left camp in order to try to reach them. When they met Sherpa Sundare, he told them the awful news. As he was also near to death from exhaustion and obviously badly frostbitten, the two climbers immediately took him back to camp.

I had to hear about all of this while stuck in Camp 2 under the South West Face of Everest, unable to do anything at all to help. I was so bewildered that I could only vaguely understand the tragedy and the consequences of what had happened.

Of course, you hear again and again of tragic accidents that abruptly put an end to a close human relationship. But to be affected myself in a place so hostile and in such an extreme situation, was beyond my comprehension. Hannelore and I had been inseparable for 20 years, not only in our daily life together, but also in dangerous situations in the mountains of almost every continent.

Despite my dismay, I was forced to continue what Hannelore had done with such enthusiasm. In the camps she knew exactly where everything was in the chaos of boxes and sacks. I was the expedition leader, but I had no idea of the small but important details. In my extreme grief, I was forced to carry on her job.

Our long, successful, but extremely tragic journey eventually came to an end, and the team arrived home. I could claim to have climbed the world's highest mountain, but that same mountain had claimed my wife and my friend. They are still up there, high among the mountains that so enriched all of our lives. In every image of Everest I see, there is Hannelore…

junko tabei

everest's first lady

In 1975, Junko Tabei became the first woman to climb Everest. She was the leader of the first all-female attempt on the mountain, at a time when merely obtaining a permit took time and tenacity. She was able to sustain her single-mindedness on the climb itself, reaching the summit to set one of the most important landmarks in the history of women's mountaineering. Tabei proved that in the mountains, women could achieve anything that men could, even the highest point on the planet. Her ascent shattered masculine misconceptions, paving the way for the many outstanding climbs made by talented women climbers since then. It would only be a matter of time before a woman climbed Everest solo and without the assistance of supplementary oxygen.

It was March 1971 when we first applied for a permit to climb Everest for our expedition, which would consist only of women. We were well aware of the numerous applications being submitted to the Nepalese government each year and of the unfortunate reality that they would only issue a permit for two expedition parties each year – one for the spring and one for the autumn. Prepared for this lengthy process, we

joined the queue and waited our turn. (Fortunately, the situation has changed in recent years and many parties can obtain permission simultaneously even for mid-winter expeditions.)

A year and a half later, in August 1972, when my daughter was just five months old, we eventually received the news that our application had been approved for spring 1975. I thought the timing was good as my child would be three years old then, so my absence should not be a problem. I began, therefore, to seek extra climbing partners. Although nowadays we see middle-aged and elderly people in the mountains, at that time there were mainly young people at Shinjuku and Ueno (railway terminal stations in Tokyo) taking trains to the mountain areas. We tried to find women in climbing gear at the railway stations or in the mountains and we asked around, "Wouldn't you like to join us in an ascent of Mount Everest?" Whenever I heard of mountaineering clubs with good women members, I went to see them.

Most of the women exclaimed, "It's a wonderful idea to go to the Himalayas. I want to see Mount Everest once in my life!" Then they continued by saying, "I wish to go, however, I do not have the climbing skills, physical strength, or money." This was the most common response among the women I surveyed. Of course you need physical strength and climbing skills for Himalayan climbing, but there are other essential factors, including an extremely strong desire to keep going whatever happens and the mentality to find a way out when you get into the deepest kinds of trouble.

It was really difficult to collect donations for the expedition at that time, since 1973 was the year when the Japanese economy was suffering as a result of the oil crisis. We tried to economize in every way possible, such as by restricting the size of our cups to small ones – using a big mug would have made us drink more tea and so consume more fuel in making it. We made heat-insulation bags for batteries from old woollen sweaters; the wool was put into a nylon cloth cover, which was originally a part of the plastic cover for cars. Batteries that had been put into these bags, and then inside our sleeping bags, could be used for longer. We converted empty plastic mayonnaise bottles into water bottles. We wanted to restrict the weight of our gear as much as possible, so we even removed the cardboard core from toilet rolls and took the wrapping papers off cakes and candies.

We did everything we could to minimize the size of our baggage and our budget. Everything we took was carefully considered, no matter how small it was. We knew that all the small things would easily accumulate in size as well in terms of cost. We spent 1400 days carrying out our full preparations and working out our strategies. The actual time we spent on the climbing expedition itself was just 130 days, which was less than 10 per cent of the total time. Then we were on the summit for just a few hours, which, in spite of its significance, felt like the most fleeting of moments.

left Carrying the Japanese flag, Junko Tabei climbs the Lhotse Face during her historic first female ascent of Everest.

right This rare view from the top of Lhotse shows the South East Ridge of Everest with the South Col at its base.

yasuko namba
her last diary

On 10 May 1996, Yasuko Namba became the second Japanese woman to summit Everest, completing her Seven Summits at the same time. Tragically, she perished during the descent, together with seven others in one of Everest's worst disasters.

15 April The religious Nepali ritual "Puja," which prays for a safe climb, was conducted today. It was a very pleasant ceremony. I almost feel that it is enough for me to just enjoy the life at the Base Camp.

19 April The view from Camp 2 is as excellent as everyone said. Now I know why people are attracted to come to Everest. At the same time I feel a little scared to think of climbing the bitterly frozen Lhotse Face, which rises high in front of me. Why does one climb a mountain? It might be essential for one to have some dream of an objective to accomplish. Climbing mountains is one of the easy ways to do so and we could also have the joy of being in nature.

21 to 25 April Rest at the Base Camp.

26 to 30 April Climbing up and down to Camp 3 for acclimatization.

26 April It is indeed true that Everest is a tough mountain. I admire everyone who has climbed this mountain, however they did it.

2 May Why am I here? I wish that the expedition would end as soon as possible whether or not I reach the summit. I am thinking about everything negatively today. I should think in a more positive way.

5 May (A fax in reply to her husband, Kenichi):

My dearest Ken, Thank you for your fax with your kind words of advice. While I was reading the fax tears filled my eyes. You are the only one who thinks about me and really speaks to me. I really am moved deeply in my heart. So once I am back home, I will be "more" generous to you than ever before. Your fax made me so relaxed. It seems there is more snow than usual in this season and even the very strong Yugoslavian party could not reach the summit. The next time I can fax you is when I return to the Base Camp. I am always thinking of your gentle face and the spring greenery of Tokyo. Lots of love and a big hug from the Base Camp of Mount Everest. Yasu

6 May Started from Base Camp at 5am and arrived at Camp 2 at 12.50. Some seracs were melting and the crevasses are becoming deeper. I am feeling much lighter and I pant less than before.

7 May Rest day; Scott Fischer of the American expedition came to see us.

That was Yasuko Namba's last diary entry. She reached the summit at 2.30pm on 10 May. During the descent she was caught in a devilish blizzard and collapsed on the South Col. One year later her body was found and carried down to Base Camp. Her remains were taken home by her husband, after a cremation with Tibetan Buddhist rituals in the foothills of Mount Everest.

The freight we brought from Japan amounted to about 11 tons, while the extra food that we bought in local markets reached nearly four tons. So we had a combined total of 15 tons that had to be carried by yaks and porters to the Base Camp, pitched at 5350m. Then our gear was carried up to the higher camps by Sherpas and the party members. From one camp on to the next, we climbed step by step in order to become acclimatized to the high altitude. Some of us were caught by avalanches but survived and, in spite of our acclimitization, quite a few of us suffered from altitude sickness.

With the blessings of good weather, Sherpa Ang Tsering and I eventually reached the height of 8848m. I shouted into the radio: "Please convey my full appreciation to everyone in the party and the Sherpas," and in my mind I appreciated the solid foundation of the 1400 days of preparation.

"We wanted to restrict the weight of our gear as much as possible, so we even removed the cardboard core from toilet rolls..."

Kilimanjaro
Marangu Route
23.8.84

jeff shea
the spirit of tibet

Though the Tibetan side of Everest is regarded as a tougher climb than the Nepalese side, many climbers still prefer Tibet. Barren and windswept, with the striking pyramid of Everest visible for many miles, Tibet makes a lasting impression. In spring 1995, climbers enjoyed unprecedented good weather on the Tibetan side. By the time the monsoon spilled over the mountain from Nepal, 67 climbers had succeeded on the North Ridge. But Everest was no pushover, as Jeff Shea explains...

After sailing across the ocean and travelling many miles by land, I reached the ridge above Namche Bazaar in Nepal and spied the windblown cap of Mount Everest for the first time in my life. During the weeks that followed, I had vague aspirations about climbing the mountain, but they seemed like pipe dreams. My first grapplings with Himalayan altitude, as I panted up a 6000m peak a few weeks later, emphasized Everest's unattainableness. The Himalayan magnificence was upon me, more impressive than I could have imagined, the sheer size dwarfing any other mountain range in the world many times over.

On that journey in 1983, I stood at Kala Patar and surveyed the grand vista of icy peaks; I huddled in the warm emptiness of a mess tent at the South Col Base Camp at 5200m, in awe of those men and women who were actually on an Everest expedition; I breathed in the Tibetan culture at Thyangboche Monastery during the Mani Rimdu festival, delighted, marvelling over the colour and richness of the costumes of the masked dancers. As a child might view it, it was all new and exciting. Unable to sleep and lured by the moonlight, I stepped into the crisp December night, scrambling above the rooftops of Thyangboche. In the vast canyon formed by Ama Dablam and the Everest massif, the perfect silence was suddenly broken by the echoing trumpet of the monastery's ancient horns, dispelling evil spirits and resounding with the purity of good intent. Magic! I came away from my first Himalayan trip knowing why the local animists attributed god-like powers to the mountains. Indeed, they seemed to have a spirit of their own.

Twelve years later, I found myself lured again by the Himalayas. Except this time I went to the North Side of Everest, and this time I was not a trekker, but a climber. On the journey from Lhasa — at the top of the astonishing monastic ruins of Xegar — Cho Oyu, Shisha Pangma, and Makalu appeared amid the clouds. While there, a Xegarian monk portended, "You see Everest, good luck. You no see Everest, good luck. You no see

Everest, no good luck." Just as we gathered to leave, the clouds cleared to reveal Everest in its all glory, towering over the rest of the landscape.

Jumping off the back of the gear truck, dusted from head to toe, and nauseous from the drive to 5200m, I set up my tent, where it would remain for two months. It was 12 April 1995. At Base Camp, I wrote:

"Last night was the worst night I've had. I was dehydrated and was still adjusting to the altitude here. At times like that, the mental battle is worse than the physical one. To resist thoughts of despair takes a strong will, and yet to discern when it is advisable to abandon a project takes good judgement. I do not feel it is, on one hand, necessary to make the summit of this mountain, but still, to abandon it now would render all the effort I took to get here a folly. I have risked an awful lot to climb this mountain...The greatest part of this journey is not the climb but in

right Strewn with colourful prayer flags and frequented by climbers, the Rongbuk Monastery in Tibet provides breathtaking views of the North Side of Everest.

			1995			

| Aconcagua
Normal Route
29.1.93 | McKinley
West Buttress
30.5.93 | Everest
North Ridge
24.5.95 | Kosciuszko
Normal Route
2.5.96 | Elbrus
Normal Route
29.8.96 | Vinson
Normal Route
22.1.97 |

all the other combined sights and sounds. The people here are a rather amazing collection of accomplished individuals. Some are great mountaineers. Some are adventurers and photographers, others doctors, or women attempting firsts in the climbing world."

The Base Camp affords a sweeping panorama of Changtse, the North Ridge, the Great Couloir, the North Face, and the summit pyramid, with the jet stream sailing off in a vaporous plume. The route winds clockwise around Changtse, through the ice pinnacles of the East Rongbuk Glacier. Twenty-one kilometres of trail ends at Advanced Base Camp (ABC) in full view of the North Col and the summit pyramid.

Resisting the trend to rush headlong to ABC, I followed the advice of Australian Jon Muir, who reckoned the best way to acclimatize was to simply take it easy and hang out at Base Camp. For 12 days I did so.

I arrived at ABC on 25 April. Two days later, I traversed the glacier to the foot of the precipitous slope leading to the North Col, a picturesque mass of tumbling house-size blocks of ice that must be negotiated to reach the Col itself. Light avalanches rumbled off to my left from the flanks of the North East Ridge. A seldom-discussed Everest disaster occurred in June 1922, on the second-ever expedition to the mountain, when the slope I was about to climb avalanched, taking the lives of seven porters. In all, avalanches from the slopes below the North Col have killed at least 16 people, nearly as many as the far more notorious Khumbu Icefall.

My acclimatization schedule sent me to the Col four times. Although in some places it was steep enough to make an unroped fall fatal, the snow was soft and felt secure. Wending my way around the blocks of

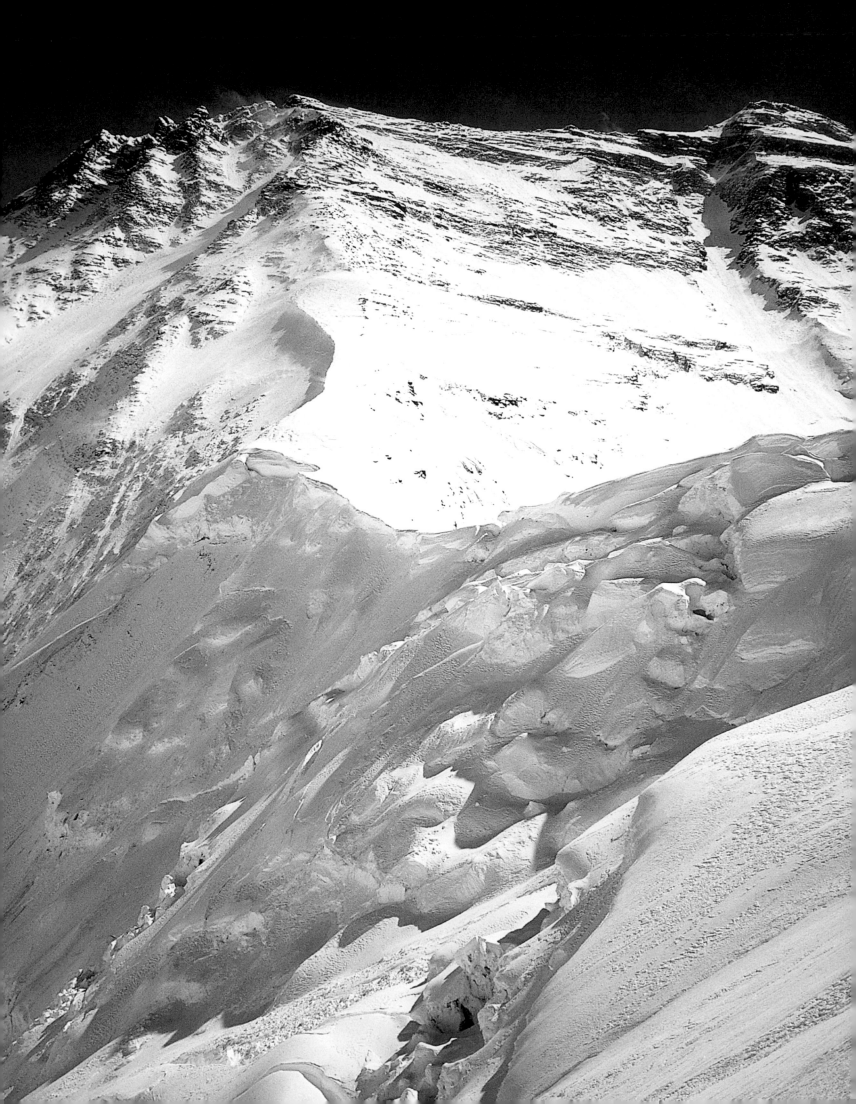

ice brought me to the Col at 7050m, affording a clear view of the North Face, its enormous Great Couloir ending in an ice cliff of unimaginable dimensions. The summit seemed as if you could reach out and touch it. The tents were nestled on the leeward side of an ice buttress, sheltered from the 70 knot winds that scoured the North Face.

On 30 April, I climbed to Camp 2 at 7600m. From the North Col, the route continues on a wide, gradually steepening saddle of snow. At first, I was comfortable as the sun was out and the wind was just a breeze. Almost imperceptibly, the conditions deteriorated. Visibility shrank to a few metres and the chill crept through my heavily insulated boots. The dwindling of my inner core's heat became a concern. I had been using the fixed ropes to safeguard a fall, only to discover that the top snow stake holding them slid easily out of the ice. At the top of the snow saddle, I arrived at a pair of tents flapping violently in the wind.

My partner Fred Zalokar and I feebly made unappetizing soup, and then scooped our spilled water from the tent floor. I slept restlessly, constantly aware that the wind was blowing like crazy. I wondered what might happen if the tent ripped apart. The next morning, Fred and I took seemingly forever to get ready to descend. Thoughts of putting our boots on occasionally roused us from our altitude-induced stupor long enough for us to look up from our sleeping bags, then we would slide back into a senseless haze. It took me 11 days at lower altitudes to recover from my visit to 7500m, most of it spent at Base Camp. I wrote:

"I have been like a zombie since I returned from up above. I have been bothered by dry throat, lethargy, shortness of breath, stomach aches, diarrhoea, and feelings of claustrophobia since I arrived back here at Base Camp. My lower lip is a blistered mess. I must have forgotten one morning (just one!) to properly protect it, and now it is a maze of blood, blisters, and puffiness. Also, I have been coughing since I have been here. It is like trying to scratch an itch that I cannot reach.

We sit down here at Base Camp day after day watching the weather change. In the morning it might be clear, and by afternoon, snowing. The weather above all scares me when it comes to this mountain. If I am going to make a summit attempt, I will only do so, as I now see it, when the skies are clear and calm for as far as you can see. I figure this is the only day that has any chance of being 'reasonably safe' to climb Mount Everest."

On 12 May, I was back at Camp 2. I felt stronger, the minor miracle of one month's acclimatization. Above Camp 2, the route ascends through a patchwork of rock and packed snow. I climbed alone enjoying the sunny, windy solitude. When I reached 8000m above a 30° snowfield, I considered my acclimatization completed. It was time to descend and shore up my strength for a summit attempt. I spent a solid week eating at ABC to regain some of the 14kg lost from my 82kg frame.

One evening during my respite at ABC, a buoyant Alison Hargreaves popped into our mess tent for a visit – she appeared as fresh as she did on the flight to Lhasa at the beginning of the expedition, when I absurdly mistook her for a non-climbing companion of another climber! She had just successfully completed an unassisted climb without

"It is rumoured that in 1952, when the North Side was off-limits to Westerners, six Russian climbers were literally blown off the face of the mountain."

above With the last of major difficulties surmounted, Lama Dorje makes his way towards the final summit pyramid.

left The avalanche-prone slopes of the North Col lead to the North Ridge, rising left of centre to the skyline with summit to the right.

oxygen. Her goal was to climb the three highest mountains in the world in one year. Three months later she was dead, having been caught in a storm on her way down from the summit of K2.

On 20 May I was back at the Col with Yves Detry, Patrick Hache, and Andre Tremouliere. The next morning, radio reports informed us that two climbers were blocked by high winds for the third day in a row at Camp 3. Given it was late in the season, I concluded wrongly that this year's unusually good weather was at an end.

The next morning, I laced up my crampons and grabbed my ice axe, preparing to descend. Yves, a constant source of good cheer, inquired where I was going. When he reminded me of their special stockpile of French cheese, sausage, and crackers, my resolve to abandon camp vanished. As if to validate my gastronomical instincts – and Yves' experienced advice – the winds died down during the night, allowing us to move up the saddle the next morning. Arriving at Camp 2, my French companions declared that the wind, having brewed up again, was advising us against continuing. I "leaned into it" and moved up a few hundred metres to camp with Lakpa Gelu and Lama Dorje of Nepal.

The following morning, in fine weather, Lakpa, Lama, and I, first passed the 8000m snowfield, then climbed a snow gully to arrive at Camp 3 by early afternoon. The sloping high camp lay at the rocky base of the so-called Yellow Band, a place where finding protection from the wind was extremely difficult. It is rumoured that in 1952, when the North Side was off-limits to Westerners, six accomplished Russian climbers were literally blown off the face of the mountain from the Camp 3 area.

We took a meal in the late afternoon and bedded down while the sun was still shining. After six weeks of restless nights, I now used supplemental oxygen for the first time. My frigid fingers and toes felt a sudden rush of warmth, and I slipped away to dream-filled and euphoric slumber.

At 10pm I awoke, my lungs pulling vainly for air on an empty bottle. We drank tea and checked our gear, departing just after midnight. It was pitch black. Our vision was confined to the narrow beams of our headlamps. We moved straight up through the snow and rock gullies, seemingly for hours. I longed for an end to the incessant upward effort. We then began traversing down and to the right, signalling that we had arrived at the North East Ridge itself. The air was remarkably still. Horizontally traversing an exposed patch of snow to a fixed line, we jumared up and around the First Step. Approaching the fabled Second Step, we ascended sloping terraces of crampon-scratched shale only a boot wide. I used my axe like a walking stick to balance on my crampon points. Perhaps fortunately, the moonless darkness rendered the drop-off invisible. Seventy-one years earlier, in 1924, Mallory and Irving were last seen alive in this area. The shelves of shale supported old loose ropes, dubiously secured by pitons, in some cases no more than flat, rusting iron anchors placed into cracks of eroding, stratified rock. The ropes' false security was worrying. However, a week later another climber, while coughing up bowlfuls of lung matter on descent, was held by them when he slipped.

> **"I glanced back, shaken by the commitment I had made. If I fell, could I self-arrest? More likely I would hurtle uncontrollably down the North Face."**

At about 4am we scrambled up rocks to the foot of the Second Step, a high, ungainly outcrop of rock at 8600m. Visible from Base Camp, this was the crux of the North Ridge Route. In 1975, the Chinese left a relic of their epic ascent: the "Chinese Ladder." Lakpa stepped onto it and climbed to the top rung. Then, wrapping his forearm around a half dozen fraying ropes that dangled from above, he hoisted himself up and out of view. As I came over the edge of the Second Step, I was transfixed by the awesome view. The North East Ridge was bathed in the golden light of dawn and the summit pyramid looked remarkably close.

After passing the Third Step, the final rock obstacle on the ridge, the route came within one metre of the East Face. I could not resist leaning over it to check it out. Space catapulted, near-vertically, thousands of metres to a valley that spread out eastwards towards Kanchenjunga.

At 8750m, a final snowfield separated us from a platform from where, I had been told, the summit was an "easy walk." Near its top, Lama disappeared to the right among some rocks. I followed Lakpa up to the left, remaining on the snow unroped. My ice axe flew back at me, having hit solid ice just under the surface. I glanced back and was a bit shaken by the meaning of the commitment I had made. If I fell, could I self-arrest? More likely I would hurtle uncontrollably down the North Face. It being an exceptionally fine day and only about 8am, I afforded myself the luxury of chopping steps for security. After labouring for half an hour, I came to a frayed remnant of rope. Lakpa peered over the platform and motioned to me that it would hold. I clipped in and climbed the remaining 20m to the platform.

The summit of Everest was in full view, shimmering, dream-like, about 100m away. I warned myself not to let my guard down. As a testament to the need for vigilance, a few days later Bob Hempstead slipped on this "easy ground" and rocketed head-first on his back to the brink of the North Face. Swiftly reacting, he caught himself with outstretched arms on rocks. He peered over his shoulder, staring down the awful 3000m precipice. Greg Child and Ang Babu found stray rope and pulled Bob to safety.

As I approached the highest point on the globe, I felt as if the spirit of the mountain touched me. At 9am, Lakpa radioed, "T'ree people summit! T'ree people summit!" During 40 minutes of celebration and photography, I reminded myself that the day was not done. At least 15 people have died while descending from the top of Everest.

During the eight-hour descent I suffered extreme dehydration, which was made worse by the effects of the dry ambient air and bottled oxygen. When I tried to swallow, I gagged, then flew into a fit of dry retching. Later, the condition grew serious. I reached inside my mouth and extracted a strange brownish gel that had formed over my teeth and gums; I discovered later that some of the enamel of my teeth had flaked off. The mixing bag of my oxygen mask became a deflated sack of ice. About 100m above Camp 3 I ground to a halt, my oxygen having run out completely. At 6pm I laid outside the tents, stretched to my limit, revelling silently that I had made it. I spent the night without dinner, then headed to the North Col the following day.

After our expedition, at an American Himalayan Foundation event, Bob Hempstead and I found ourselves sharing an elevator with another Everest summiteer. We were shaking hands with Sir Edmund Hillary! Bob blurted out, "We summited Everest." I naively added, "From the North Ridge!" A man of impressive stature, Sir Edmund smiled down on us, as if beaming approval on the progeny of his pioneering. But I sensed his mind was far away. Perhaps he was thinking about the speech he would give that evening, covering his climbing career and his school building programme in the Sola Khumbu. Somehow I sensed that long ago he had recognized that reaching the summit of Everest was secondary to the effort of helping those people who had helped us to get there in the first place.

The thrill of reaching the top of Everest is equalled by the privilege of having been to Tibet, and I will never forget its landscape and its native people. Later that year, I dedicated my Seven Summits adventure to the Dalai Lama's dream of Tibet as a World Park, a wildlife refuge, and non-nuclear Zone of Peace.

right Mask off and hood down, Jeff Shea stands triumphant on the summit of Everest while climbing companion Lakpa Gelu, a Sherpa from Nepal, looks on.

aconcagua

The "Stone Sentinel" of South America, Aconcagua is the second highest of the Seven Summits. While Everest is the world's highest mountain, Aconcagua is a worthy number two. It is not only the highest mountain on the South American continent, but in the whole of the Americas.

Aconcagua is also often referred to as the highest mountain in the western hemisphere; of similar importance, but much less reported, is that it is the highest mountain in the southern hemisphere.

The Andes is the longest mountain range in the world with over 7000km (4500 miles) of continuous waves of peaks, from the shores of the Caribbean in the north to Cape Horn in Chile in the south. Technically, Aconcagua lies to the east of the main Andean chain, in the smaller Frontal Range, just inside Argentina's border with Chile. This is a barren region and snowfall is comparatively light; Aconcagua is not adorned with the spectacular corniced ridges and fluted ice faces that are so striking on other South American mountains.

Aconcagua is shaped rather like a wedge. The gentle slope faces northwest, ending at an enormous col known as Nido del Condores (the Condor's Nest). This col can be gained from the Horcones Valley to the west or the Vacas Valley to the east, and it provides the easiest route up the mountain. The rocky West Face of Aconcagua is a huge expanse of loose gullies and buttresses – it is not good for climbing but is a splendid sight when bathed in the red light of the setting sun. The east side is much colder and the large Polish Glacier flows down sharply from near the top of the South East Ridge. The steep side of the wedge is the colossal South Face, a 2400m (8000ft) wall of rock and ice which is capped by Aconcagua's wind-beaten North and South Summits.

Aconcagua can often be mistaken for an eroded volcano and is actually built up from layers and layers of volcanic sediments, which were thrust up in the forming of the Andes. Interestingly, the relatively close proximity of Aconcagua to the Chilean Trench in the Pacific Ocean creates the biggest "wrinkle" in the face of the Earth, with a significant difference in altitude amounting to almost 14,000m (46,000ft).

Weather

The best months for climbing Aconcagua are December to March, though November is quickly becoming a popular time. During the winter months from May to August, most of the area is snow covered and is extremely windy. At times the road between Santiago, Chile, and Mendoza, Argentina can be impassable due to the major snowstorms and their effects on roads. Even during the finest months, December to February, wind can be quite extreme above a height of 5000m (16,400ft). It is not too uncommon to see a big lenticular cloud around the summit, indicating extremely high winds. This weather phenomenon is referred to as Viento Blanco (White Wind) and a summit attempt is extremely dangerous and nearly impossible under such circumstances. Viento Blanco has been known to blow for days on end.

Vegetation and wildlife

The arid climate in the area makes the valleys leading up to Aconcagua look barren and desolate. In the lower areas, below 2500m (8000ft), only hardy bushes and grasses are found. Only a few areas have any trees, and these are usually eucalypti, planted by man. The wildlife is similarly sparse. Lucky climbers may see the alpaca, a smaller cousin of the llama. The mountain lion, or puma, is present, but also very difficult to see. Birds are just as sparse, but a sudden flutter of a hummingbird is quite common. Above 4000m (13,000ft) the area is almost

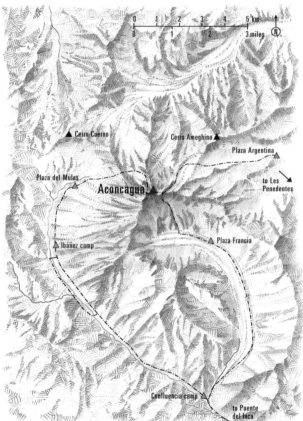

"Aconcagua's proximity to the Chilean Trench in the Pacific Ocean creates the biggest wrinkle in the face of the Earth."

Messner's South Face Solo

In January 1974 Reinhold Messner led a team to attempt a direct route on the South Face of Aconcagua. The team, which included Oswald Oelz, climbed the original French Route to the base of the summit headwall, where the French Route moves right towards the South East Ridge. Messner and Jörgl Mayer then set off up the ice slope which leads directly to the col between the North and South Summits. Mayer was climbing too slowly to reach the summit and still have time to descend the same day, so he waited on a ledge while Messner climbed the last 600m (2000ft) to the summit alone.

Climbing Routes

① **Normal Route** (not shown)
This, the most popular route on the mountain, poses few technical challenges, apart from the obvious ones of altitude and weather. Two to three camps are used on the way. The final section of the climb is a steep scree-filled gully, the notorious Canaleta.

② **Polish Glacier**
This fine line climbs the left side of the Polish Glacier on the East Face of the mountain. From a camp at about 6000m (19,700ft), the route is climbed in one day. A more direct version has also been climbed.

③ **South Face, French Route**
This route takes the central spur of the Face. It involves rock climbing on far from perfect rock and steep snow, and mixed climbing to reach the South East Ridge, close to the summit. At the top, the 1974 Messner variation (④) is often used, finishing at the ridge between the South and North Summits.

devoid of any kind of life and the environment is desert-like. There are, however, smaller flowers, that are naturally camouflaged to resemble small rocks. They show an amazing adaptation to the tough climate in which they live.

Exploration and Climbing History

The Inca Indians started to explore the high Andes long before Colombus discovered the New World. They were drawn to the summits for religious reasons, and many burial sites and artefacts have been found in remarkably high places. The highest such discovery to date is on the summit of Llullaillaco, a mountain a few hundred kilometres north of Aconcagua, at 6720m (22,050ft).

On Aconcagua itself, the skeleton of a guanaco (a wild animal related to the llama) was found on the ridge connecting the North and South Summits. It is unlikely that a guanaco would have climbed there by itself, but no other evidence has been found that would indicate that the Incas were responsible for its demise. In 1985 a mummy was discovered on one of Aconcagua's outlying peaks, at an altitude of about 5200m (17,000ft). Although there is no evidence to suggest that the Inca Indians climbed to the summit of the mountain, it is not beyond the realms of possibility that they did so hundreds of years before the first recorded ascent was made. The name Aconcagua comes from the word

South Face

quechua, which in the language of the Inca means stone sentinel.

In the early 19th century, the area was visited on many occasions; once by Charles Darwin. The first serious attempt to climb the mountain was in 1883, when the then well-known alpinist Paul Güssfeldt approached the peak from the Chilean side. He made a determined attempt, reaching 6560m (21,522ft) on the North West Ridge.

In late 1896 an expedition led by the Englishman Edward Fitzgerald, camped at the head of Horcones Valley, close to today's Base Camp for the Normal Route. With him was another English climber, Stuart Vines, and several Swiss guides, including Matthias Zurbriggen. After weeks of building camps and reconnoitring up the northwestern slopes, Matthias Zurbriggen managed to reach the summit alone on 14 January 1897. Other members of the expedition reached the summit a month later, though not Fitzgerald himself.

The next important ascent of the mountain was made in 1934 by a group of Polish climbers. On 9 March four of them climbed the glacier on the upper part of the East Face. Despite the wind and the low temperatures, they reached the summit from a camp at 6300m (20,200ft). The whole climb was done alpine style – without fixed camps – making their ascent particularly impressive for its time. The glacier is now known as the Polish Glacier.

In the 1950s, attention was drawn to the impressive South Face. This incredibly high face is both difficult and dangerous, with steep loose rock between ice cliffs and glaciers, layered like a treacherous birthday cake. As Aconcagua is in the southern hemisphere, the South Face receives little sunshine and is like a North Face in the Alps or the Himalayas. In 1953 the western boundary of the South Face, the long South West Ridge, was

East Face

climbed. A year later, a French expedition led by René Ferlet established a Base Camp on the Inferior Horcones Glacier, below the South Face. After a month of preparations, six climbers reached the summit, taking a line up the right side of the face. Several climbs have been added to the South Face since then, including Reinhold Messner's direct finish to the original French Route.

Approach Routes

Three approaches, each taking two to three days from the main road, lead to the three different Base Camps, from where all routes on the mountain start.

From Puente del Inca (on the Santiago–Mendoza road), through the Horcones Valley, one route leads to the Plaza del Mulas Base Camp at 4230m (14,000ft) and the start of the Normal Route on the northwest side of the mountain. Also starting from Puente del Inca, but turning to the right up the Lower Horcones Valley, is the approach to Plaza Francia, the Base Camp used for the South Face.

The approach to the east side of the mountain starts from Punta de Vacas, approximately 15km (9 miles) from Puente del Inca on the road to Mendoza. The Base Camp, Plaza Argentina, can be reached from the Vacas Valley and Relinchos Valley.

Climbing Aconcagua Today

Nearly 3000 climbers a year now attempt Aconcagua, but the success rate is less than 50%. Most climbers follow the North West Ridge from the Horcones Valley, which provides the best chance of success. But this means that camps are crowded at the height of the season (December and January). The Base Camp is manned by a doctor and a hotel is a short walk away. Climbers must register with Aconcagua National Park and pay a peak fee. Though the summit can be reached in three days from Base Camp, climbers should allow a week to adapt to the altitude before making an attempt.

Conservation

The management of Aconcagua's environment has undergone an amazing transformation over the last 25 years.

Having been a "dirty" mountain, with litter blanketing the trails and campsites, today it is well cared for and clean through a simple but effective waste management programme.

In order to control garbage and waste, Park Authorities now give every climber a garbage bag when they enter the Park. This bag has to be presented, full of garbage, at the end of the trip. If not, the visitor will be fined on the spot.

Meanwhile, toilet facilities are being developed and placed around the Base Camps of the two major approach routes in an effort to solve the growing sanitation problem that exists in and around these big camps.

Agirre's Flight

On Christmas Day 1995, José Ramón Agirre reached the top of Aconcagua to complete his continental summits. The day after returning to Base Camp, he climbed back up to the bottom of the Canaleta with his parapente. At 6pm he took off to make an unforgettable flight: "I was facing the sun; to my back Aconcagua, and below my feet the dark valley which awaited me. All the while I enjoyed this dance without music, a melodious swaying motion which was only interrupted by the touch of firm ground and the hugs of my friends."

below Bathed in the red light of the setting sun, the rocky West Face of Aconcagua is crowned by a halo of lenticular clouds, which can indicate extremely high winds.

Elbrus
Normal Route
6.92

david keaton

chasing the modern grail

When David Keaton completed the Seven Summits in February 1995, he was the youngest person to do so. At not quite 30 years old, the realization of his ambition came almost too soon. It takes tremendous drive and commitment to climb the Seven Summits, and completing the final peak may leave a gaping void that is hard to fill. Keaton could see this coming, and here he provides a glimpse of the inner conflict that he faced on his seventh summit.

Cold sweat bleeds from pores. Like Chinese water-torture in reverse, it gathers on my chin then falls away to the dusty trail. The high peaks spin in a daze as I ditch my pack and take a seat. As in diving, when you rise gradually to avoid the bends, the best climbs are a series of adjustments. Today it is a mire of imbalance, with each step a considered effort. A few more like this and I can forget about ticking off the oddly modern grail of the Seven Summits.

Slipping back from the self-absorption, I realize that today's scenery has been impressive. On our walk-in from Puenta del Inca, the Horcones Valley was dry and barren, but not the colourless rubble zone that others have recounted. Rows of impressive 4000m and 5000m monuments dwarfed our approach and, passing beneath, we seemed like the minuscule guests of an ant farm.

It was late in the afternoon when our three-person group began to set up camp in a dry wash just below Cerro Almacenes, an impressive and wildly stratified peak about 5000m in height. After a few tepid spoons of freeze-dried dinner, I wander up an adjacent ridge and watch

the setting of the sun. I tell myself, tomorrow will go better, first you'll make Base Camp and then you'll acclimatize; this is important, now just concentrate.

The next day we wake and pack up as sunlight bounces off the mountain tops. We head for the main trail at Confluencia, and at the Horcones River, we each pick a different spot to cross. I watch as Mitch ploughs through the heavy current. Five months ago, I had talked him into this over-inflated hike, then he dropped out. A month and a half before I was heading for Aconcagua alone, he surprised me by again saying he wanted to go.

Before the new plan went into second gear, it quickly hit reverse. My sister had been an "item" with Mitch for the last 18 years, and my family began to hound me to get a guide. They seemed to argue that taking Mitch to Aconcagua was like strapping a civilian into the pilot's seat of the space shuttle. Not exactly a stirring vote of confidence, but I could hardly return home alone if Mitch walked off the South Face or lost the tent in a moonlight walk. Insurance was required, so I faxed the "Mule King" Señor Grajales, the multi-decade Aconcagua entrepreneur, who answered in Spanish saying that I wouldn't need assistance having accomplished the normal "yak route" on Everest. With a translator I again tried, mentioning Mitch. His second fax agreed to secure a local guide and, by coincidence, the requisite mules for the Normal or "Mule" Route. At this point I just wanted to be able to tell my family and all ther concerned neurotics that we would climb with a person who had seen the mountain before.

> **"The mountain's biggest blows are known as the Viento Blanco and through the years they have steadily filled a cemetery full of victims."**

On the way to Aconcagua, over *cervezas* in a Mendoza street café, we learned that our guide, Guillermo, or Willie, had guided and climbed Aconcagua for several seasons despite being only 25 years old. He is the product of a Connecticut-born mother and an Argentinian father, Rafael, who climbed with Señor Grajales many mules ago.

Late that afternoon, Mitch, Willie, and I reach the end of the Horcones Valley and walk into Base Camp, Plaza del Mulas (4050m). In the Mendoza permit office we were told that more than 2500 individual permits would be issued during the 1994–5 season. But as we stand gawking at the unlikely boom town ahead of us, it is still a surprise.

Across a rocky pitch from the Grajales camp is a large white tent with an array of plastic café tables, lawn chairs, and a banner advertising "Pepsi and Hamburgers." Dropping our packs, we wander around the alpine shanty town, seeing signs offering Japanese beer, adventure clothing, and various ethnic meals. The new Aconcagua Hotel, a 20-minute walk away, offers hot showers and oxygen tanks.

After two days of Mulas acclimatizing and socializing, our first carry is to Camp Canada (4878m) located shouting distance below the next highest, Camp Alaska. We pitch a tent, dump gear, then return to Base

Camp along the North West Ramp way, which is clogged with climbing groups ascending and descending in regimented columns.

On the way down, we pass an American commercial expedition that has turned back from the summit. If Aconcagua sounded like a good way to "rough it for awhile," they evidently got their money's worth. Two members of the group are slumped haggardly over ski poles and the rest look like they've been thrown over a log and flogged. Out front, their Latin guide strides ahead with a huge grin hanging off his jaw. He'll be home a week early.

As we reach the Grajales mess tent, Willie greets his friend Stephen Sustad, who is an American Himalayan climber and part-time carpenter transplanted to rural England. Stephen, in charge of a large commercial group, is currently dry-docked with frostbite.

Stephen looks sceptical every time the Seven Summits is mentioned, and I don't blame him. When I decided to throw myself onto the circuit, only a handful of climbers had completed the Carstensz version and no Americans were among them. Since then, the concept has threatened to become trivial, with media personalities and rock stars alike helping to turn the idea inside out.

That night, while gathered in the mess tent, no one mentions the Seven Summits, and I watch as Stephen repeatedly attempts to square his rounded spectacles on the bridge of his nose. After some persistent but gentle prodding and two cups of tea, he reluctantly unravels his epic and tells me what happened on the formidable South Face a few weeks before.

After soloing two-thirds of the original French line, he was caught in a violent Aconcagua squall. Over the course of the next three days he forced his way down through several metres of new snow and an avalanche, that carried away most of his equipment including his ice tools. He managed the last few pitches, some on vertical ice, by gripping spare picks in frozen hands.

As he wraps up his narrative, I ask if I can take a look at his toes. Without hesitation, he reaches down and pulls off his shoes. I crouch down and tap the lignified big toe. Having seen the ends of my own feet look the same way, I think, "Not too good." I scan Stephen's face for signs of anxiety, but the situation doesn't appear to bother him in the slightest. If you've been clawing your way up big mountains for 20 years, you probably don't need to have the rules explained.

Two days later, Willie, Mitch, and I leapfrog Camp Alaska and settle ourselves into Nido del Condores (5635m), a plateau the size of a moderate city park. We find that there are plenty of good tent sites available, even considering the Aconcagua hustle and bustle. Directly above our campsite lies the broad scree slope of Gran

above Aptly described as "an alpine shanty town," the Plaza del Mulas Base Camp lies at the head of the Horcones Valley on the trail up Aconcagua.

left A group of climbers sets off up the Horcones Valley with the snowy South Face of Aconcagua towering above surrounding ridges.

chasing the modern grail

63

aconcagua david keaton

Acarreo, which the Swiss climber and guide Matthias Zurbriggen must have duck-walked up to make his first historic ascent of the mountain in 1897.

At Nido we have a chance to visit with climbers from all over the world. Most of them have set their personal altitude record in the last day or so. A couple of them firmly disdain the use of guides, but at the same time appear to shadow every movement of the commercial groups. There is room for just about everyone on this mountain.

Nearly 100 years after Zurbriggen boarded a return steamer for Europe, Cerro, Aconcagua's Normal Route, has netted status as a kind of hypoxic Cirque de Soleil luring an international circus of record breakers. Subtract a few million tons of ice, add half the altitude, and what you have is a South American Mont Blanc. Outside of Mars, it is also the only place in the solar system where hikers can nudge 7000m without snow.

On Aconcagua's muscular shoulders, would-be conquerors have pedalled bicycles, prodded horses, and throttled motorcycles. Others have pitched from the heights via parapente and hang glider. And one man even passed an entire season on the mountain top trying to discover just how many brain cells could be lost in a single outing.

"I have ample time to question my motives. A few hours from a goal completed, I ask myself, what if I just turned around? Something deep inside relishes the thought. After all this, would it be pure courage or cowardice?"

We take the following day off and the weather finally begins to fall apart. Willie and I watch as a shiny new VE-25 tent sails past our plateau camp. "Where did that come from?" I rasp, before sprinting after it. Hunched over trying to catch our breath, we watch as the yellow bauble bounces off toward the Vacas Valley. An hour later three members of a well-sponsored American "Aconcagua Clean-Up Expedition" stomp up from Camp Alaska inquiring sheepishly if anyone has seen their tent.

In the next hour the wind reaches trumpet pitch and our neighbours scatter to wait it out. Mitch and I sit melting snow and listening to the storm draw intensity. Willie offers his tent to the "Clean-Up" team and joins a crew of rangers to help rescue stricken climbers at the Berlin Camp (5951m).

Throughout the next day and night, wind pounds our tent with the backbeat of murderous intent. The mountain's biggest blows are known as the Viento Blanco, and through the years they have steadily filled an entire cemetery. As a morbid testament to disaster, one need only walk the headstones lining the Cementerio del Andinistes on the outskirts of Puente del Inca. More than 50 victims can be found there.

With Willie's return the next morning, we hear the story of the "white wind's" latest victim, a 27-year-

right Like some eerie lunar landscape, this barren col on the way to the summit of Aconcagua, known as Nido del Condores (Condor's Nest), is swept by bitter winds.

aconcagua david keaton

above A climber makes his way along the summit "Guanaco" Ridge of Aconcagua. Behind him the South Face plummets nearly 3000m downwards.

right David Keaton celebrates his moment at the top of South America with Aconcagua's lower South Summit on the right.

distance out of sight. As if delivering a sermon, the panorama begs the conviction that mountaineering is both worth the effort and the downside.

That night Mitch asks me what it will be like to finish the Seven Summits. I tell him that "maybe I can re-enter society as a reformed citizen," but truthfully I don't have any idea. Years ago, I had set the goal as some fuzzy unattainable mark, but now, one day away, I'm not sure what the point is. In 1991, as the inhabitant of a grey corporate cubicle, I had sat at my desk and thrown together a spreadsheet on what it might cost. The monitor in front of me was filled with steady rows of numbers based on least-costly estimates. But as I sit here at 5800m on number seven, I realize that life experiences can rarely be quantified. There are no easy bargains and most dreams won't fit easily into the columns of a balance sheet.

Up at 6am, I methodically tape and pad my feet in a post-frostbite ritual that I have settled into over the last six months. I slink clumsily into my Gore-Tex bibs and a couple more layers then squeeze on boots. Now just the water. The stove hums away reassuringly but its total lack of progress is alarming.

I try to stay relaxed, confident. I force myself outside and peer up at the distant summit block. It is still and clear. When I dip back into the tent it is 7am, and still no water from the stove. I choke down half a chocolate bar, lean back, and wait.

At around 7.40am the three of us are reclined in a semi-doze, listening to the stove. I nod off and wake with a start. "Let's go!" I bark.

The trail runs clear as it winds up to the next highest camp, Playa Blanca, a sort of over-spill parking lot for Berlin. It's no great mystery why most avoid this eerie wind-blasted shelf. We plod on working upward in a frigid breeze.

Rambling along this insatiably high walk, I have ample time to question my motives. A few hours from a goal completed, I ask myself, what if I just turned around? Something deep inside relishes the thought. After all this, would it be pure courage or cowardice?

I forget about it as I top the next pitch and a big icy blast of wind blows up, courtesy of the Vacas. Nearby is the tiny Independencia Refugio (6500m) thrown together by the Argentinian military. It's said to be the highest mountain shelter in the world. We sit and put one wall of the hut between us and the wind. At nearly 7000m, there's not a hamburger or lawn chair in sight. The Barnum and Bailey feel is gone.

A 10-minute break and we strap on crampons to plod up another snow slope. An ominous stone pillar, the "Martinez Rock," marks the northern shadow and more protected side of the mountain. We pass it and the wind-chill ricochets back to comfort zone.

old French man. Reportedly he stumbled into Berlin from another route, but died on the spot. A French woman made it to camp but, according to the rangers, frostbite will claim most of her fingers and toes. Willie finishes the narrative, and Mitch glances at me. No further warnings are needed.

That evening, the winds and cloud dissipate in spectacular fashion. Hailing the shouts of our neighbours, I roll outside to catch the sunset in a final explosion of colours over South America. Through a maze of lower peaks, orange and yellow clouds drift like cotton, and minutes later the Pacific Ocean swallows the sun from the other side of Chile. Our group stands silent, reverent. "It's official," Willie says with fervour, "the mountain is open for climbing again."

Next morning, we make a leisurely ascent to high camp in blue, calm weather. Plodding into Berlin we find the three small huts all in various stages of ruin. Behind the far structure, on a mound of rocks, lies the body of the French climber wrapped in a clear plastic tarp. Someone has added a few blocks of snow to help shield it from the intense glare of high-altitude UV.

Willie calls me over, and I help him hack away with axes at a snow bank. We lay more chunks of snow on top of the makeshift pyre.

"Some rangers have volunteered to bring him down," Willie explains to me, "and if the weather holds he'll be off the mountain in a few days."

At the edge of Berlin, I scan the expanse before me, trying to clear my head. To the north, the Vacas Valley carves out a trench in the direction of Mercedario, and, left to right, a line of rocky summits kicks the

david keaton

66

In minutes we reach the infamous Canaleta, the 400m elevator shaft dead-ending at the summit ridge. Filled with horrendous loose scree, it is the crux of this non-technical climb. Common knowledge asserts it's a grunt, more effort and determination than technique, but as we look into the heart of the Canaleta, it's as if someone has left the back gate wide open. To our surprise, much of the couloir is plastered with snow offering a straightforward crampon to the top.

At the bottom though, the snow is piled up and very steep, and I wonder how Mitch is going to handle it. As I watch Willie move ahead, reaping the benefits of about two months of altitude training, I think maybe we should have brought a rope. I holler down to Mitch, "I'm not sure you want to do this!" He's only worn crampons once and this is a fine place to work on technique. "No problem!" he says, and I watch as he confidently "French steps" up the steepest section.

Above the snow I move back onto the 35° scree that has given this chute its notorious reputation. The summit ridge, the Cresta del Guanaco, is just ahead and the summit itself higher to the left. There are some decisions about which way to go, and I veer right towards the small tracks at the centre.

Reaching the summit ridge, my heart pounds through the effort of breathing in such thin air. The top of this prized lump of firmament is capped with snow, and bulky cornices drool out over the South Face.

It's a different mountain up here – pure inspiration. I take a seat to wait for Mitch. Twenty minutes later clouds move in close and I shiver. I wedge my pack between two boulders and carry on up the ridge joining the North (6962m) and South (6930m) Summits.

Not much to go, but still a tough plug. An energetic scramble carries me up and over one last outcrop then a levelled terrace. The well-photographed aluminium cross sits among a cluster of gritty brown rocks tilting earthward. No place left to go. With an ounce of pride and a dose of humility, I find the end of a journey. Someone once told me that on the longest trails there are always things that must be left behind. They were right.

As I sit on top of Aconcagua, a wave of something not unlike regret pours through me. Life is about decisions, and most mountaineers, I think, learn a thing or two about them. I pull out my water bottle, screw off the cap, and take a sip. At my fingertips, large grey clouds drift past the summit. Maybe climbing is a metaphor for life, but there is nothing really like it.

The weather is becoming increasingly cold again. Just as Mitch climbs up to the summit's cross, I reach out to shake his hand and congratulate him for standing on top of the western hemisphere. I take one last look around. "Seven Summits." Time to go down, time to go home.

ricardo torres nava

reflections on the ice

Mexican mountain guide Ricardo Torres Nava has climbed Aconcagua many times, but here he describes his first visit to South America's summit. His ascent of the Polish Glacier was an eventful and moving experience, causing him to reflect on life, death, and what the mountains mean to him.

Aconcagua, the highest peak in the American hemisphere, was my door to the Seven Summits. Its summit can be reached by various routes, but the first of my 12 climbs on this mountain was via the Polish Glacier. Climbing Aconcagua is a challenge because of high altitude and low pressures. Coveted by many, this giant has claimed the lives of experienced climbers who have tried to reach its summit, so it cannot be treated lightly.

When I arrived in Argentina I was dazzled by this land of Gardel, Eva Peron, the tango, maté tea, and its world-famous steaks. Most of all it confirmed what I was told by friends: Argentinian women are gorgeous and it was impossible to avoid falling in love every 10 minutes. From Buenos Aires we flew to Mendoza where we obtained the necessary climbing permit from the Tourist Department. At the local market we bought some fresh food for our approach to Base Camp. Next day we took a bus to Puente del Inca, to start acclimatizing. For two days we hiked around nearby mountains. Then we travelled by bus to Rio Vacas, located on the edge of the main road connecting Argentina with Chile. We began our approach on this less-travelled route rather than the North Face or Normal Route. Only the guanacos (cousins of llamas) accompanied us, making us feel close to nature in its wildest form. We crossed the river as we followed it up-stream, and finished our journey soaked from many falls in the icy, turbulent waters of the Vacas River.

When we arrived at Leños, we made camp, carrying water to the site and preparing dinner. We met the *arrieros* (muleteers) carrying our loads, and drank maté tea together. The concoction, made out of an indigenous herb, tastes bitter, but I came to like it. After that we slept like babies!

Very early in the morning we were woken up by the noise of hammering, produced by the muleteers as they shod the mules and horses. After

"At a rocky place I was shocked when I stepped onto a dead body. Staring, I noticed he was nearly naked, but still wore his gold wedding band."

breakfast we continued following the river upwards. It was a very long day with strong winds and constant rain. We finally arrived at the confluence with the Relinchos River where we camped, following the same routine as the previous night. Before sunrise the next morning, we set off on our last day of the approach march. We walked rather slowly but gained altitude very quickly. It was a strenuous day but we reached Base Camp with enough energy to set up a large tent that would become our dining room, pitch our individual tents, and build a comfortable

above right Ricardo Torres Nava takes a brief break on his ascent of Aconcagua, the first of his seven continental high points.

right Formed by the sun, these striking daggers of snow or *los penitentes* are a common feature seen along the route up Aconcagua.

1995

| McKinley West Buttress 13.7.94 | Elbrus Normal Route 15.8.94 | Kilimanjaro Heim Glacier 4.9.94 | Vinson Normal Route 17.11.95 | Carstensz Normal Route 24.2.99 | Kosciuszko Normal Route 6.3.99 |

latrine with a good view. The muleteers went back with the animals to lower terrain as there was no pasture for feeding them. We collapsed like potato sacks.

Next day we rested all day as an important part of the acclimatization process. We used the time to read, listen to music, play chess or cards, or just relax. Before retiring we left all the loads ready, so we could take them up to Camp 1 next morning.

At the crack of dawn we started ascending to Camp 1, each of us carrying incredibly heavy loads up to 60kg in weight. In Argentina there are no porters to help out. This didn't trouble me as I had become used to carrying heavy rucksacks when I was very young. But some of

above A climber sets off up the Polish Glacier, with the avalanche–prone slope above in sunlight.

right High among the clouds of Aconcagua, at around 6000m, a member of Ricardo Torres Nava's team stands at an exposed campsite along the Polish Glacier Route.

my friends were struggling with 20kg loads. On arrival at Camp 1 we hid and secured our stuff and went back to sleep at Base Camp. The next day we returned once more to Camp 1. We moved up and down the mountain in order to acclimatize, increasing the haemoglobin level in our blood so we could absorb enough oxygen from the thin atmosphere.

We repeated this routine again between Camp 1 and Camp 2 with a rest day in between when we had a terrible storm. This was our first taste of the feared White Wind, which could be so foul that it could tear your tent to pieces.

The storm subsided and we climbed to the foot of the Polish Glacier. To make the climb safer we divided into two groups of four climbers each. I led the second group, which left two hours after the first. While my friends were climbing the glacier, I decided to take some pictures of

them, so I moved to a rocky place in order to get a better angle. I was shocked when I stepped onto a dead body. Staring, I noticed he was nearly naked, but still wore his gold wedding band. I had seen corpses before, but this depressed me, and I began to imagine how he died. As I recall this, many years later, life and death have a different meaning because I have lost many friends with whom I have climbed. They were some of the best climbers in the world – Pierre Beghin, Scott Fischer, Rob Hall, Gary Ball, Chantal Mauduit, Adrian Benitez – and, more recently, a dear friend who I took by this same route to begin his Seven Summits in January 1998: Constantin Niarchos. One of the richest men on earth, he climbed Everest and later died in a London hospital at the age of 37. Though other causes are reported to have contributed to his death, I can't help but think that his Everest climb was a major factor.

But what is death after all? Some say it is the true beginning of life, but I wouldn't wish to die to find out. If I could chose, I would rather die in the mountains on these trails so far away from power, ambition, hate, wars; standing up with dignity and fighting for what I believe. But not all climbers feel the same. While talking about the subject in Antarctica, another climber once told me, "This all sounds very romantic but I would rather die in bed, drinking beer after making love with a beautiful woman or maybe two." On reflection, yes, that would be a good death also!

After recovering from my grisly discovery among the rocks, I set off again, switch-backing slowly up the snow. It was hard going due to the heavy loads we were carrying, and especially for me because I was breaking the trail through the snow for my group.

More than 10 hours passed before we arrived, completely exhausted, at Camp 3. Like mechanical zombies, some of us installed the tents and others cooked and prepared tea. At that point in my mind I started climbing towards the summit. We could barely sleep at all due to the high altitude, tiredness, and worry as we speculated about the weather next day. Also the snoring of my tent-mate made that night hell. It was not ordinary snoring, he made noises as if he were possessed. The trick was to be patient while we waited for the big summit day!

At 3am, freezing to death, we prepared breakfast which consisted mainly of cereals. Two hours later we were on our way, criss-crossing to the left and upwards on the Polish Glacier. Dawn came when we were below the séracs not far from Punta Banderas. That day seemed to be one of the best of the whole season. Due to rising temperatures, we peeled off our clothes as if we were onions. We could have chosen a direct climb through the glacier but the depth of snow probably would have impeded our chances of reaching the summit.

I was leading my four-climber group. Behind me I could see three unknown climbers and, below them, the four remaining climbers of our group. I was traversing when I heard a distinctive rumbling sound. I felt electrified when I looked up and saw an avalanche approaching in full flow. By a sheer miracle it passed below us, just touching the last climber of my group. With horror I watched as the group of three unknown climbers was swallowed up and taken, tumbling down the glacier, without touching our other team of four.

At that point I stopped to see where the avalanche left the bodies at the foot of the glacier. We saw some dots moving and I felt relieved that at least they were alive. A little later we saw some tiny figures moving slowly downwards until they disappeared on their way to Camp 2. Some days later we found out they were not badly hurt.

We recovered our breath and started again. We were climbing light, carrying only the bare necessities, but our pace was slow. Finally we reached the ridge overlooking Aconcagua's South Face – majestic, beautiful, and so dangerous. We walked along it until we found a long plateau from where we could see the summit far away. Though I quickened my pace it was a long time until we reached the top. There we saw the characteristic aluminium cross, placed many years ago.

We cried out of sheer joy, embraced, and congratulated each other. Someone produced a bottle of champagne, we took pictures (a de rigueur ritual), and drank while contemplating the magnificent view. I thanked God and the Stone Sentinel for finally allowing me to touch his head.

The descent was quick but careful. My group passed several very steep sections without any problems and finally reached Camp 3, where we spent the night, tired but happy. We woke up ready to leave the mountain, carrying all our stuff as if we were mules bringing back our rubbish. Sadly not all expeditions do the same and our mountains have become the worst dumpsites. Days later we were back in Mendoza celebrating and thanking God for our coming back alive.

Speaking of God, I've heard that someone once asked a Talmud Rabbi, "What does God do now that he has finished creation?"

The rabbi answered, "He makes staircases so that men can reach heaven and he can reach us through his messengers, the angels."

For me, the mountains are staircases that take me high up in order to bring me back alive to my everyday world with a broader knowledge of what life, death, love, and humbleness mean. I don't climb mountains for the sake of my ego, I climb them because doing so teaches me more about my weaknesses, fears, and strengths – and there I renew my spirit in order to serve my family, my country, my friends, and, above all, God, in a better way.

mckinley

The view of McKinley from Wonder Lake, north of the mountain, is one of the most majestic mountain scenes anywhere in the world, as McKinley and the Alaska Range rise abruptly from the Arctic tundra and surrounding lowlands. This is the view that inspired the native Inuit people to call it Denali, the "High One."

Mount McKinley, the highest mountain in North America, is the second hardest climb of the Seven Summits, only surpassed by Everest. It is a mountain of grand scale, standing head and shoulders above its neighbours, and presents a tough challenge. Lying just south of the Arctic Circle in Alaska, at 63°N, it is one of the coldest mountains in the world and the elevation gain from the foot of the mountain to the summit is almost 6000m (20,000ft), one of the greatest vertical gains in the world. Also, because it is closer to the pole, the lower barometric pressure makes an ascent comparable to climbing a 7000m (23,000ft) peak in the Himalayas.

McKinley is the apex of the Alaska Range, stretching from the Aleutian Peninsula, through central Alaska, to curve southeast to meet the Mount St Elias Range in Canada. Three major glaciers radiate out from it: the Muldrow to the northeast, the Ruth to the southeast, and the Kahiltna to the southwest. It has two summits, the South Summit 6194m (20,320ft) and the lower North Summit 5934m (19,500ft), separated by the lofty Denali Pass.

This wild, untamed region is surprisingly accessible – only 240km (150 miles) north of Alaska's largest city, Anchorage. The nearest town is Talkeetna, from where a 40-minute flight takes climbers into the mountain's icy embrace.

Alaskan Weather

The weather in Alaska is notorious for being dramatic and changing quickly. Stable months are April to June, while late July and August usually provide poor weather for climbers on McKinley. April is cold, so the most popular months are May and June. Even so climbers must be prepared to be stormbound for days at a time. Temperatures can plummet to −30°C and below with the wind-chill factor. The secret of success on McKinley is to ensure that you are poised for the summit when the good weather arrives.

Flora and Fauna

The flora and fauna of the higher peaks is almost non-existent. Birds, such as ravens and finches (which can be a nuisance if they find a food stash!), and some lichen or mosses on rocks can be encountered, but above 2000m (6000ft) is a virtually sterile kingdom of snow, ice, and rock. The surrounding arctic tundra consists of lowland vegetation dominated by forests, peat-bogs, and montanc moorlands, which in summer offer a feast for the eyes with luxurious bloom of flowers. Wildlife such as moose, reindeer, bear, and wolf abound, as does the most blood-thirsty of all animals – the mosquito!

Exploration and Climbing History

The mountain, visible from the sea, was discovered as early as 1794. The name Denali was always used for the mountain, but in 1897 it was also given the name McKinley, after presidential candidate William McKinley. In recent years, Denali has returned to vogue, and the mountain's National Park has taken the same name.

The first serious attempt to climb McKinley came in 1903. Approaching from the north, the expedition gave up below the Wickersham Wall, named after the expedition leader. A group led by Dr Frederick Cook, first circumnavigated the peak later in 1903.

Three years later, Cook returned to climb McKinley. He went up the Ruth Glacier from the southeast and attempted the East Buttress. He came back with a picture of himself flying the American flag from the "summit." His claim was later revealed to be false, and the peak in his summit shot was found to be only 1600m (5200ft) high. This remains one of the greatest controversies in climbing history.

> "The secret of success on McKinley is to ensure that you are poised for the summit when the good weather arrives."

Climbing Routes

① West Buttress or Normal Route

This most popular West Buttress Route starts from the South East Fork of the Kahiltna Glacier at 2100m (7000ft). From Camp 3, at the "Basin" 4330m (14,200ft), the crest of the West Buttress is reached via the crux 45° headwall. From the top camp at 5200m (17,000ft), a rising traverse to Denali Pass and a long haul over Archdeacon's Tower leads to the summit.

② The Messner Couloir

A direct variation on the West Buttress, going from the Basin directly to the summit.

③ West Rim

A difficult variation on the West Buttress, taking the elegant ridge from the North East Fork directly to the Basin.

④ West Rib

This beautiful route starts from the North East Fork. An ice couloir gains the crest of the rib which leads, in a superb position and without great difficulty, directly to the summit plateau.

⑤ Cassin Ridge

A major prize for mountaineers. The usual approach is from the North East Fork, where the 60° Japanese Couloir is climbed to the ridge crest, with few deviations, to the summit.

⑥ South Face; Scott/Haston Route

This very serious route picks a way up the impressive 3000m (10,000ft) South Face. The route traverses rightwards from the base of Cassin Ridge, across the lower half of the face, to a hanging glacier, which is followed trending leftwards towards the summit.

⑦ Muldrow Glacier (not shown)

Approached from Wonder Lake, this long route follows Muldrow Glacier to its top. There the Karstens Ridge leads to Harper Glacier and Denali Pass to join the West Buttress.

A few years later a team of gold miners, so called "sourdoughs," made a bet that they could climb McKinley. Starting in December, they approached the mountain from the north with horses and dog sleds. By early April they had spent over a month in a camp at 3350m (11,000ft) on the Muldrow Glacier, making one abortive attempt. On 3 April 1910 they set out and climbed the North Peak in a remarkable 18-hour round trip. They carried a 4m (14ft) spruce tree pole, which they planted among the summit rocks. This later supplied proof of the achievement, when the pole was sighted by the first team to climb the main summit three years later.

The higher South Peak was finally climbed in 1913 by Harry Karstens, a local guide, Walter Harper, Robert Tatum, and Hudson Stuck, an Englishman who was then the Archdeacon of Yukon. They climbed the mountain by the Muldrow Glacier, following the Sourdoughs Route, and then climbed directly to the summit from the Harper Glacier.

In 1951 the West Buttress Route was pioneered by Bradford Washburn, Bill Hackett, and Jim Gale, with another five members following a few days later. Following the introduction of ski-equipped light aircraft access to the Kahiltna Glacier, this became the Normal Route up the mountain. The name of Bradford Washburn is inextricably linked with McKinley because of his record keeping and photography. His crystal clear aerial photographs of the mountain and other Alaskan peaks have provided a valuable source of information for a generation of mountaineers. In 1947 his wife Barbara became the first woman to stand on top of McKinley. In 1954, the massive South Buttress was climbed

and the same team descended by the Muldrow Glacier, to complete the first traverse of the mountain. From the late 1950s to early 1960s attention turned towards the formidable 3000m (10,000ft) South Face, the steepest and highest face on the mountain. In 1959 the West Rib was climbed, a route which starts below the South Face, but climbs along its western edge. In 1961, the renowned Italian climber Ricardo Cassin led an expedition to the blunt ridge which divides the South Face. The team completed the climb having faced difficulties never before

above Queues on the crux ice slope of McKinley's West Buttress are common during May and June.

West Side

South Face

encountered on McKinley. Named after the team's leader, the Cassin Ridge is perhaps the finest route on the mountain.

With the ascent of the East Buttress in 1963, all major flanks of the mountain were climbed. Then attention turned to more difficult climbs, with many new routes and variations in the 1970s and 80s.

The first winter ascent of the mountain was made in February 1967 by the West Buttress Route. The climbers endured temperatures down to –100°C, including wind-chill factor. In 1970 Naomi Uemura became the first to climb McKinley solo, using a long bamboo pole tied to his waist to prevent him from falling down crevasses. He returned in 1984 to make the first solo winter ascent. He reached the summit but got lost in a storm. His body was never found.

Climbing McKinley Today

Since 1980 McKinley has increased in popularity, and now attracts over 1000 climbers a year. More than 80 per cent of these use the West Buttress Route for its low level of difficulty and ease of access. All expeditions to the mountain must register in advance with the Denali National Park Service, and climbers' experience is scrutinized with regard to their chosen climb. Only six guiding companies are permitted to operate on McKinley. They offer climbs up the West Buttress, the West Rib, and Muldrow Glacier Routes.

Conservation

Most climbers on McKinley use the West Buttress Route, and any environmental problems, mainly related to litter and sanitation, are concentrated along this route and its camps.

The National Park Service (NPS) on McKinley is well-organized and minimizes the environmental impact of the many visitors to the mountain each year. Climbers are instructed to carry out all litter and broken equipment, and to throw human waste into deep crevasses. Offenders are fined on the spot, and the fine is big enough to deter any further attempts to break the rules. It's tough, but it works!

On more technical routes, like the Cassin Ridge, abandoned equipment and fixed ropes are one of the major sources of litter. Occasional clean-ups, by the NPS or volunteers, remove much of it.

Doug Scott's Climb

There was quite a stir in Alaska when two of the world's top mountaineers arrived to climb McKinley. Doug Scott (left) and Dougal Haston, fresh from their epoch-making first ascent of the South West Face of Everest, boldly set off up the South Face in May 1976. Tormented by bad weather and frequent avalanches, they battled up previously unclimbed and often dangerous snow slopes, throwing away food and equipment in an effort to climb faster. They had five grim bivouacs before reaching the summit in bitterly cold conditions. On their descent of the West Buttress, they climbed 1000m (3000ft) back up the route to assist in a rescue, eventually returning to their camp after eight nights on the mountain. This was the first time a new route had been climbed in alpine style on McKinley.

below A six- to eight-hour climb takes climbers from the top camp on the West Buttress Route to the summit ridge on this rare perfect day.

arne naess

unmasking the king

Preparation, training, and trust between climbing partners are vital to any mountain ascent. As Naess says, a lack of any of these can lead to the "mountaineer's equivalent of Russian roulette." Here Naess and his team discover just what it takes to make it up McKinley.

There was less than a year left until we were to climb Everest. Ralph Höibakk and I wanted some altitude training. Running in London was not enough. Our plan was climb the highest mountain in North America, McKinley, and the highest one in South America, Aconcagua, immediately before our departure for Everest. It would be a good order of progress. Ralph's job meant that he often had to go to the West Coast of the USA. The detour to Alaska and McKinley was therefore not so far.

Ralph met an energetic and stocky little character called Dave. He and Ralph fell into conversation about mountains and climbing. Ralph was mightily impressed by what Dave had told him. His accomplishments made both Ralph and my climbs seem like Sunday excursions. He had done the most difficult rock climbs on El Capitan in

Yosemite. He had climbed the dangerous and difficult South Wall of Aconcagua. He had climbed the difficult Cassin Ridge on McKinley. He knew most of the climbers about whom Ralph and I had only read.

"It just wasn't possible! Ralph looked carefully. No doubt whatsoever. Dave had put his boots on the wrong feet."

Dave asked if we could possibly take him along? He wanted to make a trip to McKinley again and, living nearest, could co-ordinate the preparations.

Dave introduced two new names: Nathan Smith and Bill Davidson. Bill was an accomplished mountaineer who had climbed McKinley before. He could assume the responsibility for organizing everything that concerned formalities and supplies. We agreed, although admittedly it was unusual to climb with people we had never seen or heard of before.

All five of us met for the first time at a hotel in Alaska. Nathan was of middling height, slender, and seemed young for his 30 years. He had coarse, curly hair, soft eyes, a friendly, slightly reserved manner, almost un-American. He had climbed a lot. He, too, had been on Aconcagua. Then, he had only been 18 years old. He did not seem to have rough edges. Pleasant company, we thought.

Bill was a robust type in his mid-20s. He seemed strong and had experienced good training. His manner was more open than Nathan's. His language suggested that he had seen many Westerns on TV. He

seemed a mite too hearty, but he was obviously well prepared. All of the food and equipment he brought were absolutely in order.

Dave was very keen for Ralph and me to see his equipment. We went with him up to his hotel room. All the equipment that he showed us looked new. His boots appeared to not have covered many steps and his anorak was free of marks from rubbing against rock. His ice axe and crampons were without any scratches or specks of rust.

Climbers continue to buy new equipment throughout their careers. Love of equipment is a part of the love of climbing. Even after they have finished serious climbing, the pleasure of taking out a new, extra light

1990		1995

Vinson
Normal Route
11.11.88

Elbrus
Normal Route
6.5.92

Carstensz
Normal Route
24.5.92

Aconcagua
Normal Route
15.1.94

ice axe or strapless crampons is a kind of substitute for the climbs that family, job, or age have made infrequent or eventually put a stop to.

Small aircraft brought us to the foot of McKinley in two stages. First we flew over a flat tundra landscape, then in among the mountains of the Alaska Range. The tundra was completely covered in green, threaded with rivers and lakes. The deciduous forest had the lushness of summer, but the conifer forest seemed jaded. Out on a marsh, just a few hundred metres from the airport in Anchorage, a well-developed elk stood in water and mud up to his knees and revelled in sedge and birch branches.

The encounter with untouched wilderness was almost a shock. Beyond the city limits there were no roads or houses and scarcely a path. There were animal tracks where bears, wolves, and foxes hunt for elk, deer, and hares. Rivers, regulated by beavers, were rich in salmon and rainbow trout. Over all this, the eagle watched for anything that moved.

The approach flight in between the summits of the Alaska Range made an even stronger impression. The mountains were too close for comfort, their grey, polished granite a mere 50m from the wing tips.

above McKinley, "the King," rises high above the surrounding Alaskan plain. It takes 18–20 days to trek from Base Camp to the summit and back.

mckinley arne naess

above Hanging back on his ascender, Arne Naess takes a breather while climbing the crux headwall on the West Buttress at around 4600m.

right Ralph Höibakk (left) and Arne Naess enjoy the view from the crest of the West Buttress, just below the top camp at 5200m.

There were gaping chasms between sky-high rock towers. Interminable, dead-white glaciers flowed between the mountain ridges, turning into rivers towards the tundra.

But McKinley itself made the greatest impression. Called Denali, the High One, by the Indians, no mountain dominates its surroundings quite like McKinley. There is nothing feminine about it; it is a man with self-certainty and gravity, a stable father-figure, no swaggering Rambo with a macho-complex.

While Everest is the first among equals and Kilimanjaro is lonely guard over the savannah, McKinley is king and autocrat of his kingdom, the Alaska Range. Denali holds court, but the king's council remains at a respectful distance. Neighbouring Mount Foraker and Mount Hunter have withdrawn well away and are 1000 to 2000m lower. This, together with its huge shape, makes McKinley immeasurably high and massive.

McKinley is grand from all sides, but is perhaps finest from the north when you walk over the tundra in the bright sun and see the summit soar 6000m above. Then your gaze wanders down along the dead-white Muldrow Glacier nestling between ragged mountain ridges, a milky avenue the like of which I have never seen on other mountains.

McKinley lies at 63°N, the same latitude as Trondheim, but there is no Gulf Stream to mitigate the arctic climate. The mountain range and McKinley itself are the climatic divide. Storms are frequent and violent.

The wind howls and the snow pours down. The periods of fair weather are short. Nobody can count on climbing the mountain in good weather the entire way.

From the Base Camp at 2500m to the top and back again normally takes 18–20 days. During that time climbers must allow for several stormy interludes. From 5000m up to the summit, all campsites are unprotected. The winds can exceed hurricane force and tear everything to pieces on its way. Climbers must crouch well down to avoid being swept off the mountain.

The great quantities of snow mean that only the steepest parts of the mountain are bare. McKinley also possesses the finest glaciers in the world. They are dead-white, ermine paths reaching almost to the horizon, but they are treacherous. Under the velvet-smooth surface, hungry jaws gape. The frequent snowfalls cover the crevasses. The low temperatures mean that the snow bridges do not become strong, so the weight of a human being is enough to collapse them. All of this makes McKinley a challenging mountain – not technically difficult, but dangerous. One who approaches it must do so with respect, have good equipment, and be experienced.

McKinley has great magnetism and climbers from around the world fly in to the Base Camp on Kahiltna glacier; nearly 1000 each summer. Not all come back. In 1992, the worst year for fatalities, 12 people died in storms, glacier crevasses, or of altitude sickness.

It is always exciting to land with a little aircraft on a glacier. Since the main glacier was severely crevassed, the Base Camp lay on a tributary glacier some 100m higher. The pilot circled several times between Mount Foraker and Mount Hunter before depositing us. Base Camp was full of people. A "camp warden" allotted us a tent site. It gave me a strange feeling of mass tourism in one of the uttermost corners of the world.

It was boiling hot in the afternoon sun, like an oven. We grasped that in such good weather we would have to transport our baggage at night and rest during the day. We had the choice of carrying everything at once, or shuttling back and forth. The latter suited us best, because it gave time for acclimatization to the altitude.

Ralph and I lay in one tent, while Bill, Nathan, and Dave camped in another one. We agreed to get up at 3am and carry our first load to the next camp. The night was cold and clear. It was light and the snow crust was hard when Ralph and I prepared to start around 4am. Bill and Nathan were up and about, while Dave still had not emerged from his sleeping bag. Ralph shook the tent and shouted: "Dave, time to get up." "OK Ralph, I'll be out in a minute."

Ralph and I started off on skis, each with a sledge. On the crust down to the main glacier, it was splendid going. In the first rays of morning, Mount Foraker was a golden cupola. Along the Kahiltna Glacier we set a good pace. It was lovely to be moving. Mount McKinley, which had been hidden by an obstacle, became visible again. A narrow valley ran in under the south wall. The view took my breath away: an expanse of sheer cliffs, hanging glaciers, and gaping crevasses.

Our climb went surprisingly quickly up to the next camping area where a big Swiss group was preparing to depart. They told us that death had already visited McKinley. Someone had died of altitude sickness, another had been saved at the last moment, and two men had been brought down with severe frostbite. In the burning sun down on the Kahiltna Glacier it was easy to talk about this. It did not seem to concern us. In one way, it did not concern McKinley either. At least not our McKinley. We are all immortal until it is our turn. Precisely like the gnu grazing peacefully, even if it knows that the lions are lying hidden in the grass close by.

Ralph and I made a depot and went back. At the foot of the slope up to the Base Camp, we met Bill, Nathan, and Dave. They were roped up, with Bill in the lead. In the rear, I glimpsed Dave in his brand new fibre fur suit. Bill motioned us to him when we met. "There's something wrong here," he said. "It was almost impossible to get Dave out of the tent. He fumbled for an eternity with his equipment."

Dave seemed to be in real trouble. Ralph went back to him. He had sat himself down on the sledge. "Hi Ralph, I've got trouble with my feet. These new boots are hurting horribly. I'm getting blisters." Ralph bent down and looked. It just wasn't possible! Ralph looked carefully. No doubt whatsoever. Dave had put his boots on the wrong feet. When we all finally came back to camp, Dave was absolutely worn out. "I don't understand anything, Ralph," he said, "I think it's due to conflict at work and lack of training. I'm taking the first plane out." Nobody protested. We helped him pack and a few hours later loaded his belongings on board. He came, he saw, and he disappeared.

The impression made by Bill and Nathan improved the further civilization receded. For my part, I do not really care about equipment and technology. It is always the development that interests me. For that reason, I am easily impressed when I see climbers who master equipment and craftsmanship. Bill and Nathan represented American precision at its best. Everything had its fixed place in labelled and taped bags, holdalls, and cases, and everything – sewing materials, first aid equipment, patches, tool sets – was in its place. I always take the minimum of equipment. It weighs too much. Nathan's rucksack towered over the man. It was incredible what that slightly built boy carried. He had one weakness:

he moved slowly. It was not only on account of the big rucksack, it was his rhythm. It was torture for Ralph and me, as we have a quicker pace.

Ralph and I have climbed many mountains together. We are good partners. We are at ease with each other on the mountain, in the tent, and in life-threatening situations. We are a good balance. I hate to carry and never bring enough equipment or food. Ralph likes to carry. He always has a heavier load and brings what I leave behind. Very convenient for me. We both have the attitude things will work out, so don't take things too seriously. Bill and Nathan were methodical and more careful, so as a foursome we were well balanced.

Preparation and training are vital to any mountain ascent. A lack of either can be the mountaineer's equivalent of Russian roulette. It is vital that members of the team trust each other in these respects as in all others. Our climb up the Normal Route was uneventful. We did almost get lost in a fog and had to sleep out without tents, but that was all. We climbed to the summit and descended in nine days. There is no honour in following the ordinary route up McKinley behind a caravan of tourists. You break no new ground – neither your own, nor others. But nature and the magnificent mountain gave us a wonderful experience and we did get some altitude training, although of little or no benefit for Everest, which still lay nine months ahead of us.

Though the events in this account are factual, some of the names have been changed.

Kilimanjaro
Heim Glacier
1.2.87

steve bell

a date with denali

Steve Bell returned to Alaska 17 years after his first visit, to climb McKinley and complete his Seven Summits. During his climb he considered what was important about mountaineering, but it took a personal loss to understand the real answer.

One blustery day in 1980, I made my date with Denali. Roger Mear and I stood on the summit of Huntington, having climbed a new route up the East Face. Towering above us, just a few miles to the north, was the huge South Buttress of McKinley, leading upwards through the ragged, wind-torn clouds to the top of North America, some 8000ft above us. It was an awesome and spine-chilling sight. We were out on a limb, facing an unknown descent down the opposite side of the mountain we had just climbed, but my thoughts had already turned to future climbs. As the wind roared and the clouds swirled against McKinley's precipice, I knew with certainty that one day I would have to climb it.

We survived an epic descent from Huntington's little-trodden summit, but it was many years before I had the courage to return to Alaska. Roger was made of sterner stuff. Unperturbed by our first harrowing view of the High One, he chose to climb McKinley by one of its harder routes, and in winter. In February 1982, he climbed the Cassin Ridge with two Americans. This was only the second time that the mountain had been climbed successfully in winter. It seemed a crazy thing to do, but I was duly impressed.

right Heavily laden, Ulf Carlsson takes the lead at the start of the long haul up McKinley – from the airstrip to the main route up the Kahiltna Glacier.

below An airborne view of the Kahiltna airstrip, launch pad for the majority of teams climbing McKinley.

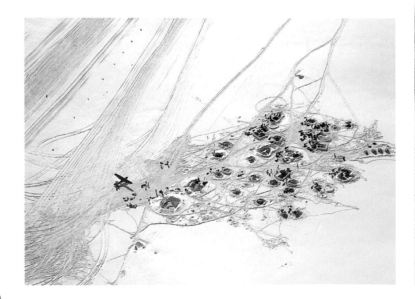

| Aconcagua Normal Route 25.1.93 | Elbrus Normal Route 26.6.93 | Everest South Col 7.10.93 | Carstensz Normal Route 20.11.94 | Vinson Normal Route 1.12.95 | McKinley West Rib 29.5.97 |

Years passed and, after what seemed an interminable wait, the future eventually arrived. The need to climb McKinley had become critical, as it was the only continental summit I had not climbed. Finally, I would have to face the High One. Ulf Carlsson and I had designs on the Cassin. What a great looking route! A classic 10,000ft spur up a vast, unwelcoming face, leading directly to the summit. It looked like a beautiful and fitting way to complete the Seven Summits.

"Any elation I felt was short-lived as sadness, and perhaps even guilt, welled up inside ."

We acclimatized on the West Buttress Route, sharing it with several hundred other people all intent on standing on the roof of America. The weather was awful, but we didn't mind, as long as it was good on the Cassin. It was fun slogging up the trail, shooting the breeze with other climbers, or reading a good book while McKinley's relentless wind and snow hammered the tent walls. We left a small stash of food and fuel at the top camp to aid our descent, then plodded all the way back down to the North East Fork of the Kahiltna Glacier, where the route to the Cassin branches off to the right.

On the way down the weather was perfect, everyone else was going up, and we faced a dilemma. Should we be going down, or should we be using the rare good weather to bag the summit first then think about doing the harder route? We might not get another chance to get to the top. Wouldn't it be more sensible to claim the summit by any means rather than increase the odds against success by attempting a difficult

route? Ulf and I stopped against the tide of upwardly mobile sledge haulers to deliberate. What was more important, the summit or the route? Was it success that counted, or the *quality* of success? Ulf was not riding the Seven Summit train, so the imperative to reach the top was less acute than it was for me. As we thought about our reasons for being there I looked back up the hill towards the High One. Denali the giant was asleep, serene yet magnificent against the clear blue sky, and gently fanned by a soft breath of wind. I thought of all the climbs I had done, and which of them meant the most to me. And there was the answer. It wasn't reaching the summit that was important, it was how the summit was reached. We continued our downward journey.

The next day we were poised at the mouth of the "Valley of Death," the less than fond nickname for the North East Fork. Threatened by avalanches from both sides, the narrow, steep-sided valley was the gateway to our chosen route. Suddenly fear and self-doubt were weakening my resolve, aided by a gripping photocopied account of a nine-day ascent of the Cassin by two Americans. I tried to be rational. Roger had said the Cassin was easy, but then he would. It was a matter of balancing great British understatement against all-American hype; somewhere in between them lay the truth.

Ulf was also having second thoughts about the Cassin, but his doubts were based on sound judgement. He was concerned about the weather. We had used two fine days to descend the West Buttress and prepare for the climb, and soon Alaska's weather would awaken the giant. We reckoned we had two good days left, if we were lucky. Not enough for the Cassin, but enough for the easier West Rib. If we were quick. I grabbed at the excuse and, at midnight, we entered the Valley of Death, bound for the West Rib.

The snow was firm and we made good time in the Alaskan twilight. The walls of the valley were frighteningly avalanche prone, but there wasn't a sound, as though the world had been frozen solid by the cold of the night. Behind us Mount Foraker was beautiful, bathed in a soft pink alpenglow that gradually turned to orange. As the sun touched the top of McKinley, we meandered between the crevasses and séracs of an icefall to find a large, hidden snow couloir. Now in sunshine, we put the tent up and made breakfast, then slept for a couple of hours. After our sub-zero nocturnal journey, the warmth of the sun was wonderful. But Alaska is a country of extremes, and it was soon stiflingly hot. We repacked and by 9.30am we were on the move again, with Ulf leading the rope up the couloir.

The West Rib is a fine climb. Bounding the South Side of the mountain on its left (west) end, the rib rises from near the top of the North East Fork in a series of icy waves. The initial couloir leads, after about 1500ft, to the crest of the rib, which is followed until it is absorbed by the blunt mass of the mountain. Then either snow slopes or the rocky crest of the rib lead disjointedly to the summit plateau, a vertical 10,000ft above the start of the climb.

Moving together with the occasional running belay, we got halfway up the couloir when I had a fright. Directly above us, very high up, I heard the rumble of an approaching avalanche. Straining to look upwards, there was no sign of it, but the noise was there, loud and ominous, coming from above the rocks to our right. I couldn't remember any potential avalanche hazard from the photos, but I still expected to be engulfed by high-velocity snow at any second. In a futile gesture, I buried my head in the snow, thinking, "that's the trouble with Alaskan mountains, they are always trying to wipe you out." The rumbling built to a crescendo that exploded above our heads, and two low-flying jet planes streaked across the sky. My relief was instantly replaced by anger at my stupidity. I shook the snow out of my face and stole a glance at Ulf, 50m away from me at the other end of the rope. He was still climbing; the jets had not fooled him!

The top half of the couloir steepened to about 60° and the snow became water ice. We pitched it for a while, then reverted to moving together for the last few hundred feet to the crest of the West Rib. We passed an American couple who were moving slowly, without the benefit of prior acclimatization. In contrast to the crowded West Buttress, they were the only others we saw on the whole route.

The crest was spectacular, a series of ice domes providing alternately steep then easy climbing. The last dome to be climbed was the steepest, being 100ft of soft 70° snow that led to a large, almost level snow shelf halfway up the route. Further up we

left Ulf Carlsson leads the initial 1500ft ice couloir which gives access to the crest of the West Rib.

right Enjoying the sun, Carlsson relaxes at his and Steve Bell's first camp on the West Rib of McKinley, with the North East Fork in the background.

found an accommodating bergschrund where we called it a day. Pleased with our progress, we brewed up and took in the view, down the length of the treacherous Valley of Death toward Foraker and, in the opposite direction, across the face towards the Cassin Ridge, where at least two teams appeared as tiny dots. "You're braver than I am," I thought. We had a comfortable night, despite our little Gemini tent being considerably shorter than Ulf.

The weather continued to be perfect the next day, when we reached a perfect perch at 18,000ft. It felt strangely warm as we ate in the open, looking across the Alaskan Range, higher than everything around us, except for the High One, on whose shoulder we sat. Behind us was the snow slope known among mountaineers as the Orient Express, which led to the summit plateau. Just beyond was my last continental summit, only a few hours away.

The next morning was also perfect, but not for long. The sun wore an opaque halo and, as we set off, we knew the honeymoon would soon end. Two hours later we pulled ourselves onto the summit plateau, just as the giant awoke. Visibility was down to 150ft and the wind beat us

mckinley steve bell

above Ulf Carlsson takes a breather during the last day of good weather on the West Rib.

right Feeling naked without his rucksack, Steve Bell stands on the summit of McKinley, the last of his continental summits.

they leaned breathlessly into the wind. Last of the summit-bound teams were three British Army lads whom we'd got to know while acclimatizing on the West Buttress. Their leader, Mark, congratulated us and we shared his flask of tea. At 3pm it was late to be still going for the summit, and there was no doubt that the weather would get worse before it got better. Mark shouted a question through the wind, "How far to the summit?"

"About three hours," I said. But I thought, "Are you sure you want to continue?" I wish I had said it. Soon after moving off in opposite directions, I looked back up at the three of them just as they disappeared into the storm.

It was snowing hard when, at 8pm, we reached the sanctuary of the 14,200ft camp on the West Buttress. That night, more than three feet of snow fell on McKinley. One of the guided groups we passed was benighted on the summit plateau. They survived by digging themselves into the snow, but some did not escape frostbite. The British Army guys were less fortunate. After one of them gave up his attempt and descended safely back to the top camp, Mark and his remaining team mate reached the summit late in the day. On their way back across the summit plateau the blizzard reached its peak and visibility dropped to zero. Losing their way, they tried to descend too soon, getting into difficulties on steep ground. When they fell, they had no idea where they were. They were found the next day after a rescue party climbed up from the ranger station at the 14,200ft camp. Mark was dead and his friend was helicoptered to hospital with fractures, frostbite, and hypothermia. They had fallen about 4000ft down the Orient Express.

This news was a body blow. Why didn't I say something when we drank their tea? I felt sick and appalled at my lack of foresight. Ulf, as rational as ever, said that it wouldn't have made any difference. Perhaps he was right, but how can I be sure? Two days after reaching the summit, Ulf and I wrote our names on the ceiling of the West Rib Bar in Talkeetna. Over a few beers we bantered and back-slapped over our climb, and I tried to be in a celebratory mood. But somehow, our achievement felt empty.

from every direction. Walking on a compass bearing, we found and followed a line of marker wands to the invisible summit. We both felt tired now, the effort of the last few days was beginning to take its toll. Despite knowing that you should never be separated from your equipment, we left our rucksacks at the foot of the final slope. It could have been a fatal error, but we wanted to move quickly before conditions prevented movement altogether. At the foot of the summit ridge a solitary climber passed us, on his way down. His clothing was a patchwork of sponsor badges and from the top of his rucksack a large Korean flag fluttered loudly in the wind. In a hurry, he waved briefly before disappearing into the gloom.

A deep trail led upwards along the left side of the ridge crest. In the intensifying blizzard it was impossible to tell how far it was, but soon there was no more mountain to climb. I had imagined looking across to the North Peak, down the opposite side of the mountain, and across the endless tundra of the Inuit towards the North Pole. But all we could see was a few feet of snow-covered ridge, spindrift, and cloud. All smiles, we embraced, took a picture of each other, and headed back down, hoping we would find our rucksacks along the way.

Reunited with our packs, we crossed the summit plateau and slogged up the exhausting slope behind Archdeacon's Tower to descend the West Buttress Route. Several other teams were on their way up, including a couple of guided groups whose clients looked miserable as

"Losing their way, they tried to descend too soon, getting into difficulties on steep ground. When they fell, they had no idea where they were."

Postscript: In the summer of 1999, Ulf Carlsson lost his own life in a fall in the Pamir mountains of central Asia. His friends buried him there, a long way from Sweden, and from his home in Nairobi where his wife, Vanessa, was expecting their first child. Now I understand. It is not the summit that is important, nor is it the route. It is the comradeship of those you climb with. This is what makes a climb special, and none more so than my climb on Denali with Ulf.

kilimanjaro

Kilimanjaro is perhaps the best-known mountain in the world that has a peak attainable by those with little more than walking experience. It is without doubt one of the easiest to climb of the seven continental summits and an increasing number of climbers and walkers are travelling to Africa with this in mind.

One of the easiest of the continental summits to climb, Kilimanjaro draws tourists who aim to reach the summit from all over the world, while its steeper flanks receive attention from some of the world's most accomplished climbers.

The mountain is like an island. Surrounded by the hot and dry plains of the Masai steppe, it rises almost 5895m (19,340ft) from the base to its icy crown. The comparison with an island goes much further than mere appearance, however, for suspended above the ocean of the African plain there exists a whole new world that is radically different from anything else on the continent. It amazes all with its widely contrasting vegetation: in the lower reaches, there is rainforest, a tropical alpine zone, and beautiful unspoilt moorland. Above this tower the cliffs and glaciers that can be seen from hundreds of miles away.

Kilimanjaro is a dormant volcano and lies 400km (250 miles) south of the Equator, just inside Tanzania's border with Kenya. In 1886, Queen Victoria gave the mountain to her German grandson Wilhelm as a birthday present. This explains the kink in the otherwise ruler-straight boundary between the two countries. As a result of this regal whim, virtually all of the early exploration of Kilimanjaro was carried out by the German colonials of what was then known as Tanganyika. After World War I the mountain became a British asset once again until Tanganyika's independence and the birth of Tanzania in 1961.

Climate

The vast slopes of Kilimanjaro are unique, as they pass through many different climatic worlds. Climbers must travel through tropical rainforest, heathland, desert, and finally tundra before reaching the ice-bound summit, all in the space of a few days. The best times to climb Kilimanjaro are between December and early March and from June to October, to miss the two rainy seasons. Climbers should always be prepared for cold weather and sudden storms, as the upper reaches of the mountain are very cold, especially from June to August, which is the East African "winter." It is often very windy, which can make the temperatures that reach as low as −10°C feel even colder.

Flora and Fauna

The many climatic zones on the mountain also mean that there is a vast range of flora, some of it unique to the East African mountains, making Kilimanjaro a place of particular interest to botanists. One of the most spectacular of plants is the giant groundsel (a species of *Senecio*), whose tree-like stems hold large rosettes of leaves as high as 6m (20ft) in the air.

Kilimanjaro is the backdrop to some of the world's most famous game reserves, so it is not surprising that its flanks are roamed by a diverse array of wildlife. Each zone on the mountain has its own permanent inhabitants, but, forced together by the rapid gain in altitude, some animals can be found in places other than their normal surroundings. The discovery of a frozen leopard near the summit of Kilimanjaro is a well-known example of this phenomenon.

Much of the wildlife on the mountain is elusive, so many visitors take the opportunity to go on a nearby safari before or after climbing. A herd of elephants with the snows of Kilimanjaro in the background is an unforgettable sight.

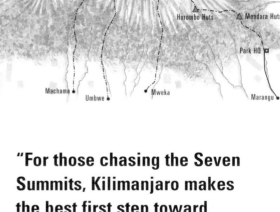

"For those chasing the Seven Summits, Kilimanjaro makes the best first step toward completing them all."

The Mountain and its Climbing

Kilimanjaro offers a huge range of experiences to those who are prepared to venture from the ever-popular Marangu (Tourist) Route. As well as the testing climbs on the glaciers and Breach Wall, there is a host of moorland routes leading onto non-technical ascents of the summit cone. For those who prefer the company of lots of people, the Tourist Route will not disappoint!

The mountain has three peaks, Kibo, Mawenzi, and Shira. Kibo is the highest with its instantly recognizable volcanic cone and a summit crater some 2.5km (1½ miles) across. It is on this, the major feature of the mountain, that most of the climbing is focused. East of Kibo stands the jagged spire of Mawenzi, the second peak of Kilimanjaro, which offers numerous rock climbs. Shira lies to the west of Kibo and is so eroded that it is little more than a plateau of rolling heathland.

Kibo's crater rim is intact except for the mighty gash of the Western Breach and some much smaller notches on the eastern side. These notches provide the easiest access to the crater and rim. The highest point of the rim and mountain as a whole is Uhuru Peak, the summit of Kibo, whose cliffs rise steeply for some 180m (600ft) from the floor of the caldera. Uhuru is the apex of the great Southern Glaciers that spill down the south side of Kibo, providing some of the most challenging climbs. Between the glaciers and the Western Breach is the Breach Wall, a 600m (2000ft) precipice of friable overhanging rock.

On the opposite side of the mountain is the Northern Icefield, a single expanse of ice that drapes over the crater rim, its shimmering whiteness visible

high above the Amboseli National Park in neighbouring Kenya. Other glaciers lurk languidly in the shallow crater, like beached whales hopelessly waiting for the next tide, or ice age, to secure their survival. All of the glaciers on Kilimanjaro are in retreat, and some have already disappeared altogether.

Climbing History

The records of human endeavour on Kilimanjaro begin with western missionaries whose travels took them by the mountain in the 19th century. As yet, there is no evidence that native Africans ventured on to its slopes, or reached the summit, before Kilimanjaro first appeared on the horizon before western eyes – but it may well have been climbed by these early residents of the region. No doubt the great volcano with its strange white cap would have been enmeshed with the reigning superstitions and folklore, perhaps compounding the intimidating physical barriers of Kilimanjaro's dense jungle and high altitude with myth-induced terror.

In 1887 missionary Charles New became the first person to reach snow on Kilimanjaro when he climbed to the saddle between Kibo and Mawenzi. The first ascent of Uhuru Peak (then named Kaiser Wilhelm Spitze) was made in 1889 by the German geographer Hans Meyer with his Swiss guide, Ludwig Purtscheller. In 1898 Johannes Korner opened the now popular Tourist (Marangu) Route.

Built in 1932, the Kibo Hut heralded the age of mountain tourism on Africa's highest peak. The hut became the springboard for thousands of ascents. There is a complex of huts in the area today and also lower down the trail at Mandara and Horombo.

The first recorded ascent of the Western Breach was made in 1953 by a Sheffield (UK) University team. In 1957, A Nelson, H Cooke, and D Goodall made the first ascent of the classic Heim Glacier Route. Most of the other major lines were climbed during the 1970s, mainly by visiting teams from the Mountain Club of Kenya. In 1978, Reinhold Messner and Konrad Renzler climbed the formidable Breach Wall Direct Route.

Climbing Kilimanjaro Today

While Kilimanjaro continues to be a playground for high-altitude alpinists, new route activity has virtually ceased. More so than on any of the other

Trekking Routes

There are six moorland approach routes to the base of Kibo: Marangu (shown above), Mweka, Umbwe, Machame, Shira, and Rongai. These provide access to climbing routes. Only the Marangu, or Tourist Route, leads all the way to Uhuru Peak, ascending steadily for 34km (20 miles). The other routes gain the Kibo Circuit Path which links to the start of all routes to the summit, including the Marangu. A one-way system on some routes is in place to reduce erosion.

The Marangu aside, there are other climbs up Kibo that do not require technical mountaineering skills, namely the Barafu Route and the Western Breach Route (③), but the latter can become difficult when covered by snow.

Climbing Routes

The two technical routes that are known to have been climbed by Seven Summiteers are:

① The Heim Glacier

This once amenable route (which was skied by Ronald Naar in 1984) is now a taxing climb on steep, mixed ground until the upper glacier is reached. Difficulties are concentrated in the first 600m (2000ft) with vertical ice and loose rock.

② The Breach Wall Direct

This route gains and climbs the giant icicle which links the Balletto and Diamond glaciers on the Breach Wall. Believed to have been climbed only once since Messner's first ascent, it is probably the hardest and most serious climb on the African continent.

③ The Western Breach Route

South Side

left Kilimanjaro, known for its beautiful game reserves, overlooks several national parks including Amboseli, across the border in Kenya.

Seven Summits, Kilimanjaro's great glaciers are receding, making them steeper and more prone to stonefall. Additionally the loose rock makes for unappealing climbing. In light of these conditions the once frequently climbed Heim Glacier is now a tough proposition for climbers and other more difficult glaciers, such as the Kersten, are no longer climbable at all. As the ice retreats still further, the great ice routes of Kilimanjaro may disappear altogether. Meanwhile, the walking routes are becoming ever more popular, putting pressure on the environment.

Conservation

With more than 50,000 visitors per year, Kilimanjaro is on the verge of being loved to death. The mountain is showing all the signs of overuse, with eroded trails, waste, and litter accumulation – especially around camps on the lesser-used routes, since these are not managed by caretakers – as well as deforestation, caused by the cutting of trees for firewood in the camps. Sanitation is not yet a major problem, but the toilets at Kibo Hut have upset even the strongest of stomachs!

Despite the fact that Kilimanjaro is a National Park, very little is being done to address these problems. Trail restoration and management,

banning use of firewood and encouraging the use of gas and kerosene stoves, and visitor education on carrying out all litter are solutions which will need the combined co-operation of the National Park authority, overseas and local guiding agencies, and each individual visitor. This would go a long way towards ameliorating the environmental problems on this very popular mountain.

Messner's Astounding Feat

The Breach Wall on Kilimanjaro is a formidable climb. Its crucial section is a 90m (300ft) vertical pillar of ice that links the Balletto Icefield to the summit slopes. It had been attempted on several occasions, once by Doug Scott, but it was the prolific Reinhold Messner (below) who finally succeeded on this daring climb. With Austrian Konrad Renzler, Messner astonished the climbing world by completing the 1500m (5000ft) route in only 12 hours in January 1978. Messner regarded it as one of his most dangerous climbs – a telling statement from the world's most renowned mountaineer.

chris brown
a farmer's odyssey

In 1995 Chris Brown took a week off from growing potatoes in northern England to climb the highest peak on Africa. Although it is a straightforward climb and the Tourist Route provides a number of amenities, he found that it still has its challenges: altitude, cold weather, and extremely slippery conditions.

I was 49 years old and Kilimanjaro was to be the second of my Seven Summits. Mike Potter, a neighbouring farmer from North Yorkshire, and I joined a commercial expedition. Being busy farmers, we aimed to climb Kilimanjaro and be back at work within a week. We decided not to take much technical climbing gear because the mountain presents a straightforward hard walk. Altitude would be the significant challenge.

Arriving at Kilimanjaro Airport in January, we were amazed at the difference in temperature from our native Britain. At 35°C, it was unbelievably hot and humid. Once we were transported to the Mountain Inn, we met up with our eight expedition companions, who had been together on safari to the Serengeti.

An open-topped truck took us along the dusty road to the entrance of Kilimanjaro Park where we registered and met up with our mandatory eight porters and two guides. We then set off towards the Mandara Hut

at 2743m, through really green, lush rainforest. Everything is provided for climbers taking the Tourist Route, including the huts, each of which sleeps about eight people, and electricity, which is supplied by solar panels. These comfortable facilities are an encouragement to climbers, helping them to forget about the discomfort that can often be induced by Kilimanjaro's altitude.

After breakfast we set off at a leisurely pace, through trees that occasionally parted revealing spectacular views across the African plain. As we progressed, fewer trees were seen and vegetation became increasingly sparse. We arrived at the Horombo Hut at 3760m after a five-hour long walk.

The following day was an acclimatization day and, in spite of the wet conditions, we walked up to the saddle on the plateau below Kilimanjaro at about 4115m. Mike developed a headache and became dehydrated – signs he was suffering from altitude sickness. As we set off the following day, he took some medication to help. I had once done the same but wouldn't do so again on principle as I think it's best to wait and let the body adjust naturally, though the medication did provide Mike with some relief. This was a big day because it was extremely evident that we were at altitude. Kibo Hut is at 4730m and without a day to adjust to the height, climbers get sick and can't go for the summit.

After a long trek we arrived at Kibo at 3pm. I was extremely tired and Mike was experiencing altitude sickness again. We drink together at home and, to me, the effects of altitude on him seemed very much like that of excess alcohol. He was falling all over the place and couldn't manage to put more than two words together. More medication seemed to help.

Mike wasn't sure that he would be able to go for the summit in light of his condition, but when we woke at about 10pm he decided he would at least try. Our team of eight left at 1am in the pitch black that precedes the dawn. Before we started, the guides gave us a little lecture, telling us we had to be at a certain point by a certain time, otherwise they would need to turn us round. When we started walking they kept saying, "poli, poli," – slowly, slowly. But we were going so slowly that I suddenly realized we were in danger of being turned round without reaching the summit. So I broke away without a guide, following an Irish team some distance ahead, finding the route with my headtorch. I climbed on dry, frozen scree that was quite steep, though just how steep I didn't fully realize in the darkness. Thirsty, I stopped frequently to drink water, but the weather was so cold that the water eventually froze. Some

climbers aren't prepared for the extremely cold temperatures. Experiencing the heat as we did on our first day, it's easy to see how some can mistakenly get the impression that it's going to be hot throughout the climb to the summit.

The sun began to rise at about 4am, revealing a magnificent view across Africa. An amazing orange glow lit the fertile volcanic soil across the plain. I reached Gillman's Point on the lip of the crater at 5670m nearly five hours later, enjoying the spectacular view across the south facing glaciers. I knew that Mike was behind me and was probably suffering, but being only about 90 minutes from the top and within easy reach of my goal, I focused myself on going for the summit, alone to the Uhuru Peak.

Snow and ice presented quite a difficult and slippery climb down into the crater, making me wish that I'd brought my crampons and ice axe after all. Managing as best I could in the unbelievable cold, I climbed around the edge of the crater for nearly five kilometres, amazed at the enormous hole in the volcano on one side and the glaciers on the opposite side. I made my way steadily up and at last reached the summit of Kilimanjaro, feeling exhausted but elated. Taking a few celebratory photographs, I basked in the moment, enjoying my view from the top of Africa and the completion of the second of my continental summits.

Twenty minutes later three members of our team arrived with a guide, telling me that they'd left Mike at Gillman's Point. Tired and with some difficulty, we descended the slippery slope. I once again wished that I had brought my ice axe and crampons.

At Gillman's Point we met Mike, who was desperate for a drink since his water bottle had frozen. Undaunted and determined to go for the summit, he and two others set off with a guide. Meanwhile I descended, reaching the Kibo Hut at 11am. After some time Mike returned in good spirits, tired but exhilarated by having stood on the top of Africa. Exactly one week after we left Yorkshire we returned home— proving it is possible for busy farmers to climb Kilimanjaro in a week!

above Chris Brown's aerial view of Kilimanjaro's crater shows the Western Breach at 12 o'clock and Uhuru Peak just to the left, on the crater rim.

left Brown enjoys the second of his continental summits, with the shrinking glaciers of the summit crater in the background.

a farmer's odyssey

91

gary pfisterer & ginette harrison

unwitting variations on the heim

American Gary Pfisterer and British Ginette Harrison had never met before they arrived in Kathmandu at the start of an Everest expedition in 1993. But when they walked the last few steps to the summit hand in hand, they knew it would not be the only mountain they would climb together. Finishing the Seven Summits became a shared objective. In 1994 they went to Kilimanjaro, and being competent technical climbers, chose a route that would challenge them – the Heim Glacier. They found the guidebook description to be somewhat obsolete.

Gary

The four of us met up in Nairobi. Ginette was the common thread, joining an otherwise unacquainted team together. A medical doctor, Ginette was an active and adventurous traveller who found her way to Australia in 1991 to pursue her career. There she met Yorkshire climber Richard Bamfield, and Terry Stubberfield, an Aussie paediatrician, through her work. An accomplished mountaineer, Ginette was the most experienced member of the team.

Ginette and I had just climbed Elbrus together, and we were now off to Africa to attempt another of the Seven Summits, Kilimanjaro. We first met on Everest in the autumn of 1993 and, after reaching the summit hand in hand, decided to pursue both the romance and the remaining continental summits together. We had both previously climbed McKinley and Aconcagua, and I had been to Kili's summit in

1991 via the Marangu Route. We therefore decided to attempt a more challenging route on this particular occasion. After thoroughly researching the possibilities in Iain Allan's 1981 guidebook, we settled on the Heim Glacier, which we felt would be a challenging but achievable objective.

The drive to Tanzania provided a gentle immersion into the ambience of East Africa. Along the way we were imbued with the dusty tans and desiccated greens, and captivated by the giraffes, zebra, and gazelles visible along the roadside. It was also an exhilarating ride with the pedal to the metal. Brakes were unknown to these drivers, who maintained speed at all costs in total disregard of the deteriorating road conditions and welfare of the passengers. Any vehicle going even fractionally slower was overtaken, with right of way assumed as a birth right.

We attributed our safe arrival in the late afternoon more to good luck than good management. We were delivered to the Marangu Cottages where we met our guide and cook, Abel, with whom we discussed our plans. We would take the Machame Route to the Shira Plateau, then traverse eastwards to the Baranco Hut. From there Ginette, Richard, and I would gain the Heim. Terry and Abel would climb the Barafu Route and camp on the crater floor, where we would join them for the night. Meanwhile the porters would take the kit and descend to the Mweka Hut where we would meet them on our way down.

As we set off the following morning, any vestige of civilization quickly gave way to primordial jungle, with trailing begonia vines and fiery Kili impatiens. We arrived at the dilapidated Machame Hut (3000m) late in the afternoon. The porters arrived shortly afterwards and we pitched our tents, crashing out after a hearty meal.

The weather had cleared overnight. We set off in tee shirts under blue skies with clouds below in the lowlands, walking through cloud forest festooned with Spanish moss to reach desert-like terrain leading to the Shira Plateau. Each footstep now raised a small cloud of dust, which parched the throat and caked the nostrils. We moved upward into the eerie environment of the giant groundsels and lobelia, flora unique to this region of the world and elevation.

Emerging onto the plateau we were rewarded with our first view of the Heim, which only bore a slight resemblance to the photograph that we had seen in the guidebook. The glaciers on Kilimanjaro are in retreat. While this may sound like a gradual process, the changes we observed since the guidebook was published 15 years previously were dramatic, with nearly 300m of the lower glacier having disappeared. We pressed on, heading towards the Breach Wall, reaching the Shira Caves (3840m) where we spent the night.

The route the following day was a long undulating traverse, contouring the southeast of the mountain with little net gain in elevation. As we progressed, the Heim and glaciers beyond came more directly into view, resulting in frequent stops to assess the route that we were taking and to examine the difficulties that we would have to overcome. With the retreat of the glacier, the snout and lower slopes

appeared rotten and likely to present us with the most difficult challenge. Arriving at the Baranco Hut (3900m) in the early afternoon, we had the last of Abel's mega meals and anxiously awaited the next dawn, when the climbing would begin in earnest.

above In the 1970s the Heim Glacier reached the base of the mountain, but since then has shrunk to half its size and the climb is very different.

left The Heim Glacier flows down the middle of the most impressive side of Kilimanjaro, overlooking the unique vegetation of the East African highlands.

Ginette

We said goodbye to Terry and set off at first light for the base of the Heim Glacier. Two hours later we changed into our plastic boots and climbing gear and bid Abel and the porters farewell. We reduced gear and kit to the minimum essentials, setting off with a Spartan two-days' worth of food, one stove, one litre of fuel, one 9mm rope, eight screws

unwitting variations on the heim

93

and runners, a couple of snow pickets, bivvy gear, necessary personal kit, but no tent. Our loads were a comfortable 15–18kg. It took three hours to reach the snout of the glacier itself. Starting up the glacier without ropes, the angle quickly increased, forcing us to rope up. We climbed three pitches of debris-covered ice which proved to be alternately wet or frozen, depending on whether each was in sun or in shadow. It brought us to a position in which we were supposed to traverse left. Unfortunately this option was blocked by a waterfall that promised dangerous footing and a good soaking! The landmarks and guidebook references were less than apparent, so we decided to avoid the unexpected obstacle.

Exploring to the right we found a short, steep, friable rock pitch that offered access to the ice above. We put Richard on the sharp end by majority vote. He met the challenge admirably with nothing more than a couple of slings for protection. Scrabbling up behind, Gary's unclipped ice hammer fell from the gear loop of his harness. He managed the Gumby move of the century to retrieve it from a small ledge beneath the pitch.

It was already early afternoon and we were not out of the woods with our route-finding difficulties. Gary led out to the left around a prow of steep ice, belayed, and set off to the right, leading lines of weakness on 50° and 60° terrain and trying to gain altitude. The mental clock was ticking louder as the day slipped away. We moved together for a couple of pitches to save some time but with only eight screws he couldn't go too far without regrouping to regain the gear.

It was at one of these stops that we spotted the way to the top of the difficulties we were working through. The final pitch was about 70° with an awkward bulge at the top as a final obstacle. It was a good end to what was becoming a long day and it brought us out on the top of what is known as the Window Buttress (estimated 4800m) just as the sun was beginning to set. Richard located the bivvy, a small flat area encircled by a low stone wall just big enough for the three of us. We got in, got settled, and fired up the stove as darkness became complete. Too tired to cook, we each just had a few brews and then went to sleep with lightning flashing in the distant lowlands, and brilliant stars above.

Gary

Ginette was restless and started the stove while it was still dark. As the dawn emerged, the initial rays of the sun struck the summit of nearby Mount Meru, and Kilimanjaro's cone-shaped shadow stretched westward on the top of the cloud layer below. As we packed up, we had a bit of porridge and a hot drink. I led out across a low-angled snow slope with running belays. Although this was easy terrain the surface was hard and the run outs extreme. We were climbing directly towards the Breach Wall and into what appeared to be a box canyon. A small notch allowed our passage to another snowfield from where we could see there was easy access to the glacier, which was now 100m below us. I favoured an uncertain upward route to the left. My route-finding decisions were receiving heavy and direct fire at this point, but descending hard-won ground is an anathema to sanguine mountaineers. This swung the balance to reluctant acquiescence of upward uncertainty, with the unspoken promise of serious retribution in the event of failure.

We made rapid progress over moraine, negotiating minor difficulties until we arrived beneath a 10m ice cliff studded with stony debris. This obstacle was our

"My guts fluttered and bowels turned to jello as adrenaline flooded my system. I knew if I came off it would be a grounder."

gary pfisterer & ginette harrison

final challenge to gaining the glacier. On belay, I set off upwards. Protection was difficult to place as screws wouldn't penetrate the rock-impregnated ice. I tied off a poor placement about halfway and pressed on. I was nearing the top of the vertical section and success appeared assured. I decided to keep going, rather than try to hang on and place another doubtful piece of protection.

Now making the transition from vertical to horizontal, I loosened my right tool and began to straighten my knees, creating the upward momentum I needed to reach up and over the top for a tool placement. Unfortunately, the pick of my axe struck what felt like a feather pillow with no purchase whatsoever, and the whole manoeuvre came undone in a heartbeat. What was a vertical wall turned into a deep layer of horizontal ash-like gravel. My guts fluttered and bowels turned to jello as adrenaline flooded my system. I knew if I came off, it would be a grounder.

Hyperventilating and with heart pounding, I managed to maintain my balance and slowly back down to where I could get both tools back in the ice. I was trying to maintain some composure to avoid getting totally gripped while I bashed a screw into the ice with my hammer. With the benefit of this largely psychological protection, I took a deep breath and virtually leapt upward. With this momentum and clawing furiously with both tools in the gravel my rear end followed and by the time my crampons hit the gravel my tools were in something more substantial. I had made it. As the tension and fear of the moment drained through the soles of my feet, it was replaced with a giddy sense of well-being. I clipped into a bomb-proof belay and brought the others up on a tight rope. From here we followed a large melt-water runnel onto the glacier.

Just as we gained the glacier proper, the weather took a turn for the worse and the clouds rolled in. Visibility was often limited to the length of the rope, and although the angle was only 30–35°, the surface was hard, making an unroped self-arrest difficult. I was alternating leads with Richard as the leader ran out of screws every 200m. We repeated this process six or seven times and arrived at the top of the Heim Glacier as the weather began to clear. Improved visibility made obstacles clear in every direction. Our initial distress focused on getting off the glacier, which ended abruptly in a 10m ice cliff. We abandoned one of our screws and abseiled to the rock below.

It was almost 6pm now and the mountain was beginning to turn orange in the setting sun. There was nowhere to bivvy. We kept going, to find ourselves just where we wanted to be, on the lower slopes of the Southern Icefield. We climbed straight up the 20–25° slope, then it was dark. Following our torch beams, we found a nearly flat spot and decided to bivvy where we stood. Too exhausted to think about food we crawled into our sleeping bags. Just as I was dozing off, an incredible shooting star arched across the heavens.

We woke to a cold, clear dawn in time to see a line of hypoxic zombies plodding listlessly toward the summit in what appeared to be a scene from *The Night of the Living Dead*. We were amazingly close,

about 100m distant and 25m below the summit. We stayed in our bags until the sun warmed us, then wandered up to Uhuru Peak, the highest point in Africa. The weather and views were perfect.

Seeing Terry and Abel's tent on the crater floor far below, we hurried to join them, and descended to the Barafu Hut (4600m). There we ravenously consumed a huge breakfast and then continued to the Mweka Hut (3000m), finally collapsing in the warm sunshine, satisfied.

above With the short equatorial dusk approaching, Ginette Harrison abseils down the 10m step to escape the top of the Heim Glacier.

left Gary Pfisterer climbs near his and Ginette 's Window Buttress bivouac as evening descends upon the mountain.

Postscript: Dr Ginette Harrison died in an avalanche on Dhaulagiri in Nepal on 24 October 1999. After completing the Seven Summits, she established herself as Britain's most outstanding female mountaineer by climbing five 8000m peaks, including Kangchenjunga, on which she made the first female ascent. Dhaulagiri, on which she was a member of an international team led by her husband Gary, would have been her sixth.

elbrus

The rehabilitation of Elbrus as Europe's highest mountain has been swift, assisted in no small part by its relatively easy ascent route and its status as one of the seven continental summits. But prior to Gorbachev's opening up of the Soviet Union in 1985, things were very different for Elbrus.

Western mountaineers had not forgotten that Elbrus was 835m (2739ft) higher than Mont Blanc, they'd just forgotten that Europe extended into the USSR. Perestroika and glasnost allowed unrestricted access after 1985, and the Caucasus were soon reconfirmed as one of Europe's two major ranges, ending more than 70 years of introspection and semi-isolation.

Squeezed between the Black and Caspian Seas, the Caucasus chain is nearly 1500km (940 miles) long and some 130km (80 miles) wide, and contains 14 mountains higher than Mont Blanc at 4807m (15,770ft), and 100 or so above 4000m (13,120ft). The height of the Caucasus accounts for the range's considerable snow-cover and although there are many glaciers – crevasses can be a problem on Elbrus – they are generally smaller than those that are found in the Alps.

Distinctive among the other craggy peaks of snow and ice, Elbrus is a massive two-headed extinct volcano, plastered in ice. Some 70 glaciers, large and small, cover the Elbrus massif with 145sq km (56sq miles) of ice, in places hundreds of metres thick. The peak is often referred to as "Little Antarctica."

Geographically the Caucasus mark the delineation between Europe to the north and Asia, in the form of Turkey and Iran, to the south. The fascinating ethnic and cultural diversity of the Caucasus region reflects this fusion between East and West, but has led to conflict since the break-up of the USSR.

Chechnya, Georgia, Azerbaijan, and Armenia have fought against their political masters, 1600km (1000 miles) to the north in Moscow, and between themselves, with varying degrees of success. Civil unrest continues, most notably in Chechnya, and the whole region remains politically unstable. While accessing the Caucasus from Georgia to the south remains difficult, Elbrus and the high mountains of the central Caucasus are normally easily and safely accessed from Russia in the north.

Climate

On a similar latitude to the Pyrenees, the climate of the Caucasus is quite different. The mountains are practically land-locked, although the Black and Caspian Seas are so huge that they have a significant effect on climate and precipitation. To the north is the Russian steppe and beyond that forest and the Arctic Circle. To the south is the desert and semi-desert of the Middle East and Arabia. Sandwiched between are the forest and alpine pastures of the High Caucasus – the southern slopes of which are dry and sub-tropical in contrast to the much cooler northern slopes.

Above the treeline of the region, temperatures quickly fall, and above the permanent snowline, which is higher than in the Alps, they rarely rise above freezing. On summer nights temperatures can fall to –8°C, giving excellent snow and ice conditions. But temperatures above the snowline can fall to a treacherous –30°C, even during the day.

Although the end of July and August offer the most stable weather, afternoon thunderstorms are frequent, and longer periods of heavy rain and snowfall do occur. Elbrus is notorious for its cold and violent wind and its sudden weather changes, and the peak offers little shelter from the elements. Its uniform, icy wastes make disorientation a very real danger in poor visibility, and once off the main trail the glacier is riven by frequent deep crevasses.

In technical climbing terms Elbrus is a straightforward ascent on moderately angled snow and ice, but weather, altitude, and demands on stamina prevent many from reaching the summit.

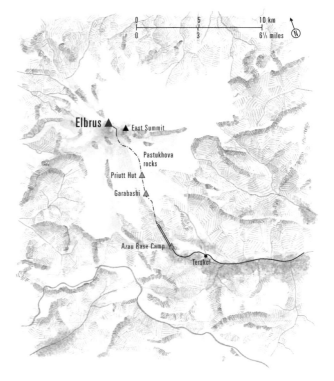

"Elbrus is distinctively different – a massive two-headed volcano, plastered in ice."

above A group of climbers lean into a savage wind on Elbrus, inching their way through the blinding spindrift.

opposite, bottom right Climbers traverse the icy slopes of Elbrus's East Summit on their way towards the Sedlowina Saddle, using ski poles for stability.

Climbing Route

① **West Peak, South East Face**

From the barrel huts a 90-minute walk up the dry glacier leads to the site of the old Priutt Refuge. A steady ascent passes the shattered Pastukhova rocks at 4700m (15,420ft) from where the route climbs leftwards around the rocks of the East Peak and up into the massive snow basin between the West and East Peaks. Above the ruined bivouac shelter on Sedlowina Saddle the ascent leads up a steep snow and ice slope past rocks to cross the horizontal ridge crest to the summit. It is also possible to ascend the West Peak via the South Face of the South West Peak, 5600m (18,372ft).

Flora and Fauna

In many respects the flora and fauna are similar to those of the European Alps, but with a few notable exceptions. Even beyond the treeline a wide variety of wild flowers and plants can be found, especially berries of all kinds and the forest belt is known for its giant shrubs, some five times their normal height.

Goats, ibex, and chamois are fairly common, as are golden eagles, wolves, and bears. The bears are shy, usually avoiding confrontation, and the wolves are less frightening than the wolfhounds used by shepherds to keep them away. Small predators such as lynx, wildcat, and marten can sometimes be seen.

The Mountain and its Climbing

Elbrus can be climbed from most directions and the mountain's uniform nature has produced a variety of similar routes. Consequently, ease of access from the valley and decent accommodation have established Abau Alm as the most popular line of ascent.

South Side

Accessed from the village of Terskol in the upper Baksan Valley, Abau Alm provides easy access to a modern cable car and a less modern chairlift that take climbers a good distance up the mountain. This used to leave a walk of an hour or so up the glacier to the Refuge of the Eleven Hut, better known as the Priutt, but in the summer of 1998 the refuge burnt down in a fire that killed one climber and injured a number of others. Since then climbers have been using half a dozen barrel-shaped huts located at the top of the chairlift. Each hut sleeps six, but the accommodation is considerably smaller than the Priutt, which slept up to 200. Until a new hut is built, accommodation and sanitation problems, rubbish removal, and access to clean water are sure to cause increasing concern.

While the cable car and chairlift give easy access to Elbrus and allow an acclimatized party to ascend to the huts, climb the mountain the next day, and descend to the valley all within 24 hours, a swift ascent can be dangerous for the unacclimatized. Elbrus's summit is 3500m (11,482ft) above Terskol and most climbers will need four to six days climbing and walking at increasing altitudes in the region to be sufficiently prepared for an attempt on the peak itself.

Climbing History

Once most of the high mountains of the Alps had been climbed and categorized, Britain's Victorian mountaineers started to look further afield. Interest grew in the big unclimbed peaks of the Caucasus and of the 10 highest mountains in the range, nine were first climbed by members of the Alpine Club (AC).

The first ascent of Elbrus's lower East Peak, 5621m (18,441ft), is a matter of dispute. The Russians claim it was climbed on 22 July 1829 by Killar Khashirov, the leader of a Russian military scientific expedition. However, in Western mountaineering circles it is credited to D Freshfield, A W Moore, C Tucker, A Sottajev, D Datosov, and F Devouassoud in July 1868. The higher West Peak, 5642m (18,510ft) was climbed in July 1874 by F Crauford Grove, F Gardiner, H Walker, A Sottajev, and P Knubel.

Prior to the 1917 October Revolution the peaks had only seen ascents from 20 or so groups of Russian and foreign climbers. Little climbing took place until 1928, when German and Austrian climbers started returning to the Caucasus. Over the next decade they established a number of new routes and some long ridge traverses. During this period both of Elbrus's peaks received winter ascents from German and Austrian teams.

Russian climbers became more active in the 1930s and this continued into the early 1940s, stopping as the USSR was drawn into the war in Europe. After the war Russian climbers returned to the mountains, climbing many of the hard North Faces and making some spectacular traverses of the long, high ridges that are a feature of the Caucasus. As mountaineering and sport became increasingly politicized in Soviet society, mountaineering camps grew in the area, many of which continue to offer valley accommodation to today's climbers. Although foreign teams continued to visit the Caucasus over the decades, entering the USSR required an expedition mentality and a willingness to suffer endless red tape with a smile. The majority of climbers turned to areas with fewer restrictions, such as the Alps, the Andes, and Alaska.

The opening up of Russia in the 1980s changed everything and paved the way for an open and unrestricted Elbrus to take its rightful place in world mountaineering.

Climbing Elbrus Today

With its demands on stamina and altitude acclimatization, Elbrus gives the would-be seven summiteer a small taste of what is to come. Although the route is technically straightforward, it is a long day with little respite – some seven to nine hours from the huts to the saddle and a further one to two hours to the summit, and then there is the descent.

Kilimanjaro, at 5895m (19,340ft), might be higher, but an ascent of Elbrus on a mediocre day with a wind blowing will give a clearer indication whether you have the stamina to reach the summit of Aconcagua, and the endurance and will power to push yourself to the summit of McKinley and perhaps, ultimately, Everest.

Conservation

Elbrus and the Caucasus have a long history of human habitation and over 100 years of mountain exploration and climbing. The area also has several skiing resorts with a long history. In the Soviet era the huts, and skiing and other tourist facilities were

kept well maintained. Unfortunately, this has ceased to be the case in the 1990s – the facilities have widely fallen into disrepair.

Today the mountain huts are badly managed and collection points for garbage and litter have been neglected, affecting sanitation facilities. The famous Priutt Hut, which had previously been the Base Camp for climbing Elbrus, burnt down in 1998 and the ruin has become a garbage dump.

Though Elbrus is in a National Park, authorities are not adequately funded to manage waste disposal. Instead individual climbers, guides, and tourist operators must take responsibility, carry out waste and tread lightly to minimize impact on the area.

The Priutt Fire

On 16 August 1998, fire swept through the Priutt refuge (here shown behind a passing climber) at about 4200m (13,800ft) on Elbrus. One climber died in the blaze and a number of others were injured, some seriously, as people jumped from the building to safety. Built in the 1930s and designed to withstand the fluctuating mountain temperatures, the three-storey aluminium-clad hut was capable of sleeping up to 200 climbers. There were about 100 people inside at the time of the fire, which completely destroyed the building. Briton Chris Pearson was in the building when the fire broke out: "We got out, but there was someone banging at one of the windows on the top floor we had just come from. We tried to throw rocks to break the window, and we gathered rucksacks together to form a landing cushion, but the smoke was everywhere around us and after a short while we had to leg it. We went up a few days later and all that was left was the remains of the caved-in aluminium shell and smouldering timbers. The walls had acted like an incinerator."

At present there appear to be no plans to rebuild the hut, but with Elbrus's growing popularity the issue of accommodation on the mountain needs to be addressed soon.

Kilimanjaro
Marangu Route
15.8.86

josep pujante
stairway to the seven

When compared to the great mountains of the world, Elbrus may seem uninteresting. The climb is a monotonous snow plod that, once you are acclimatized, only takes the climber a few hours. But the mountain and the region can provide rich experiences, as Josep Pujante describes. In 1994 he climbed it with several friends, including Ramón Agirre, the Spanish Basque who completed his own Seven Summits later the same year.

Seven months after reaching the top of the world, the summit of Chomolungma, we climbed Carstensz Pyramid, the highest mountain in Australasia. Then we immediately started to prepare for another expedition to McKinley to try our luck again, after the setback of the previous year. But, for the second time, we were foiled by Alaska's stormy weather, although we did reach Archdeacon's Tower, not far below the summit. So we returned home to Spain after what had been a long trip. A week later, two friends and I left Barcelona and flew to Moscow aboard an old Tupolev. To Elbrus…

In those days, no Spanish person had climbed the Seven Summits, and I was running towards my destiny. I was well acclimatized from

"To me, Elbrus seems less relevant than the other six continental summits, but the experience was a great lesson in life, culture, history, and ethnology."

Alaskan altitudes of nearly 6000m, but my friends, Louis Lopez, Ramón Agirre, and Emili Civis, came from the Alps and they needed to climb slowly to adapt to the height. As a medical doctor, I was all too aware of the importance of adapting gradually to this kind of altitude, but Elbrus is not incredibly high and is technically easy; some would probably say deceptively easy.

To me, Elbrus seems less relevant than the other six continental summits, but the experience was a great lesson in life, culture, history, and ethnology. It was a very impressive human experience, more than an alpine achievement. After the meltdown of the Soviet Empire, the heterogeneous mosaic of Caucasian republics re-appeared with all their traditions. After many generations of enforced political protection, the new situation has taken the lid off a simmering pot of trouble. Elbrus is located in a republic named Kabardino-Balkaria, not far from Chechnya. In fact, I was not all that surprised to learn that a few weeks before our trip to the Caucasus and Elbrus, a group of terrorists kidnapped several foreigners, demanding helicopters and weapons as a condition for their release.

This is one of the world's unstable regions, with all of its countries feeling the cold wind of abandonment after years of being in the cradle of a possessive parent. Perhaps they look back to their seclusion within the Soviet Union with fondness, even yearning, as then they had many facilities and services. Now, Russian policy has forgotten them, and most of its people stand on the threshold of the 21st century and look towards an uncertain future.

We arrived in Moscow one evening in July and spent the night in an ancient dacha on the outskirts of the capital. The next day we flew to Mineralny Vody and made a long journey by truck to Terskol, the main town at the head of the Baksan Valley. A ruinous hotel was our headquarters from which to attack Elbrus, the "double-headed giant." The extinct volcano has two summits, almost twins, separated by a col known as Sedlowina Saddle. The Oriental Summit is a little lower than the main top, the West Peak (5642m), the highest ground of our old and dear Europe.

The valley of the river Baksan, as well as adjacent valleys, is wonderful, with alpine forests of beautiful tall trees, green meadows full of multicoloured flowers, and dozens of magical butterflies. Above all that, towards the vertical horizon, icefields and glaciers are the gateway to impressive walls of pure granite, to the universe of rock and snow, to the big mountains and summits. This is a paradise of green, white, and grey, capped by the blue dome of the sky, pure and clean as a sapphire.

At last, here we were in the Caucasus. But my main thoughts were not with the mountain but the people. I was troubled by the social and moral order, and the bleakness of their lives. I reflected on the fact that in old times, Elbrus was known as Mingui Tau, which means "White Mountain." What a contrast to the almost black future that so many of these people now contemplate.

On 11 July, the weather was clear and dry, so we went to explore the Cheget Valley. The tiny winding paths among trees were like a precious stairway to the heavens. We relished the thousands of smells from the trees, the flowers, the bushes, from the streams, and even from the stones under the sun. We walked towards Dungussorum Pass (3198m), a snowy col on the wild border with Georgia, with the aim to climb an acclimatization peak. We looked at Dungussorum Peak and its icefall shaped like the number seven, and at a splendid mountain called Nakra Tau. But not all was poetry. Suddenly, from behind a bend in the trail, a patrol of three soldiers with weapons cried out to us: "Halt!" Their Kalashnikov machine guns encouraged compliance. We all stopped, not daring even to blink. The three men were wearing old military uniforms and carrying old rifles, though perhaps the bullets were new. They ordered us to halt and then they asked us for some "presents." Despite their turning us back, we felt a deep pity for them and their kind of life.

Following another route that was free from interrogation, we managed to reach Dungussorum Pass at last,

right To aid acclimatization, some people climb up to enjoy the view from Pastukhova Rocks, at 4600m, about an hour above the old Priutt Hut, the day before making their summit attempt.

stairway to the seven

where we greatly enjoyed the mountain landscape. That evening, back in Terskol, we met up with the renowned British climber Doug Scott and some of his friends. He told me that they had been climbing a new route on the impressively steep mountain called Ushba, and other peaks. We drank together and said "cheers" for the mountains, and I gave Doug one of my books. The following year, Doug Scott completed his Seven Summits just five weeks before I finished mine.

Next morning we went to the Shkelda Valley, where we followed the edge of the Adyl Su River and climbed up on to the Shkelda Glacier, below the wall of peaks from the Akhsu to the Yusengi. Finally, we reached the summit of Gumatschi and stood for an hour on the top, admiring the marvellous Tcheget Tau, a difficult summit 4190m high. The following day, we made our first contact with Elbrus, using the highly precarious cable car to reach the Priutt Eleven Hut. This odd-looking bunkhouse gained its name many years ago, when an expedition of eleven climbers survived a major storm by staying there. We continued up the slopes of Elbrus until we arrived at Pastukhova Rocks (4690m), before returning all the way to Terskol for a good night's rest to prepare for our climb to the top of the highest mountain on the European continent.

On 16 July, we ascended to Priutt Eleven again, where we found a bunk for the night. At 3am the following day we set off for the top. We walked steadily, wearing all of our high-altitude equipment, with crampons biting the snow and using our ice axes like walking sticks.

> **"We were both on very private journeys, looking for our inner selves, but the pleasure and satisfaction of climbing were best shared."**

Some clouds hid the stars and eclipsed the moon. The sky was not the best, but the weather seemed stable. We reached Pastukhova Rocks before 5am. Climbing in silence, and enveloped in the darkness that hid everything beyond our headtorch beams, I thought of the first people who had come this way – the pioneers Gardiner, Crauford Grove, and Walker from Great Britain who, with their Swiss guide Peter Knubel, reached the summit of Elbrus for the first time in history.

I was feeling happy, but just because I was on the mountain, not because of the kind of climbing. The motivation was not the summit, but the possibility of one day fulfilling my personal challenge of climbing all of the Seven Summits. I prefer mountains like Everest, K2 or Cho Oyu, Manaslu or Annapurna, my favourite mountains in the Himalayas. Elbrus is one of the Seven, so it had to be done, but it was a pleasurable experience.

When we stopped to drink some water from the thermos, we finally began to notice the extremely cold weather. The temperature was around −15°C. However, we soon forgot the unpleasantness of the freezing cold as the colour of the sky began to change and take on the distinct pearl tones that precede the sun's rising. Later, a line of red, like a

left In the pastel haze of the early morning, two climbers plod up Elbrus as the mountain's shadow stretches across the Caucasus Mountains.

blaze of fire, announced that sun and warmth were on their way, with a marvellous halo of mallow and amethyst, reminding me of a Van Gogh painting.

Ramón and I increased our climbing rhythm and arrived at the Saddle at 7.30am without great effort. We drank hot sweet tea with a lot of sugar from our thermos bottles and one quart later, we continued up the mountain. My friend and I swapped leads to share the trail breaking. Free of ropes and other climbing paraphernalia, we advanced up the snowy hill making steps in compact snow. The sun was high on the horizon and we could see already that the sky wasn't too clear. Several clouds hung from the blue dome and the wind began to blow with force.

"In front of our eyes was the whole of the frozen crater, shaped like a half moon."

Arriving at the edge of the crater, the ridge became steeper. Looking below, we saw our friends Emily and Louis progressing very slowly with two other climbers. There was nobody else on Elbrus. Half an hour later we gained the cornice of snow overhanging the snow slope. A quick pull on the axe and we were both enjoying a very nice view from the balcony. We could feel the wind blowing with increasing force.

"Now the job is done," said Ramón, "look over there, at the end of the snow slope. You can see the silhouette."

"Yes," I replied, "the outline is very close, I think this ridge and the other meet at this hill. Let's go."

"OK, here we go!" my friend exclaimed in happiness, smiling. "Ahead to the summit."

After climbing the short prominence, which was almost vertical, we saw – oh what a surprise! – a panorama that we did not expect. Before our eyes was the whole of the frozen crater, shaped like a half moon, at the opposite end of which was the true summit pinnacle. So, we were not on the top after all, but an almost horizontal 500m from the crown of rock and snow.

We breathed deeply, taking air, then exploded in laughter, laughing in guffaws as we enjoyed the landscape that opened under our feet. We were level with the East Summit of Elbrus, just across the Saddle. It was comforting to see it there, perhaps it was there to keep the West Summit company. We started marching again and finally reached the last little steepening in the terrain. Now there was only blue sky above us! We covered the distance from false summit to real summit by walking along the mouth of the extinguished volcano. At 9am, we finally reached the West Summit of Elbrus. The highest point of Europe was marked by a squat monolith of about waist height, made from volcanic stone.

Certainly, Elbrus is not a difficult peak, it is not a steeple or the sharp spire of a beautiful tower, but it is what it is. Creation made Elbrus like this and our

right "At the threshold of the Old Continent's doors to heaven," Josep Pujante enjoys the fifth of his Seven Summits.

below Climbers follow a well-beaten path to Sedlowina Saddle, the col separating the east and west summits of Elbrus.

mission was to climb to its highest point. At the threshold of the Old Continent's doors to heaven, at 5642m above sea level, we embraced each other and took photos to immortalize the moment. This was not a particularly special summit and there was no great emotion, but we were the same two guys that had climbed the top of Everest the year before. Here we were sharing another summit, while on our own personal quests for the Seven. We were both on very private journeys, looking for our inner selves, but the pleasure and satisfaction of climbing are best shared.

We enjoyed the magnificent panorama and admired the double-pointed arrow of Ushba, its inaccessible summits poised to strike at the heavens. And further south stood the disquieting mass of Dungussorum and its loyal sentinel, Nakra Tau. On the opposite side of the hill, our view of the Russian steppe was diffused by mist and the fog of dawn. In the morning there was a sea of clouds beneath us, floating at mid-height, covering the valleys. It wasn't very windy or cold.

The view was wonderful, but in other ways, Elbrus was empty. Our victory was almost sour, a curious mixture of happiness and deception. We were glad we had done it, but we had not experienced the flavour

and the smell of adventure like in other mountains. I had been involved in more difficult challenges, more complex and risky climbs on peaks that had resisted more; I had escaped dangerous situations with the help of the Goddess of Fortune. But still, this climb had to be done. It was one more stop on the long stairway to the Seven, and from this came a satisfaction that might otherwise have been missing.

Half an hour later we began our trek down. Before we reached the balcony at the end of the semi-circular crown of the crater, we met Luis Lopez and two friends, so I climbed back up with them to the summit. An hour later, the four of us reached the top. We took more photographs, and then descended, noticing that bad weather was on the way. Not far above the Saddle, we saw Emili climbing up, slowly because he had some problem with his boots. My friends quickly continued their descent, due to windy and cloudy weather. I decided to help Emili and two hours later we reached the top. For the third time that day, I stood on the apex of Elbrus, in honour of friendship. Although the storm was coming, I took a can of beer from my rucksack and, without haste, the two of us quietly savoured the delicious taste of the cold, frothy liquid.

vinson

The interior of mainland Antarctica can truly claim to be the last great expanse of real wilderness. It is the world's highest, coldest, and, perhaps surprisingly, driest continent, with valleys that in all probability have not received any precipitation for the last two million years.

In Antartica, mountain ranges rise from seas of polar ice and the environment, devoid of all flora and fauna, is perhaps the most unforgiving in the world.

Vinson Massif, often erroneously called Mount Vinson, is situated at 78°S, in the southern half of the Sentinel Range and some 1200km (750 miles) from the South Pole. Unlike most mountain groups in Antarctica, the Sentinel Range, home to the six highest summits on the continent, is primarily a collection of slender jagged peaks with narrow arêtes and steep rocky faces up to 2500m (8200ft) in height. Vinson Massif is less spectacular and more bulky, with eight peaks rising a short distance from the 90sq km (35sq miles) summit plateau.

Named after Carl Vinson from the state of Georgia, USA, once Chairman of the House Armed Services Committee and who from 1935 to 1961 put considerable pressure on the US Government to support Antarctic exploration, Antarctica's highest mountain was the last continental summit to be both discovered and climbed.

In November 1935 the American Lincoln Ellsworth, already in the record books for completing the first transarctic ocean crossing, joined with pilot Hubert Hollick-Kenyon to make the first transcontinental flight over Antarctica. Setting out in the single-engine aircraft, Polar Star, from Dundee Island at the tip of the Antarctic Peninsula, they ran out of fuel after 22 days and were forced to land just short of the Bay of Whales. They walked the last 28km (15 miles). On the first day of this flight, Ellsworth caught sight of a jagged yet "solitary little range," which he christened the Sentinel Range, though he was unaware that higher summits were hidden beneath a thick bank of cloud.

Vinson Massif was not "discovered" until 1957 when it was spotted by US Navy pilots during an aerial reconnaissance for the American International Geophysical Year traverse party. Aerial and ground surveys between the years 1958 and 1961 not only established heights for all the major peaks but also found that the mountains consisted of two distinct ranges. The northern group kept the original name of Sentinel, the southern group became the Heritage Range and the entire collection the Ellsworth Mountains.

Climate

Vinson is best attempted during the summer months of November, December, and January, when there is 24-hour daylight. Unlike the climate of many of the world's great mountains, the Sentinel Range tends to be influenced by a stable air mass producing very good weather and mild, low temperatures. However, in practice life is never quite that simple. Atmospheric pressure at the Poles is lower than it is at other latitudes, resulting in air masses being sucked into these regions at high altitudes. As the air cools over the South Pole it descends rapidly and rushes outwards at high speed. Being caught in high winds on the summit plateau of Vinson is probably the most serious aspect of the climb. Temperatures can fall to −35°C on relatively calm days. Frostbite is an ever-present threat, particularly in the presence of wind, and the slightest lack of concentration can prove disastrous. Perversely, due to constant daylight and the hole in the ozone layer, the unwary can also suffer sunburn.

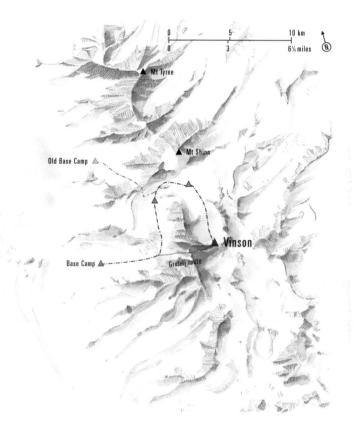

"**Mountain ranges rise from seas of polar ice and an environment, devoid of all flora and fauna, that is perhaps the most unforgiving in the world.**"

Climbing Routes

① The Normal Route via Branscomb Glacier

The Normal Route to the summit of Vinson is often likened to the West Buttress of Denali, being a long glacier expedition with no particular difficulties. From the ANI Base Camp the route climbs gently up the Branscomb Glacier for 5km (3 miles) to the base of the icefall, leading to the col between Vinson Massif and Shinn. From the top camp, placed above the icefall at 3700m (12,140ft), the route heads south up low-angled slopes of bare, wind-scoured ice to a short, steep snow/ice face leading to the summit ridge. The ascent takes six to 10 days.

② The Slovenian Route

Climbed in a single push by Viki Grošelj 's group, this route takes a steep ice couloir from halfway up the Branscomb Glacier to the summit plateau.

Climbing History

The 1966–7 American Antarctic Mountaineering Expedition was the first major project on the continent to have climbing as its main objective. The US government was keen to launch it as rumours spread that a somewhat eccentric American, Woodrow Wilson Sayre, was also planning to mount an attempt on Vinson. Sayre had already blotted his copy book with a clandestine attempt on Everest from Tibet in 1962 and the government, unhappy about Sayre's logistical organization, feared they would be forced to instigate a huge and costly rescue operation. In early December 1966 a ski-equipped US Navy Hercules landed 10 first-rate American mountaineers on the Nimitz Glacier a little over 30km (18 miles) from the summit of Vinson Massif. After establishing the three camps, Barry Corbet, John Evans, Bill Long, and Pete Schoening reached the highest point in Antarctica on 17 December, and later in the month two other ascents were made by other members of the team. The expedition stayed 40 days, during which time six peaks were climbed, including the four highest in the range. Tyree, the second highest, only 45m (150ft) lower than Vinson Massif, proved to be the most challenging and a terrific prize for Corbet and Evans, who remain the only partnership to have climbed all three highest peaks in Antarctica.

In 1979 Vinson finally received its fourth ascent, when a largely American scientific expedition was resurveying the Ellsworth Mountains. Days before Christmas two Germans, Buggisch and von Gyzycki, plus a Soviet surveyor, Samsonov, made an unauthorized ascent and left a red pennant on the summit. Though the ascent was frowned upon by the authorities, it allowed scientists on the ice cap to make a much more accurate height measurement of the summit using satellite Doppler techniques to arrive at the altitude quoted today. The third successful expedition, making the fifth and sixth ascents in 1983, included Dick Bass, the first to climb Vinson while collecting his Seven Summits.

The first new route and first true solo ascent of the mountain took place in January 1991 when an Austrian mountaineer, the late Rudi Lang, climbed

above From the col on the original approach to Vinson, a climber observes the headwall at the top of Branscomb Glacier.

West Side (North Section)

West Side (South Section)

vinson

directly from the Branscomb Glacier up the hanging glacier on the West Face. The following year the American Robert Anderson, soloed two new routes: one on the South Face (Sunshine Wall) and another via the West South West or Rolex Ridge. Since then several routes have been added to the South and West Faces, including the Slovenian Route, which was climbed very quickly by Viki Grošelj and party.

The Approach Route

The only practical means for most mountaineers to reach the Vinson Massif is by using ANI (see sidebar), the only non-governmental organization that can supply the logistical services for an Antarctic venture. In 1986 the company created the Patriot Hills blue-ice runway and tented camp at 80°S. Clients are flown there from Punta Arenas in Chile in a wheeled Hercules, which offers a reliable service, though the landing at Patriot Hills will always be exciting as it is impossible to apply brakes on the ice runway. Patriot Hills remains open about four months a year and from there it is a one hour flight by ski-equipped Twin Otter to Vinson Base Camp. In 1992 Base Camp was moved from the traditional site on the Nimitz Glacier to about 2100m (6870ft) on the Branscomb, allowing easier access to the Normal Route.

Climbing Vinson Today

Since the inception of ANI and the birth of the Seven Summits quest, Vinson has become the destination for mountaineers visiting the Antarctic mainland and there have now been more than 400 individual ascents. A few guides have each made more than 10 ascents. The majority of climbers are members of guided groups, using either ANI guides or other guiding companies who buy ANI logistical support. Because of the very high cost of operating a rescue, ANI has stringent criteria for accepting independent non-guided groups. This has caused frustration for some climbers, as the climb itself is a straightforward ascent. But the remote location and extreme cold make it a serious undertaking and a simple mistake could have dire consequences.

Until quite recently nearly all those visiting the Sentinel Range concentrated exclusively on climbing the highest summit, but over the last few years an increasing number of small parties have begun to explore other parts of the range. The rock in the Sentinel Range is mostly metamorphic and very loose, though areas of stable green quartzite do exist. The general structure of the Massif appears to preclude the possibility of creating major technical ascents, although those seeking difficult and challenging climbs will find quite a few on the more spiky succession of peaks that extend northwards along the range.

It may be several decades before there is a regular service to the Antarctic interior that the "average mountaineer" can afford. But, with more climbers willing and able to pay great sums to access this remote region and the growing popularity of the global quest to climb the seven highest summits, Vinson (and ANI) is sure to have a captive audience for many years to come.

Conservation

Under the Antarctic Treaty, inaugurated in 1959, no one country owns any part of the continent but simply administers a particular sector (the Sentinel Range lies in the Chilean sector). Countries that have joined the Treaty, and there are now more than 30, generally need to have a presence in the form of a scientific base and uphold a number of basic requirements, such as no nuclear testing or mining. The original Treaty does not mention tourism but all countries party to the Madrid Protocol, a set of guidelines that address the environmental protection of Antarctica, must uphold certain laws while visiting the continent. The International Association of Antarctic Tour Operators (IAATO), of which ANI was a founding member, was launched to promote self-regulation within the industry and to ensure that its members met the highly stringent obligations of the Antarctic Treaty. Though the protocol suggests hazardous goods be removed and bars incineration, ANI goes one step further and requires climbers to remove every trace of passage, including all human waste, from the continent. This policy provides excellent protection for Vinson and the Sentinel Range. Even though Vinson is visited by a growing number of climbers, they continue to experience a pristine Antarctic environment.

Adventure Network International

After the seventh ascent of Vinson in November 1985, three members of the summit party, Giles Kershaw from the UK, plus Canadians Pat Morrow and Martyn Williams, set up a company called Adventure Network International (ANI). Kershaw, who had worked for British Antarctic Survey prior to Transglobe and Footsteps for Scott, had been the adventurous pilot who flew in the 1983 expedition and was rapidly gaining great respect as probably the most experienced of polar aviators. All three realized that there was a potential market for a commercial organization that could supply the necessary logistical support for an increasing number of mountaineers wanting to stand atop Antarctica's highest peak. Tragically, in March 1990, Kershaw was killed in a gyrocopter crash on the Peninsula while involved in a filming project, so the running of the company was subsequently taken on by his widow, Anne. Operations were expanded to meet the growing demand by mountaineers and virtually all ascents of Vinson to date have been made using the infrastructure of ANI. The company's policy is to review climbers before accepting them for a guided ascent, and a return trip to Vinson Massif, normally scheduled to last 12–14 days, cost around US $25,000 in 2000.

1980			1985

McKinley
West Buttress
1980

Kilimanjaro
Marangu Route
1981

david hempleman-adams

an antarctic initiation

In 1994 David Hempleman-Adams visited Antarctica to climb its highest mountain. Cast from the mould of the classic British explorer, his account of this Antarctic adventure is laced with the self-effacing humour that has carried him through even more challenging Polar experiences since then, including solo journeys to both the South and North Poles. Hempleman-Adams' ascent of Vinson was clearly a formative experience.

At 4897m, Mount Vinson is not the hardest to climb of the Seven Summits, but I think that for me, without question, it was the coldest, cleanest, remotest, and, on a day rate, the most expensive. First climbed in 1966, it has probably had fewer ascents than any of the other continental summits.

The critical part of the jigsaw of getting into Antarctica is arranging a flight. This is done through Adventure Network International (ANI), now run by Anne Kershaw. Her late husband Giles was the pilot who audaciously flew the first climbing group to Vinson, in the heart of

Antarctica. Anne is a petite Scottish blonde with the face of an angel, which belies her acute business acumen. In fact, she makes adventurers' dreams happen, from solo South Pole expeditions to guided ascents of Vinson. While the flights seem expensive (at around $25,000 per person) they are, in fact, incredibly cheap when you consider the cost of organizing your own flights and the logistics of flying from either South America, South Africa, or New Zealand, and how time-consuming that would be to arrange yourself.

The expedition proper started when we arrived in Punta Arenas, at the southern tip of Chile. The town is a favoured stopover for whalers, and in times past it was a welcome haven for ships travelling through the treacherous seas off Cape Horn. On the first visit, it seemed like the edge of the world – cold, dusty, and uninviting. However, with its coloured corrugated iron rooftops, hardy yet hospitable local people, and, as you would expect of a port, disproportionately vibrant night-life, it offers a colourful contrast to the bleakness of the continent that lies to the south. Apparently it has more whore houses per capita than most places in the world, but the crab sandwiches and Pisco Sours make a second visit a must. (This is just as well, because any one visit to Antarctica means two visits to Punta Arenas!) I defy any man to drink three Piscos; it would kill anyone without the constitution of an ox.

We knew that we had to be lucky – very lucky – for our flight into Antarctica to leave within a couple of days of the scheduled departure time. The flight, in a civilian Hercules C130, and the landing at Patriot Hills, is very sensitive to weather conditions. If the wind blows harder than 25 knots, it is too dangerous to attempt a landing. Also, the flight time being six hours, coupled with the need to carry enough fuel to return, it is extraordinarily expensive to operate. To fly to Patriot and have to return because of bad weather would simply kill a whole season's profits for ANI. With this and the unpredictability of the weather, and the lack of weather stations en route, we had to wait some time for the weather to improve in order to provide safe flying conditions. This was extremely frustrating, but once we were airborne over Antarctica's desolate landscape, I was grateful for the caution.

Inside the plane there were rows of passenger seats bolted to the floor of the Hercules transporter plane, and the rear was packed with freight. For me it was one of the highlights of the trip, gradually leaving land, over Cape Horn, across Drake's Passage, and into the heart of Antarctica, with the flight crew pointing out the sights on the way. The landing at Patriot Hills was a cross between a Disney ride and a gut-wrenching nightmare. The Herc landed with wheels onto a bare blue-ice runway, which is kept clear of snow by the winds screaming

down from the Patriot Hills. Once at a halt, the plane was quickly unloaded, and we followed marker wands to Patriot Hills camp, about a mile from the airstrip. By the time we reached the huts, the aeroplane was on its way back with a cargo of passengers, kitchen waste, and barrels of human waste.

The camp was surprisingly well fitted out with a homely mess and cook tent, toilet facilities (an igloo with a 40 gallon drum wearing a loo seat), and accommodation tents. The food was brilliant and there was no shortage of booze. However, the weather was good, as it obviously had to be in order to get the Herc in, so the ANI staff did their damnedest to conserve Patriot's wine stocks and fly us straight out to Vinson Base Camp. The work horses of the Polar regions are small, robust Twin Otter aircraft fitted with skis, and one of these took us on the one-hour flight to Vinson Base Camp. As we were the first flight at the start of the season, we landed on a pristine glacier, opened the door, and the headwall of Vinson stood right in front of us. It was incredibly impressive. The first thing that hit us was the cold, −25°C ambient at 3660m. When we jumped out of the plane we knew

above This headwall at the top of the Branscomb Glacier leads to the col between Vinson Massif and Mount Shinn, the site of the top camp.

left Climbers disembark at Vinson's Base Camp after an hour long journey from Patriot Hills in ANI's ski-equipped Twin Otter.

an antarctic initiation

111

above On the summit of Vinson, a radiant sun and crystal clear skies overlook low clouds across Antarctica.

right With the bastion of Vinson behind them, climbers descend the last mile of the Branscomb Glacier on their way to Base Camp and the final flight back to civilization.

just how cold it was because the hairs in our noses instantly froze solid. It didn't take us long to learn that when you get cold hands, the fastest way to get warmth back into them is to put them in your or your partner's warmest areas – the armpits or the crotch. It was at times like these that I wished I was climbing with someone other than a bearded Antarctic explorer.

The other thing I noticed was how clean it was. The snow was actually white compared to the dirty grey stuff I had seen in other places. We hardly had time to take it all in before the Twin Otter was taking off for the relative metropolis of Patriot Hills. The sound of the droning engines faded to silence long before the plane disappeared, then we were alone. I felt incredibly isolated.

If you are fit, you could probably climb Vinson in just two days, but I don't really see the point of doing it in such a short time. The normal turnaround for the ANI aeroplane is every 12 days, and they come and pick you up from Base Camp by Twin Otter after 10 days, in the hope that you don't have to spend too long at Patriot Hills making a nuisance

of yourself. So you would have a lot of hanging around time at Base Camp, unless you had plans to climb other peaks and such. Besides, we weren't that fit.

We stayed at Base Camp for one night, then we donned skis, roped up, and set off with everything for the climb. We didn't do any shuttles like on McKinley. Moving together demands good technique for walking over crevasses with heavy weights. Invariably, if the person at the back stops they will be tugged over by the leader, who lets out a low grunt as the rope goes taut around the waist. Most people have quirks, so you need to be good friends. Things get out of control faster when travelling on skis, and if one or the other stops suddenly, they can pull the other partner completely into the air. Extreme patience is an important piece of equipment, especially for those who are tied on to the same rope as me. To ski with sledges while roped together is tantamount to testing the United Nations Charter for Peace.

We were the first team on the mountain, but breaking trail over the crevassed glacier was a lot of work and no fun. Even the innocent collapse of the top snow crust sent shivers of doom down my spine. On more than one occasion, I seriously believed that I was falling into a black hole.

We skied towards the headwall, and turned a natural left, up the continuation of the Branscomb Glacier. Just around the corner we made our first camp. The trick was to place our black bags (everyone has to bring all their waste back off the mountain in these) in the sun, and to try to keep them out of the wind. Although it got colder with each hundred metres we climbed, it was the bitter wind that bit into our bare white buttocks that gave us an experience few have encountered.

The headwall is extremely impressive, with many new routes waiting to be climbed by the adventurous. On the second day we skied parallel to this wall up a gentle sloping glacier, again roped up. We chose to camp in the sun at the bottom of the icefall, rather than the frequently used wind scoop to the right. The scoop is more protected, but it is even colder!

I was climbing the mountain with the experienced mountaineer and polar traveller, Roger Mear. One of the great things about working with some of the world's great climbers and polar travellers such as Roger, Borge Ousland, and Rune Gjeldnes, is what you can learn from their vast experience. I do tend to get set in my ways, but occasionally I would think, "Damn – that's a good idea, why didn't I think of that!" One morning Roger passed me a hot cup of chocolate while I was deep in my sleeping bag. It was the best cup of chocolate I had ever drunk, thanks to Roger's special knack for melting Mars bar chunks into the hot chocolate powder.

The icefall above Camp 2 was the only place where we had to be really careful. Here the crevasses were open, and because it is too steep for sledges, we were carrying huge loads. We were lazy and only wanted to do one carry. Jumping an open crevasse with an 36kg rucksack stretched muscles I didn't even know I had.

Climbing through a series of séracs and crevasses near the top of the 300m icefall, we started to get beautiful views of the mountains around us. The snowy pinnacle of Mount Shinn reared up to the left and behind us we looked over the tops of peaks that rose from the edge of the Nimitz Glacier, a gigantic river of ice that flows the entire length of the Ellsworth Mountains. After a long day, we finally reached the site of Camp 3.

We had an Italian tent that we were testing. An advantage of climbing in Antarctica at this time of year is the 24-hour daylight, but it can be strange to the uninitiated, and you certainly mess up your biorhythms. Waking up to set off at 1am is not uncommon. To ease this, we took a black inner tent. This was supposed to absorb any heat from the sun's rays, and help us to sleep. In fact, after spending a day in the tent, I found it quite depressing, like living in a big black hole. It might have saved some heat, but I didn't feel it, as it was hellishly cold. Both of us knocked our feet together in the middle of the night to generate some warmth.

Camp 3 was our last camp before the summit. The permanent daylight of the austral summer months was a big advantage because all we had to do was wait for clear and not too windy weather. But it was getting colder and colder. Sometimes on skis and sometimes on crampons, but always roped up to protect ourselves from the unseen crevasses that we knew were out there, we climbed into a large plateau-like valley, at the top of which was the summit pyramid. At the bottom of this I had the most incredible stomach ache, the sort of rumbling one gets after consuming four pints of lager and a curry. Roger insisted that I had to remain roped up to use the black bag that we had brought along for such an occasion, which left me with quite a problem. With a harness and crampons on, and the wind blowing off the coldest mountain in the world, I managed to relieve myself, much to the amusement of Roger.

We climbed a fairly steep snow slope, to a large cornice that I was pulled over like a flapping penguin. Then there was a long haul up the final rocky ridge that led to the top. When we reached the summit at 1am, there were no queues, just us, a ski pole, which was left by the first ascensionists 29 years before, and a view to die for. Bathed in a pink hue, the mountains all around were crystal clear, with Base Camp on the glacier below us seemingly just a stone's throw away.

That trip was one of the most memorable of my life. The only drawback was skiing back down with a bag full of excrement in my rucksack. But the retching was worth it, because Vinson was still the coldest, cleanest, remotest, and most beautiful mountain in the world.

viki grošelj
breaking records – and the rules

Even now Antartica is an expensive place to get to and, for many of the world's climbers, a visit to the ice continent is an impossible dream. But, in 1997, four of Slovenia's most accomplished mountaineers managed to get there, and they made the most of it. Super fit and highly motivated, they not only climbed Vinson in record time by a new route, but made several other first ascents in the area. Viki Grošelj here describes the stylish culmination of his Seven Summits quest.

The story of Slovene climbing in Antarctica began shortly after World War II, when the Slovene emigrant Dinko Bertoncelj climbed some of its peaks. In the 1980s, Stane Klemenc started collecting data and seeking contact with Chilean and Argentinian authorities.

> **"Boundless ice plains sown with mountains stretched before our eyes for more than 1000km towards the South Pole."**

Unfortunately, all further efforts to climb there were thwarted by the amount of money needed for a visit to Antarctica – three times more than the average Himalayan budget. Over the years, the Himalayas have won out time after time.

Only recently, when Antarctica became a glaring blank spot on the world map of Slovene climbing, did our efforts turn again in its direction. In the meantime the Canadians had established ANI (Adventure Network International), the only means of transport to Antarctica, which put an end to lengthy and tiresome negotiations with the countries that have Base Camps there.

left Viki Grošelj and his team climbed the right of the two obvious couloirs that form the backdrop to Vinson's Base Camp.

right At its highest point during the Antarctic summer the midday sun warms Viki Grošelj's Base Camp.

The first Antarctic expedition aroused great interest among Slovene climbers, but as it turned out only three of us were willing to spend our own money in addition to sponsorship: Stane Klemenc, his long time climbing partner Rafko Vodišek, and me. We had negotiated a discount with the agency, but only on the condition that our group consisted of at least five people. So understandably, we gladly accepted the offer of participation by Stipe Božić, an old climbing partner of mine from the Himalayas, and his cameraman Joško Bojić, who had been preparing a TV series on all the continents' highest peaks for over a year.

On 3 January 1997 we were to fly to Antarctica from Punta Arenas, Chile. Our departure from home was due on 30 December. I had been raising money for the journey throughout the autumn. My main sponsor was the Slovenica Insurance Company, and there were a number of other companies and individuals contributing to the best of their abilities. On the day of our departure the budgetary problems were far from solved, but nevertheless I left much more at ease than expected.

The weather was good in Antarctica, so on 3 January we boarded a Hercules to fly from Punta Arenas in the south of Chile to our longed-for destination. The flight lasted six hours, and half an hour before landing, the clouds beneath us cleared away. Holding my breath I stared out of the window taking photo after photo. On numerous mountain sides the whiteness of the wind-swept landscape was enlivened by blocks of blue-green ice. The landing was quite a thrill. The plane was jumping up and down on the wavy and slippery ice for a long time before it finally came to a halt. We descended the freight-ramp and for the first time in our lives stepped onto Antarctic ice. What a feeling!

Within just a few hours we left Patriot Hills, our home Base Camp, in a small plane and flew to the foot of Vinson. We landed on the glacier below its South Face, at an altitude of 2100m. We jumped out of the plane and unloaded our equipment. I was pleasantly surprised to find that the Base Camp was no longer where it used to be in the early years, but was now in a much better location. The mountain peak rose 3000m above us. But best of all, the base of the new route I had silently planned to climb was right in front of us.

It was past midnight before the tents were pitched and the first tea made. The sun shone nicely and the temperature was bearable; with no wind it stayed at about −20°C. I inquired of Dave, the Base Camp keeper, about the 2500m high South Face of Vinson, and he assured me that its right part – the highest – was still route-free. I decided that would be where we would try first.

By 10am we were all out of bed. We feverishly prepared our gear and food for the ascent while the members of the other teams observed us somewhat doubtfully. There is an unwritten rule that the ascent should be made gradually, with two camps on the way up. The ascent and descent usually takes five to eight days, which supposedly strengthens the possibility of success. Ah, well. We felt we had

Vinson
Slovenian Route
5.1.97

breaking records – and the rules

the experience needed and were well prepared to try it alpine style, to which we were much better suited. The weather was wonderful, so we felt we must make the best of every hour. We knew if we failed that there would be more than enough time for another attempt.

We left at noon, and three hours later we were at the foot of the face. The area in which we planned to climb our new route seemed promising enough, so we unanimously decided to give it a try. Stane, Rafko, and Stipe left their skis by a snow boulder, while I decided to take mine to the top to make a ski descent from there.

I found a way across the bergschrund and then, about 200m higher, Rafko took the leading position. We climbed unroped, hoping to continue like that all the way to the top. The snow was good and the cramponing was fairly easy. There were moments, struggling upwards on the windless slope, when I was even rather hot! We looked back and, deep down in the track, we could see Josko, our cameraman, who had accompanied us to the foot of the face, returning to Base Camp. We also spotted members of the other expeditions who were transporting food and equipment for their first camp, using sledges that were tied around their waists.

We were light and swift up there. No sleeping bags, no tents, no dishes, or cookers. We each carried a litre of liquid in a thermos in the backpack and that just had to do. The view from the face was magnificent. Boundless ice plains sown with mountains stretched before our eyes for more than 1000km towards the South Pole. At this point I felt the first pains in my calves but hardly gave it a thought as we progressed remarkably quickly. I thought to myself, "Either Antarctica affects me favourably or I must really be in very good shape."

The hugeness of the face absorbed us and the constant straining slackened our pace. At 9pm, with about two-thirds of the face covered, the first crisis set in. We were getting more and more sleepy but were afraid to rest as the sun would soon disappear behind the ridge, leaving the bitterly cold shade. I took the lead with Rafko following on my heels. The face got much steeper, but the conditions were still good so we continued climbing unroped. However, we struggled with the last and steepest 200m of height. The windpacked snow cover increased our fear of a slab avalanche so, using my ice axe, I cautiously groped my way up from rock to rock. Now and then I took a quick look downwards between my legs. What an incredible view it was. We literally hung above an unearthly landscape.

Just the final 100m remained before the summit. There was some rock climbing and then we had to make our way over a bulging snow flank where the inclination reached and even exceeded 55°. Because of the constant fear of a slab avalanche this frightening section of the face dragged on interminably – every minute felt like an hour. When the steepness eventually slackened I paused to wait for Rafko. After a hug we marched those last metres to the real edge of the face, in that ineffable mixture of morning and evening with the sun still shining on us. It was 3am.

left Still 500m below the summit of Vinson, members of Viki Grošelj's team reach easy terrain at the top of the 2000m face.

Two thousand metres of precipitous face – and finally we had made it! But the view in front of us was a great disappointment. The summit of Vinson was actually 500m above us, and felt so very, very far away. Stipe and Stane soon appeared over the edge of the face – we were all almost dying of sleepiness, but the excitement of what was still ahead drove us on.

It was morning and, at an altitude of more than 4500m and despite our excellent clothing, the biting cold cut through not only to our bones but to our very souls. We finally reached the foot of the summit pyramid. Stipe and I got to grips with the rock-hard snow in the gully above us, but the struggling seemed to drag on forever. Eventually we passed the last rocks on our left and faced a wonderful snow ridge, just like a celestial walkway high above the boundless ice plains, which led us towards the highest spot on the continent. How simple and beautiful everything seemed! We walked respectfully up those last metres to the very top. It is funny how the grandeur of the moment, the comradeship, and the overwhelming emotions made the −30°C lose its bite. I took out the Slovene flag and hung it on a ski pole stuck on the top. Then Stane arrived. We hugged. It was a magnificent completion of his many years' endeavours. Rafko followed shortly after. We were all together on the top.

So we had completed 19 hours of climbing by a new route and decided to call it Slovenska (the Slovene Route). It covers 2500m; a height gain of Himalayan dimensions. What a splendid success! As the first Slovenian to climb all of the continental summits, I silently shared my triumph with my home country.

> **"I hardly noticed that I was descending one of the most dangerous glaciers of my life – the deposit place for three avalanche slopes."**

In the rocks just below the top we found a round box with a small summit book put there by the first ascensionists of the mountain. Proudly I put down our names and the facts about the new route. Then we picked a few pieces of rock for ourselves and for our friends, as souvenirs of this incredible adventure which, at 10am on 5 January 1997, reached one of its climaxes.

We still needed a safe descent. We decided to take the route of the first ascensionists, to complete a traverse of the entire mountain. I bound up my skis with great care and climbed up to the highest point.

I took a few deep breaths to concentrate and then begin to ski. The first few metres were easy, so the whole thing seemed overly formal. Stipe and Stane both videotaped my descent. I kept close to the rocky ridge for about 100m, but then I had to head straight down the precipitous slope. A few resolute turns took me into the steepest part. The inclination far exceeded 50°, but that was not the worst. At every turn I felt the snowpack beneath my feet tremble. It seemed to me that the entire flank was going to come off any second and would roll me down the 300m in a roaring avalanche. The only thing I could do was make a traverse into the safety of a long slope alternately covered with

Instead I chose to bypass another rocky peak and then descended to the ordinary route. When the plateau dipped I started skiing zestfully, but going round the corner I stopped, completely dumbfounded: below me was an unknown valley. I said to myself, "Now what? Do I return to the col and all the way up to the summit pyramid? Or do I try to find a way along this valley hoping for a passage some place lower leading me to the ordinary route?" I was dead tired so eventually laziness prevailed. I decided to descend and, if there was no passage down there, I knew I would just have to climb over the ridge somehow.

The skiing was terrific on kilometres of steep slopes with perfect snow, but there was a nagging thought in the back of my mind; "Will it end well?" It did! A long, rounded flank led me to the valley of the ordinary route even before I reached the col between Vinson and Mount Shinn.

What awaited me there was a dangerous hanging glacier with a vertical drop of 1000m. Surely this was the hardest part of my descent. Occasional footsteps and some marking poles helped me find my way through a maze of séracs. The turns were short and sharp. It was hard and dangerous but, intoxicated by the skiing, I gradually regained my strength, skiing with perfect concentration. I hardly noticed that I was descending one of the most dangerous glaciers of my life – the deposit place for three avalanche slopes. Somewhere in the middle the sérac density decreased. The steepness remained unchanged as the séracs grew fewer, allowing me more room to manoeuvre. Floating down I forgot about the unquenchable thirst that

above Viki Grošelj stands poised on the summit a moment before taking off on his rapid ski descent.

right Looking over the tips of his skis down the other side of Vinson, Grošelj anticipates his descent down unfamililar territory to complete a full traverse of the mountain.

harder snow and patches of bare ice. My leg muscles shivered, the edges of my skis scratched against the bare ice, but I managed to control my speed. With the next turn the steepness slackened and the scary height was gone. With a shout of joy I hastened to the glacier plateau. I took another look up before disappearing behind the ridge. Rafko, Stane, and Stipe were working their way along the rocky ridge; they seemed to have found a better way for themselves. We waved at each other merrily.

I had to continue horizontally or even slightly uphill for nearly half an hour before I reached the highest spot of the plateau. On my left I could see the col below Vinson but it was too high for me to climb.

had been killing me since the previous evening. In a second I worked my way over a dangerous narrow passage at the base of the glacier, and didn't stop until I was a kilometre or so lower, and safe. I turned round and – what a view! A dangerous glacier of a 1000m vertical drop had taken me no more than 15 minutes to ski down. But for the tracks of my turns among the ice pinnacles, I would surely have thought it a dream.

There were no more obstacles. Skiing down a long, gently sloping valley at the foot of the South Face, I soon ran into the first party of three climbers, slowly pushing their way up. They offered me a drink of water – the greatest drink there is! – and then congratulated me. They spoke of our first ascent and the fast ski descent with deep respect.

In the completely level part of the valley, which I walked across in the cross-country skiing technique, all the efforts of the past two days suddenly pressed down on me. I somehow managed to drag myself to the snow boulder at the base of our first ascent route, where the glacier dipped again. The final 400m of height had marvellous skiing in powder snow. I arrived at Base Camp. And Joško and I drank and drank and kept drinking, and the world seemed so beautiful it took my breath away. I was back in Base Camp again, 28 hours after we had left it. And what a 28 hours they had been!

After only a day's rest, we were all ready for new adventures. Stipe and I climbed a nice double-peaked mountain just above Base Camp. The ascent by a snow slope took us three hours. The summit, with an altitude of 2800m, offered us an incredible view of the magical landscape. Thousands of peaks of beautiful and peculiar shapes stretched all the way to the horizon. We could have spent our whole lives and even more there doing nothing but climbing. Being the first people to climb the mountain, we named one of the peaks Slovenia and the other Croatia, took a number of photographs from our vantage point,

and then skied back to Base Camp, making long enthusiastic turns as we travelled on our way.

The following day was even nicer. We managed to climb three more peaks, all first ascents, and did many kilometres of skiing in only 11 hours. The first ascent of another peak above Base Camp was a new climax in a string of fabulous experiences. Stane and I both reached it from a different direction and named it after my main sponsor – Slovenica. We chose a third direction for the ski descent. During our trip we made over 20 ascents and descents, climbed Vinson, and conquered six previously unclimbed peaks. The sheer number and the way in which we did it were beyond our wildest plans and greatest expectations.

On 15 January two planes picked us up and took us to our home Base Camp, Patriot Hills. There had been some heavy snowfall there, so to our great delight the plane from Punta Arenas could not fetch us straight away.

We grabbed the opportunity of the four extra days to make some more great ascents on up to 500m high ice faces and ridges, as well as making some terrific ski descents, until on Saturday, 18 January, the weather conditions got better. The news of the plane coming to pick us up came rather as a disappointment.

The arrival of the plane was scheduled at 2am; our departure was at 5am. During that last evening I kept going out, just staring, taking photographs, and marvelling. I knew how difficult this parting was going to be. I did some writing, listened to some music, and talked to friends. There was a sweet sadness as I sat by the stove, warming my feet, and contemplating the incredible episode I had just experienced! It still takes my breath away to think of the beauty of Antarctica.

above Using their skis with great effectiveness, Grošelj and his friends climbed several other peaks during their stay in Antarctica.

carstensz pyramid

Had you lived in Holland in the early 17th century, you would almost certainly have joined fellow countrymen in ridiculing the Dutch navigator, Jan Carstensz, who on a voyage across the southeast Pacific in 1623 pronounced he had seen snow-capped mountains only 4°S of the equator.

At 4884m (16,024ft) Carstensz Pyramid is not only the highest mountain in Irian Jaya but also, if calculations are based on continental platforms rather than plate tectonics, the highest in Australasia. It lies, according to local tribal language, in the Dugundugoo – the high mountains of what was formerly known as Dutch New Guinea, the second largest island in the world. The Pyramid is a long, rocky fin and one of several 4000m (13,100ft) summits that make up the Sudirman Range, though the primitive inhabitants to the south refer to these peaks rather more delightfully as the Namangkawee or the "Mountains of the White Arrow." It is the highest island mountain chain in the World.

Unlike most other summits in this book, Carstensz, a remote peak with difficult access both physically and politically, received relatively scant attention until the quest to collect the Seven Summits took off in the late 1980s. Although not as demanding a climb as some others in the list, it is perhaps technically the hardest of all.

Many years ago the permanent ice cover descended as low as 2000m (6500ft), but like other equatorial mountains, glacial recession has been dramatic. Today, the ice barely drops below 4200m (13,800ft) and the highest valleys are somewhat desolate with exposed glaciated slabs and moraines.

Virtually all of the climbing on Carstensz Pyramid takes place on the the vast North Face of the mountain, a slabby angle averaging no more than 65–70°, rising about 600m (2000ft) above the Yellow Valley. Although there is loose rock in the gullies, on the open faces the rock is immaculate and can be so aggressively abrasive that wearing thin gloves or extensively taping the hands is advisable when climbing.

When the Dutch finally withdrew from the island in 1963, they hoped that the country, which they called West Papua, would be able to implement a programme of self rule. However, over the next five years the administration of the Indonesian Republic "persuaded" the people to accept a new government and from 1965 to the present day the Organisasi Papu Merdeka (OPM), the Free Papua Movement, has waged a nearly constant but so far futile guerrilla war against Indonesian rule. In 1973 the country was formally renamed Irian Jaya: Irian – an acronym from the political slogan, "the Indonesian Republic In the struggle Against the Netherlands" and Jaya – meaning victory. Enough said. The area was closed to foreigners for a large part of the 1990s due to political unrest, but by 1999 the situation had stabilized. The first climbers allowed in to the region made a successful ascent of Carstensz in February 1999.

Climate

Apart from the large financial commitment needed to make the complex approach, the greatest deterrent to climbing the mountain is the weather. It can rain at any time of the year – and usually does. However, those reaching the summit early in the day may be rewarded with a unique view south across densely forested foothills and undulating jungle to the blue of the Arafura Sea.

Climbing History

Wide disbelief in Jan Carstensz's observations continued for almost 300 years until in 1911 an expedition that included Dr A F Wollaston, a later

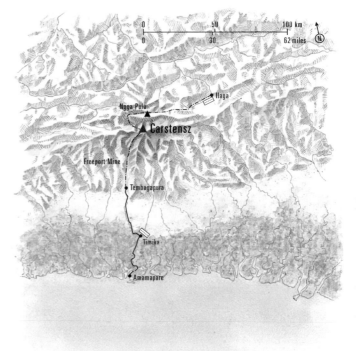

> **"The rock is immaculate and so aggressively abrasive that wearing thin gloves or extensively taping the hands is advisable when climbing."**

Climbing Routes

① The Normal Route

A line of weakness slants across the right side of the North Face to reach the West Ridge. Much of this is scrambling interspersed with pitches of V Diff and Severe (5.5). The ridge is relatively straightforward but exposed. Most parties climb directly out of the first notch via a strenuous pitch of HVS (5.9), but the first ascensionists avoided this by descending on to the South Face and following broken ledges until the crest could be regained. The average ascent time is seven hours, although the route has been completed in a five-and-a-half hour round trip from Base Camp.

② East Ridge

A long ascent in a fine position. Mostly scrambling but with several more difficult narrow sections and some loose rock.

③ The Anglo–American Route

This route climbs the North Face well left of the summit fall-line to reach the upper East Ridge. Pitches of VS/HVS (5.7–5.8) can be expected followed by easier climbing on limestone.

④ The American Direct

A direct line straight up the summit fall-line, giving superb climbing at a continuous VS (5.7) standard with two pitches of HVS (5.8) on the top headwall.

Two routes have also been climbed on the colossal "White Slab" on the right side of the North Face, although neither of these were finished to the main summit:

⑤ Aquarius

Climbs the conspicuous crack line up the left side of the slab on superlative rock to join the Normal Route after 400m (1300ft). Maximum difficulties of Severe (5.5)

⑥ Oceania

A direct line straight up the middle of the slab. Superb climbing sustained at Severe (5.5) standard, then joining the Normal Route.

North Side

Everest explorer, set out from the south coast of New Guinea. Forcing a route through swamps, jungles, and dense forest took time and effort, and after almost a year the party gave up only 35km (20 miles) south of its goal. Wollaston returned in the summer of 1912–13 and overcame considerable hardship to reach the initial ice slopes of the mountain.

In 1936 the Royal Netherlands Geographical Society sponsored Dr A H Colijn and two companions in another attempt to climb the island's highest peak. They climbed Ngga Pulu, which they thought to be the highest of the Sudirman peaks – probably due to the much thicker glacier ice that then covered the summit. With the rapid shrinking of the region's glaciers, the rocky summit of Carstensz has since been found to be higher. Later calculations revealed their mistake. War then intervened, and throughout the 1950s the Himalayas and Andes were the focal point of mountain exploration. It wasn't until 1960 that climbers began to think seriously of Carstensz once more. The following year the New Zealand alpinist, Philip Temple, and five fellow enthusiasts found a route to the foot of the North Face, only to return disappointed when their proposed airdrop failed to materialize. But Temple had the chance to return just six months later, with the legendary German mountaineer, Heinrich Harrer, a veteran of the first ascent of the Eiger's North Face. Harrer also recruited Australian rock climber, Russell Kippax, and a Dutch patrol officer, Albert Huizenga. This

time the airdrop went as planned and the group climbed 32 summits, including the first ascent of the Carstensz Pyramid by what is now the Normal Route via the North Face and upper West Ridge. On 13 February 1962 all reached the top on their first attempt, a particularly impressive achievement for Huizenga who had never climbed before.

After recovering from frostbite sustained on Nanga Parbat in 1971, the great Italian guide, Reinhold Messner, made the second ascent of the mountain via the East Ridge with a client, S Bigarella. A year later the Hong Kong-based British team of Jack Baines, Dick Isherwood, and Leo Murray were the first to venture onto the excellent limestone of Carstensz's North Face. Since then 11 routes or variations have been created on the north facing walls of the peak. In 1978 Pete Boardman and his future wife, Hillary Collins, completed Wollaston's unfinished trip by climbing the more rotten rock and ice of the South Face to complete the first south to north traverse of the mountain.

Approach Route

Carstensz Pyramid can be approached from the north or the south. Early expeditions chose the southern approach as it offered the shortest route from the nearest coastline. From 1954 missionaries opened up previously unexplored valleys to the northeast and by 1961 had established around 20 grass airstrips. The closest one to Carstensz is near the village of Ilaga at 2000m (6500ft) and approximately 80km (50 miles), as the crow flies, from the mountain. A charter flight from either Nabire or Wamena now avoids the worst of the jungle. Ilaga, a highland village of approximately 10,000 Dani inhabitants, is a six-day walk from Base Camp with local porters.

The route to Carstensz passes through rainforest and large areas of equatorial bog to reach the uneven limestone plateau. It finally crosses New Zealand Pass, descending to Base Camp by the lakes in the Upper Meren Valley and then takes an hour to reach the start of the Normal Route on the North Face. The approach can be cut to two days by chartering a helicopter to the base of New Zealand Pass. Recently some teams have been approaching from the south, via Timika through the Freeport copper mine. Special permission is required to take this much shorter route to Base Camp.

Climbing Carstensz Today

There is still scope for more new routes on the North Face and almost infinite potential for good rock climbing elsewhere in the range. Due to the time and expense needed to obtain the many necessary permits, most visitors now use the services of experienced commercial operators.

Having reached the tranquil remote Meren valley below Carstensz Pyramid, mountaineers today will be faced with the incongruous sound of throbbing machinery. A geologist accompanying the 1936 expedition was the first to notice the unusually rich copper deposits on Ertsberg, a neighbouring 4200m (13,800ft) peak northwest of Carstensz. Mining rights were acquired by a New Orleans-based company and the site is now the third largest open-cast copper mine in the world and reportedly has the largest gold deposits. Operating the mine required building a deep-water port on the South Coast, an airstrip, and construction of nearly 130km (80 miles) of access road. When the mine is receptive to visitors (which is seldom), the road provides fast access for climbers, as it is just three hours from Base Camp.

Conservation

Though Carstensz is one of the least visited of the Seven Summits it has one of the most serious problems with rubbish. Litter lines trails and camps

and deforestation is on the increase as the Dani use firewood for cooking in the camps.

Although the mountain lies within a National Park, there is little evidence of a park authority presence. Future climbing parties, therefore, need to take the initiative to protect the mountain's trails and camps.

The proximity of a major copper mine is startling. Some consider the area an environmental disaster due to reports of massive deforestation and contamination of the natural waterways. The mine is literally removing mountains to reach the valuable mineral ore. It is hoped that such devastation so close to Carstensz will not discourage a responsible attitude to the environment among its visitors.

above With the snowy summits of Ngga Pulu and Punchak Jaya in the distance, climbers make their way down Carstensz.

far left Wearing rain shawls and carrying umbrellas, Dani porters cross a bridge in typical weather, during the walk to Carstensz.

The Dani

Noted for their attire – the menfolk often wearing no more than a penis gourd or Kepewak – the Dani are traditionally a warrior nation and inter-tribal feuds took place until the arrival of missionaries in the 1950s. Now most practise Christianity and have a quiet dignified persona. They live in huts called Kanangda, which have circular walls made from bark or wood topped by a heavily thatched grass roof. Their possessions are very basic. Until the 1950s they lived in total primitive isolation without wheeled transport. Their staple diet is sweet potato, though the Dani also rear pigs and are adept at catching birds and other animals for food. The Western Dani, unlike neighbours to the east and south of Carstensz, have no recent history of cannibalism.

ronald naar

the mysterious forces of the pyramid

There is a strange aura about Carstensz Pyramid. This was clearly felt by Ronald Naar, who climbed the mountain in 1989. Sharpened by his country's long affiliation with the area, Naar's acute sense of history provides us with a fascinating insight into the exploration of Carstensz, and the unique peculiarities that make the region seem not of this world.

I am not a superstitious person but when, on Friday, 13 November, I stood on top of New Guinea's highest summit, Carstensz Pyramid, I still didn't feel truly at ease. It is true that at that moment my long-held ambition was fulfilled: climbing the highest summit of the splendid archipelago that once, as a colony, belonged to my native country, The Netherlands. The fact that I was nervous and superstitious was not absurd considering all that had happened during the previous four years. It all started in 1985 when, just before my first attempt to organize a trip to the Carstensz Peaks, my prospective climbing partner,

> **"My long-held ambition was fulfilled: climbing the highest summit of the splendid archipelago that once belonged to my native country."**

Frank Merjenberg, died under circumstances that were never completely cleared up. And three years later I had to cancel my plans to climb Carstensz for curious reasons. That year a four-man Indonesian climbing team had disappeared somewhere in the Central Highlands of New Guinea. Although it was thought to have been a political murder (one of the climbers was the son of an Indonesian general) the local government declared the Carstensz region too dangerous for Dutchmen and I wasn't allowed to enter the country.

However, on my third try I had little more luck, and was granted permission. But because of a "mistake," the telex from the local authorities had the wrong date on it for the start of my expedition. So I arrived in Jakarta two weeks early and was unable to obtain the necessary papers until a week and half later. A further delay occurred in Jayapura, the capital of Irian Jaya, simply because a chit was lost. All these incidents contributed to my unease. I started to get the idea that mysterious forces were at work around the Carstensz Peaks.

Still, it was an old love that had given me the strength to get through the years of correspondence and, when I finally got to New Guinea, the following weeks of waiting, in Jakarta and then Jayapura. It was a love for what in Holland is called the "Girdle of Emeralds," those mysterious snow-covered mountains, named after the Dutch sailor, Jan Carstensz.

When I had first started dreaming about climbing the Carstensz Peaks, the political situation made these mountains remote and extremely difficult to reach. By the early 1980s only 10 expeditions had visited these mysterious tropical snow mountains. Because of the love–hate relationship between the now independent Indonesia and its former colonial power, The Netherlands, it was especially difficult for Dutchmen to get permission to enter Irian Jaya. Even in today's era of space travel and satellite telecommunications, many parts of Irian Jaya are still in the Stone Age, with most of the local Dani people still hunting with bows and arrows and farming their land with stone axes. A journey to New Guinea's Highlands is still a journey back in time.

In the second half of the 1980s the approach march to the mountains from the north closed, so it was necessary for me to organize a joint Indonesian–Dutch expedition to enter the area. Two students of the Mapala University in Jakarta were therefore included in my team in order to get the necessary permits. After two weeks of tedious and frustrating negotiations with various officials, we were finally allowed to travel through the mine, the quickest way through the area. Above the mining town of Tembagapura we finally said goodbye to modern civilization and left for the remains of the mountains. It was at this point that I realized my dream had now come true: the mysterious Carstensz Peaks lay open before me.

The first stretch of wilderness we came across was Carstensz meadow, the grassy swamp (the same swamp that Colijn and Dozy reached after 28 days trek through the steamy mountain jungle in 1936). It only took us a few hours driving by bus and another half hour by cable car to travel through it. High above us I saw the great limestone rocks of the Carstensz summits, rising above the rain clouds. It was nearing midday and, according to the weather forecast, rain was due. But even without the rain, we were already soaking wet as the route went through swamps. In spite of the care I had taken, jumping from one clump of grass to another, I still sunk up to my knees in the mud. It wasn't long before we had been enveloped in fog and the rain started to fall. It was like a Turkish bath.

After several hours we set up camp near a flat piece of moraine. We pitched the tents in the pouring rain and Soutey, one of my two Indonesian fellow mountaineers, started to prepare our favourite meal, *nasi goreng* – fried rice with meat and vegetables.

By the afternoon it was clear that the feared thunder showers would not arrive. The clouds in the valley were blown apart by a soft breeze. I could suddenly see, for the first time, the tropical glaciers of Irian Jaya, dramatically lit by the setting sun.

right A climber leads the difficult crux pitch at 4600m on Carstensz Pyramid's Normal Route.

	1990			**1995**

| Vinson
Normal Route
24.11.87 | Aconcagua
Polish Glacier
9.1.89 | Elbrus
Normal Route
21.5.89 | Carstensz
Normal Route
14.11.89 | Everest
South Col
12.5.92 |

After so many reports by other expeditions about the long-lasting showers, I realized that we should make every second of good weather count. So, on my second day at the foot of the mountains, we started planning our climb of Ngga Pulu, the snow-covered one of the two highest peaks. I aimed to not only climb it, but also to make the first descent by skis and snowboard. It couldn't have been better.

The second objective was, of course, what is now the highest peak, Carstensz Pyramid. But mysterious forces were still at work. On our third day among the Carstensz Peaks, my Dutch climbing partner, Erik Pootjes, woke with a severe headache. Although he expected to feel a lot better after some more sleep, I didn't want to hesitate. As the weather was still good, I decided to try Carstensz Pyramid that day. Soutey didn't feel very strong either, so the only fit person left in the camp was our second Indonesian member, Didi Samsu.

As quickly as we could, we moved towards the limestone North Face of the Pyramid. As we didn't have a route description, I decided to start climbing on some gentle slabs on the western part of the face. The sun was out, but on the northern horizon dark clouds were threatening.

Under the hot sun the rock was drying quickly, giving good friction for our climbing boots. I calculated that it would only stay dry for another hour or so, so we had to be quick. But, climbing first, I didn't belay until we reached the ridge, a little under two hours later. Looking down from the ridge I could see on the other side, between swirling clouds, the canyon of the Tsing River. Until recently only two expeditions had followed this valley: Wollaston in 1912 and the American Forbes Wilson in 1960. But things change quickly in Irian Jaya; from the ridge I could clearly hear the growl of bulldozers and explosions of the advancing mine.

On the ridge, we continued climbing together. We crossed a small gap and then continued following the ridge. After a few hundred metres the joy was over: we reached another gap, but this one was 15m deep. As it was very steep, a short part was even overhanging, we decided to abseil. Didi went first. As soon as he disappeared he shouted that climbing up again could be quite difficult. "Then we leave the rope hanging here," I shouted back. "I still have a second rope in my rucksack!" Didi agreed.

From the bottom of the gap I traversed over a wide ledge on the south side of the ridge. Far below I could see patchy smears of snow, probably the remnants of the once huge ice field seen by Jan Carstensz more than three centuries ago.

From the end of the ledge we started to climb up slowly, crossing three small overhangs. There were some small rock pegs, but it was unclear if I was still going the right way. In the meantime we had returned to the Turkish bath; fog was all around us and sometimes I heard the distant sound of thunder. I felt some drops of rain, but fortunately the warm rock stayed dry.

Back on the ridge, we continued climbing with a short rope between us, almost running to the top. Then there was a third gap. Grinning, Didi shouted, "Just jump!" First I hesitated, then I took off and landed a few seconds later just on the other side. The fourth gap was less spectacular. I climbed down a short chimney for a few metres but got stuck halfway down. I thought that some of my slings had probably got caught on a rock. I carefully undid them and, thinking I was free, jumped on to a big boulder, two metres below. My flight was accompanied by a tearing noise. I looked back up to find a piece of my trousers still hanging in the chimney. A few minutes later we reached the top. It was marked by an aluminium stake and a small plaque commemorating a member of Mapala University who had died a few years before while abseiling from Carstensz Pyramid. It was a moment of great joy – the dream I had as a young Dutchman had come true and I was closer to completing the "grand slam" of the Seven Summits. Imitating Dick Bass, I shouted: "Six down, one more to go!" Didi smiled: "Why don't you finish them quickly?" "Because the last peak is Everest," I said sadly, "I've started hating that mountain, as I've already tried it twice!"

In the late afternoon, we returned to our camp. The tropical rains poured down with incredible force. I immediately ran to Erik's tent and shouted, "We climbed the Pyramid!" But there was no answer. When I zipped open the tent, I was shocked: Erik was in his sleeping bag, almost unconscious, now and then muttering a few sounds. My heart stood still. That morning, when I was preparing to leave the camp, he had said he had only a "normal" headache; on my return from the climb, it was painfully clear to me that it was no headache at all, but severe altitude sickness.

I shook my head; the mysterious forces of the Carstensz Pyramid, which I thought had taken a day off, had tricked us again.

left The mysterious Carstensz Pyramid remains enshrouded in cloud as a climber ascends one of the many rapidly shrinking glaciers in the area.

below Seen from Ngga Pulu, the rainwater run-off channels tell of the high precipitation in the region.

127

Everest
South West Face
24.9.75

McKinley
South Face
12.5.76

Kilimanjaro
Western Breach
9.76

doug scott
on the edge of civilization

In his long and eventful climbing career, Doug Scott climbed most of the continental summits without even considering the Seven Summits challenge. His single concession to this "disreputable concept" was climbing Carstensz. But the quality of the climbing, the Stone-Age culture of the Dani people, and the environmental and human rights issues he encountered, made this climb the most fascinating of all seven.

My wife Sharu, Tom Callaghan, and I flew over many miles of tropical rainforest in a missionary society's Cessna. Judging by the Australian pilot's language, he himself was not of the cloth. However he was an obliging fellow, flying off route to give us a glimpse of the Carstensz Massif, the highest point of the island of New Guinea.

Above a mass of dense white cloud, black-streaked limestone towers and crags stuck out like the broken-down teeth in an old man's head. We could make out all the main summits and smidgens of snow and glacier ice in between. "You're lucky to see anything but bloody cloud up here," our pilot informed us. We knew from conversations with a group of Indonesian climbers at Aconcagua Base Camp to expect rain. When I asked, "When do people climb on Carstensz?" the answer was, "Any time, it rains all the time." It was, in fact, that chance meeting with a group from Mapala University Climbing Club, Jakarta that was indirectly responsible for our visit to Irian Jaya. Sharu and I returned from the summit of Aconcagua to find seven enthusiastic, young Indonesian climbers camped next to our tent. They were insistent we should lecture to their university club and go climbing with them. They asked if I was trying to climb all the Seven Summits. It was the

first time I had considered such a disreputable concept as "collecting" summits. I had by then climbed Everest, McKinley, and Kilimanjaro by new routes or attempted new routes and now Aconcagua by a combination of existing routes. Since a teenager I had been curious to see new mountain ranges and had over the last 30 years been visiting them two or three times a year. The chances were that I would, in the course of pursuing this obsession, visit the Caucasus and walk up Elbrus, and also climb Vinson in Antarctica. But I probably would not have gone into the mountains of New Guinea. Peter Boardman, fresh from a visit with future wife Hillary Collins, had told me at Kanchenjunga Base Camp in 1979 of the problems they had reaching Carstensz.

After climbing Vinson and Elbrus I wrote to Norman Edwin and Didiek Samsu, the two Indonesians who were most insistent we visit. Sadly, we received letters from other team members, giving us the tragic news that both had died in a storm on Aconcagua days after we left, and the other five had suffered frostbite during rescue attempts. We continued with our plans and did give talks at Mapala University before heading off to Irian Jaya – collecting summits has the effect of moving the unwilling flesh to do what it might not do otherwise. As it turned out, this last summit was to be the most fascinating of all seven.

As the pilot flew down to Ilaga, we saw thatched huts and neat vegetable gardens scattered about, rolling downland, surrounded by dense forest. The plane bounced, rattled, and shook up the bumpy airstrip, coming to a halt by a native compound. After unloading, the pilot revved up to leave and shouted he had no idea when he would be back, and in any case the locals would probably chop our heads off and have us for dinner! With that cheery information he flew back to Nabire.

We turned to attend to our baggage. There were men, mostly wearing penis gourds and birds of paradise feathers in their hair, already sorting it out. Women wearing raffia grass skirts and little else helped to make up loads. At last, after so many hassles, we had arrived at the village of Ilaga on 3 May 1995. The local Dani carried our gear for an hour, from the airstrip into the village where we met the rest of our team. We were a group of friends from the UK – David Macrae, Chris Brown, my wife Sharu and myself; and Tom Callaghan and Mark Bowen from the US. Our reason for meeting was to climb Carstensz Pyramid and to spend as much time as possible with the local Dani people, a number of whom now act as porters for visiting climbers.

The next morning 53 such porters were assembled for a one-and-a-half hour lecture by the Chief of Police and

left Laden with supplies, Dani porters provide a helping hand to one another as they cross a swollen stream on their way to the mountain.

right The area surrounding Carstensz Pyramid contains rocky formations and lakes like this one, which lies beneath the steep northern cliffs of Punjack Jaya.

then by the Secretary of Ilaga, an Indonesian government appointee, who extolled the locals to work hard. He reinforced his message by kicking one of the villagers in the face. The villager took it without flinching. I looked on horrified, expecting some of the other villagers – young, strong, muscular men, walking about with spears and bows and arrows – to leap to his defence, but no-one moved; it was as if this sort of thing was a regular occurrence.

Except for this startling incident, the start of our journey to Carstensz could not have been more pleasant. From the airstrip we crossed a wide basin where some 10,000 Dani now live in their traditional thatched, round huts. These are set in neat walled-in cottage gardens, full of mainly potato and yam, but also just about every other vegetable you could grow here in Britain. Beyond the fields there was dense forest stretching up to ridge tops. We had seen from our flight just how much of Irian Jaya is still prime forest. To the northeast there are said to be tribes that have never been visited by people from outside the island.

By mid-morning we left our hut in the village and walked down winding lanes, passing fields of snorting pigs and grass huts, with all our porters strung out, most carrying potatoes to sustain themselves over the next couple of weeks. The women came along to help, grass skirts swishing as they walked, carrying bilum bags of sweet potatoes supported on their foreheads. Soon sweat was pouring from them, down their naked bodies, glistening in the sun. The Dani we met on the way were open, direct, happy, and secure in themselves – especially the children who surrounded us at the idyllic village of Pinapa, mostly wearing junior penis gourds or rush skirts, painted at the ends. All those Dani wearing an assortment of worn, patched, and dirty Western-style clothes were naturally not included in the photography!

After midday we entered the "heart of darkness" – the jungle – every bit as geography books describe it with long, thin tree trunks reaching up for the sun and, in the gloom below, a tangle of ferns, creepers, and spiky palms. It became apparent that jungle travelling is quite difficult, especially where there was so much rain, making it muddy and swampy in places and difficult to walk through the tangle of creepers.

We eventually came to level ground where the trees had been burned back, and the Dani together erected a long frame from tarpaulins. Inside they set up another stronger frame over a long fire on which to dry wet wood. After dinner, we sat enthralled as the Dani sang under the stars by an open fire. The music produced was like the Australian Aboriginal didgeridoo and resembled Zulu melodies. It was the finest singing I had ever heard, with all 53 Dani involved in the most sophisticated symphony of solo and chorus, welling up from deep inside themselves. David sat up late; painting by lamplight a furry marsupial that had been caught flying through the trees by a well-aimed stone.

On 5 May we began our journey early, immediately plunging back into the jungle and then went over the 12,470ft Padang Mbla-Mbla. On the pass we had a last look back at Ilaga and the airstrip before a deluge of rain had us and our porters shivering. They built a fire and lit bushes, trying to warm themselves until the rain stopped and

then we moved on. Sharp, elegantly shaped, sculpted blades of white limestone rock poked out of the mud and grass. Here the vegetation changed, becoming reminiscent of the area around Mount Kenya, with clumps of tree fern growing as high as 20ft.

"It was the finest singing I had ever heard, with all 53 Dani involved in a sophisticated symphony of solo and chorus."

We reached Base Camp by the evening of 9 May. Thirty of our porters were due to return to Ilaga, the rest would remain at Base Camp for our return. The 30 had raced off early in the morning and were now already returning from Base Camp, whooping and shouting, still full of energy after a hard eight-hour slog, barefoot on the sharpest of limestone scree and crag. From the highest col, the New Zealand Pass, we could look across at the North Face of Carstensz. Just before the mist closed in, we were able to pick out the Original Route, and others routes that we could attempt later. The path went down steep gullies and joined a well-made path that goes from Base Camp down to the area's major copper mine. We turned left up to Base Camp, reaching it in drizzling rain late in the afternoon.

The following morning, in drizzle, we reached the base of the North Wall at 6am. Mark teamed up with Chris; Sharu and I with Tom. We climbed in rock shoes and alongside a fixed rope of polypropylene for 300ft, which soon wasn't needed and wasn't used. The weather improved and Mark and Chris hared on ahead. Because of our group size and Sharu's filming, we were slower. We left the usual prominent gully route for a variation on the left, which gave better climbing than the scree of the gully. We entered the big scree basin below the summit wall and took a variation left of that too, which also gave good climbing (at about a grade of 5.6/5.7). From the summit ridge we looked down the

carstensz pyramid doug scott

far side onto a big, wide glacier, which seemed only 500ft away. The ridge was very alpine, and it was great to be there on this long and varied route. We climbed down into a notch, where Mark was struggling up the wet awkward crack. After a monumental effort, Chris followed him and hauled our sacks, which made it much easier for Sharu and myself. We marvelled at first ascensionist Heinrich Harrer, who by 1963 was quite an old man and had done a superb job getting up this bit. We climbed to another notch where there was some fixed rope. We reached the summit by 11am, the end of a fine mountain route, not unlike an alpine rock climb. I was given a standing ovation on this, my "seventh summit." We left at noon as clouds moved in and blocked out views of the mine to the west. Racing along the ridge, abseiling, and

below On the first ascent of the Anglo-American Route, the climbers enjoyed the superb coarse limestone which offered excellent placements for protection.

climbing back down to the bottom, we were back in camp an hour later, a 12-hour round trip, rounded off by a very jubilant welcome from our Dani.

On the following days, after climbing a new route to the east of Carstensz, known as Middenspits, we set out to do another on the North Face, left of the Original Route and the line climbed by Dick Isherwood. One pitch after the other, we shared leads with Tom and Mark, who climbed the most demanding sections. Each pitch was a full rope length, hovering around 5.7/5.8 (VS/HVS) on superb rock with the occasional peg belay. We found protection from wires and friends wedged in between spiky flutings. Much of the rock was covered in coalescing pockets that left spikes in between which crackled and crunched under our rock boots, but provided good friction.

At midday the bad weather came in and we raced up over easier angled slabs and climbed a steep wall into a rocky gully. As it was raining hard, we unroped and moved up the gully to exit onto the East Ridge where Reinhold Messner, or some subsequent ascensionist, had left a cairn. About 95ft below the summit and, being drenched, we had no enthusiasm to go further. We down climbed and abseiled, with water

cascading down every crack and crevice on the North Face, reaching camp before dark. The good 2000ft route (about TD or Grade V) turned to delectable high mountain limestone wherever it was steep.

Reluctantly we wandered down to the mine, which we hoped to exit through because one member had a knee injury and another a fever. We were treated to Joe Gate's hospitality, staying at his house, and ate at the camp canteen. Joe was in charge of mine rescue, and presumably was kept busy. The copper mine is a huge operation – mind-boggling in its complexity, covering several square miles of plant, gobbling up the mountainside. There would be no complaints from the workers in regard to facilities provided; food, hospitals, schools, and housing were of the highest standard. We were provided with transport down the long road to Timika. Along the way we saw the devastation caused by the rock, waste, slurry, and chemicals poured into the river. Many square miles of forest had died off, with just a few trees remaining, struggling for survival.

On my return to the UK, I heard reports that a few days after we departed from Timika, 11 people were shot by the Indonesian army at the little village of Hoea, just outside Timika. The villagers of Hoea had been living in the forest because of fighting between OPN guerillas and the Indonesian Army. At the time of the incident they were praying together. It seems that without warning, the patrol appeared and began shooting. The Reverend Martinus Kibak raised his hands to surrender, but was shot in the stomach and died along with the other 10 people.

I felt overwhelmingly that the government of Indonesia, 2000 miles away in Java, treats the Papuans in much the same way the Chinese rulers treat the Tibetans. The Dani have qualities we once had but which now lie dormant, hidden by the veneer of civilization. If human warmth, spontaneity, humour, honesty, balance, and peace are any indicator, the Stone Age may not have been a bad time in which to have lived. This is one of the world's few remaining oases of sanity. It would be a loss for us all if it were to be destroyed through greed or ignorance.

kosciuszko

Kosciuszko (pronounced Kozzie-os-ko) lies in the Snowy Mountains of New South Wales and is part of the Great Dividing Range, which straddles the state boundaries of Victoria and New South Wales. It is situated midway between the great cities of Sydney and Melbourne, about 450km (280 miles) from each.

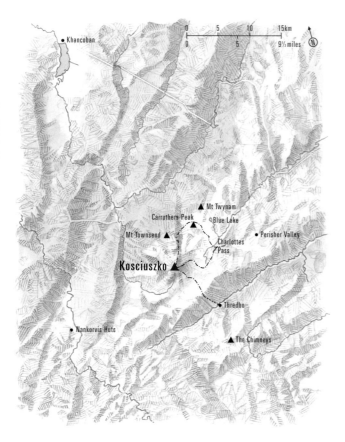

Australia has no glaciated mountains and its highest peak, Kosciuszko, is a high moorland summit with no mountaineering interest: as Dick Bass put it, "a walk in the park." In 1898 the summit was reached on a bicycle! Unlike any of the other peaks described in this book, it is unlikely to ever feature in the brochure of a commercial expedition operator. But it is the highest point in Australia and for that reason alone it has been a popular destination for many years. Were it not for its status as a continental summit the majority of the world's mountaineers would never have heard of it. However, the Seven Summits challenge itself will not have had a significant impact on the number of visitors to Kosciuszko.

Climate

On a good day, tee shirts, trainers, and a supply of suntan oil are the norm, and the ascent will definitely have the atmosphere of a family outing. The austral summer, November–February, offers the most reliable weather for a walking ascent, though March and April can also be good. June to September is best for skiers, but watch out for white-out conditions on the vast plateau areas. As with any mountain region, conditions can quickly deteriorate and danger can never be completely dismissed. In winter, avalanches have caught the unwary skier. In July 1997 a huge landslide destroyed part of Thredbo, the ski resort below Kosciuszko, killing 19 people. For one highly experienced Himalayan

mountaineer with a quest to solo each of the Seven Summits, Kosciuszko was the only peak except Everest that he failed to climb on his first attempt, thwarted by severe blizzard conditions.

Flora and Fauna

The Kosciuszko plateau is a brown treeless expanse, reminiscent of the Scottish Highlands. The various approaches pass through dense pine, then eucalyptus, and finally the ubiquitous thorny vegetation and hardy snow-gum, which becomes increasingly stumpy and gnarled as height is gained. In spring and early summer there is a profusion of colourful alpines, buttercups, and forget-me-nots. The skies are home to ravens and falcons but the higher plateau sees only small rodents, snakes, and spiders, some poisonous. Lower down, if you are lucky, you might glimpse an echidna (resembling a large hedgehog) or a brumby (wild horse).

Climbing History

Kosciuszko was almost certainly climbed many hundreds of years ago by Aboriginals, but lying in the heart of the Snowy Mountains (often referred to more liberally as the Australian Alps) it wasn't until 1824 that it was first seen by white men. In 1839 the Polish explorer, Sir Paul Edmond de Strzelecki, arrived in Australia and investigated the remote southeastern corner of the country. On 15 February 1840 he reached the summit of what he believed to be Australia's highest mountain, naming it after a famous fellow countryman because of the similarity the peak bore to the shape of Tadeusz Kosciuszko's tomb in Krakow's Wawel Cathedral.

Strzelecki reached his mountain from the northwest and left no cairn, leading historians to speculate that he may have climbed neighbouring Townsend, the second highest mountain in the range, just 18m (60ft) lower than Kosciuszko. From

"**Approaches pass through dense pine, eucalyptus, and finally the ubiquitous thorny vegetation and hardy snow-gum.**"

the northwest Townsend appears to be the highest peak, bearing an uncanny resemblance to the tomb in Krakow.

The name of the Polish patriot was first recorded incorrectly, then anglicized to Kosciusko. However, since 1940 there has been growing pressure to return the name to its correct form. With the backing of such notables as Pope Paul II and former Australian prime minister Gough Whitlam, the movement finally succeeded and in March 1997 the NSW Geographical Names Board formally added the z, though to make life easy for today's word processors did not reinstate the accented s.

Walking Routes to the Summit

Popular routes to the summit are from Thredbo to the south and Charlottes Pass to the northeast.

Easily reached by public transport, the resort of Thredbo, at 1370m (4500ft) offers the best and probably most expensive downhill skiing in the country. The Thredbo trail begins with a 600m (2000ft) ascent through forested terrain, but most people take the Crackenback Chairlift to the same point and save two hours steep walking. From there it is 7km (4½ miles) on a steel track (laid to prevent erosion damage) to the summit. A more picturesque and circuitous variant is possible to the southwest.

The large car park at Charlottes Pass 1840m (6040ft) is reached via the surfaced Kosciuszko Road. Beyond this, a gravel 4WD track, built in 1909 but now prohibited to vehicles (though not to mountain bikes), heads west. It passes Seaman's Hut, an old stone-walled, metal-roofed emergency refuge and the highest building in Australia, which is dedicated to Laurie Seaman who died of hypothermia here in 1928. The track finally circles around the back (north) of the summit to end after 8km (5 miles), only a stone's throw from the highest point. It is this route that is most commonly taken by cross-country skiers during the winter months.

Conservation

The Kosciuszko National Park ensures proper management of the area and controls visitor impact. This is essential as it is a popular area in both summer and winter, being within easy reach from Canberra. Problems with litter, sanitation, and trail erosion are minor, but there is another very serious threat. Australia is famous for its bush and forest fires during its long and dry summers. Some of these are started by hikers and campers. The most prominent rule regulating visitors is that above 1700m (5700ft) only fuel stoves are allowed and campfires are prohibited to reduce fire accidents.

above Kosciuszko offers a pleasant walk or bike ride in the summer and an excellent playground for skiers in the winter.

Tadeusz Kosciuszko

Born in 1746, Tadeusz Kosciuszko, a military engineer motivated by a passion for freedom, moved to America in 1776 and made a highly significant contribution to the Revolutionary War. In the aftermath he was awarded citizenship and the rank of brigadier general, before returning home to apply his efforts to the liberation of Poland. He pursued this goal passionately for the rest of his life, leading Polish forces against the Russians with temporary success before dying peacefully in 1817.

kosciuszko

brigitte muir
a world apart

To date, Brigitte Muir is the only Australian to have climbed the Seven Summits. Here she describes what she enjoys so much about Kosciuszko, leaving us in no doubt as to which mountain she considers to be the top of her continent.

I am a mountain lover and a forest worshipper. When the two come together, I am in heaven. One of my favorite places, in this big country spanning a whole continent, is the "High Country." It is high in contrast to most of the rest of Australia, which is at or around sea level. And it is country because there is a different world up here, a world of tall trees and thick bush and steep spurs, a world of screeching parrots and unexpected blizzards, a world of alpine meadows and snow-gums twisted by the wind.

Mount Kosciuszko, named after Polish patriot Tadeusz Kosciuszko, is the highest point of the continent and was first climbed in the autumn of 1840 by Paul Edmund de Strzelecki, a Polish world-wandering self-taught geologist. At 2228m, Kosciuszko is little more than a bump, a pimple on the high rolling hills of the "Australian Alps." But the magnificence of the region makes the climb interesting. Forget what everybody tells you: that you can catch a lift from the ski resort town of Thredbo and walk on a steel track (constructed to protect the fragile environment) pretty much to its summit; that there is a road following its final curves; that it is just a walk really, and hardly worth a mention, even as the true highest point of the continent of Australia.

Kosciuszko is a world apart. I have been to its summit three times now, always starting from Geehi Flats, a clearing lost in time and mist on the shores of the Swampy Plain River. Kangaroos love this place. Mobs of them graze the empty meadows nestled at the foot of densely forested slopes, losing themselves in clouds. Pioneers tried to settle the area, and old huts remain to remind us of the isolation and strangeness the first European inhabitants of the continent faced when settling the hills, digging for riches. No one lives here now. Only families on holiday, fishermen, cross-country skiers in winter, and walkers in all seasons stop at the campsite by the river.

Geehi Flats, at 420m, is the departure point for the Hannels Spur walk, offering the more adventurous climber an 1800m ascent to the summit of Kosciuszko. After crossing the Swampy Plain River twice, first on a bridge, then wading through (which can mean getting anything from your ankles to your belly button wet, depending on the season and the weather), we cross a plain of tall grass, having walked past an old hut that I wouldn't mind calling my holiday shack. The Hannels Spur walk proper then starts – a good trail, used in bygone days as a bridle track. Its always been wet going through the forest, from sweat, rain, or from both. But this doesn't detract from the experience: fairytale mushrooms cover the ground under majestic trees, sprinkling the shade with red and fluorescent yellow. Black cockatoos sing out their heartbreaking call and gang-gang (a type of parrot) swoop through the trees and giant ferns. Paradise lost this is, a walk in the garden of Eden, with snakes to boot but no apples to be seen.

There is a big hole smack bang in the middle of the trail: it is a wombat burrow. Rumour has it that wombats, big, square, and rather stubborn marsupials, have a rather delicate way of dealing with foxes invading their homes – they walk in backwards and squash the intruder with their large bottoms against the wall of their den!

Moira's Flat, a tiny clearing at about 1600m, is the usual stopping point for a night of laughs, a fire

left Brigitte Muir and a friend take a light break from the serious business of climbing to exchange "sword thrusts" on the slopes of Kosciuskzo.

right A beautiful sunset gilds the rocky summit of Kosciuszko while warming Brigitte at her camp site near the summit.

1995		2000

Vinson
Normal Route
28.12.94

Everest
South Col
27.5.97

hung with wet socks, and a whisky bottle swinging (purely out of tradition, of course). Then it is a stumble onto another planet as the trees get smaller, turning into thick waist-high bushes, and the heart leaps as the eye catches the view: blue ridge after blue ridge, silver patches of reflected sky shimmering in their hollows, forests and more forests, hazy with eucalyptus oil vapour, then the dry plains, where I imagine sheep bleating, their million feet lifting yellow storms from the parched earth.

Up here, I am on top of the world just after creation, everything is perfect, I understand life and the universe: a few good friends, a lot of love and tolerance, a healthy respect for nature and what she throws at us. Because there is no reason to rush, because it is so beautiful and pure up here, we usually have another two nights in the upper regions. We spend one at Byatts Camp, at the foot of rocky Mount Townsend, the second highest mountain in Oz at 2209m. The second night we camp near the summit of Kosciuszko, at the end of a day's walk across lakes on the Wilkinson Creek, and up the broad grassy ridge leading to the summit. I could stay here forever, feasting on the wind, the colours, and the space, but tradition has it that a debrief, involving food, ends every adventure in our Australia, and this one screams for a barbecue and beers by the Swampy Plain River, lying down with kangaroos and friends and nursing sore knees after the long descent through the forest.

diary contributors

Steve Bell

Steve Bell has climbed for 25 years, is a UIAGM guide and the proprietor of the mountaineering company, Jagged Globe, based in Sheffield, UK. His most memorable climb was a seven-day winter ascent of the Eiger Nordwand. Future plans include climbing in places that are still "blanks on the map."

Chris Brown

Chris Brown is a farmer from North Yorkshire, UK, who didn't start serious climbing until he was 40. He climbed the Seven Summits to raise money to set up a workshop for the mentally ill, for which he was awarded an MBE. The workshop, Claro Enterprises, is based in Harrogate and employs 15 people who produce worthwhile products which are sold to the public.

Viki Grošelj

Viki Grošelj is a Slovenian primary school sports teacher. He is the author of eight books and began his Seven Summits challenge by ascending Kilimanjaro in 1985. He has climbed ten "eight thousanders" (four in less than one year), and is looking forward to climbs at Carstensz, the Himalayas, and the South Pole.

David Hempleman–Adams

David Hempleman-Adams is a businessman with a yearning for adventure. In addition to the Seven Summits, the English explorer has travelled solo to the North and South Poles. He is actively involved in several charity organizations which make outdoor adventure accessible to young people.

Ginette Harrison

A medical doctor and experienced mountaineer, Ginette Harrison began her Seven Summits in 1983, after summitting McKinley. In 1993 she met future husband Gary Pfisterer in Kathmandu at the start of an Everest expedition and they completed the quest together. Tragically, Ginette was killed by an avalanche while climbing in Nepal in late 1999.

David Keaton

A professional photographer and writer from the USA, David Keaton has visited the 50 US state highpoints (1996), and has joined expeditions to Cho Oyu, the Cordillera Ramada, and the Ecuador volcanoes. In 1998 he completed new climbs in Tajikistan's East Pamir, including a first ascent of Zartosh West (6060m).

Brigitte Muir

Since 1976, when she first began climbing, Brigitte has completed 14 Himalayan and nine 8000m peak expeditions. The first Australian woman to summit an 8000m peak, she also climbed a new route on Shivling West (India) in 1986. Her future climbing plans include unclimbed peaks in China, and doing a new route on a 7000m+ mountain with Jon Muir.

Ronald Naar

Dutchman Ronald Naar is an adventure photographer, a lecturer, and the author of nine mountaineering books. He has completed over 550 summits in the European Alps and 40 expeditions in other parts of the world since 1968. He is currently in the process of climbing all 4000m peaks in the Alps (with 82 out of the 88 completed).

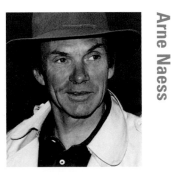

Arne Naess

After beginning climbing at the age of 11, ship owner Arne Naess was the first Norwegian to ascend the Matterhorn North Face and has led three Himalayan expeditions, including a Scandinavian expedition up Everest, cited as the most successful expedition ever. He next intends to climb the Alpine Classics.

Yasuko Namba

In 1996 Yasuko Namba became the second Japanese woman to reach the summit of Everest. It was the last of her Seven Summits. Tragically, she perished during her descent in one of the worst recorded disasters on Everest. Her last diary, kept while on Everest, highlights the determination and courage of this extraordinary woman.

Ricardo Torres Nava

Ricardo Torres Nava, a professional mountain guide, succeeded in summiting all Seven Summits on the first attempt at each. The first Mexican to summit Everest (1989), he received a decoration from the Mexican government as "Sportsman of the Year." He was also the first Latin-American to climb Kilimanjaro's Heim Glacier and Normal Route.

Gary Pfisterer

Inspired by Dick Bass's book, fellow American Gary Pfisterer began his Seven Summits quest in 1990 with his ascent of Kilimanjaro. On his way up Everest in 1993, he met Ginette Harrison, who became his climbing partner for the remaining summits, and later his wife. They completed the Seven Summits in 1995.

Josep Pujante

Spaniard Josep Pujante is a medical doctor, hospital director, diplomat, and the author of 14 climbing books. He has summited the highest peaks on the world's largest islands in addition to the classic ascents in the Alps. His future climbing plans include the "Annapurna 2000," a return to K2, and exploratory trips to the Andes, Himalayas, and Polar regions.

Gerry Roach

An American software engineer from Colorado, Gerry Roach's devotion to climbing has kept him busy since 1955. He completed the Kosciuszko version of the Seven Summits in December 1985 and eight-and-a-half years later climbed Carstensz. He continues to climb actively today, and summited Gasherbrum II in 1997.

Gerhard Schmatz

Dr Gerhard Schmatz is a German lawyer and town-councilor who began the quest for the Seven Summits in 1972, after summiting Kilimanjaro. He then went on to climb the "Seven + Seven Summits," summiting the highest peak on each of the world's seven largest islands. His major climbing plans for the future include Nanda Devi.

Doug Scott

Author Doug Scott began climbing at the age of 12, in 1953. When not climbing, writing, or speaking about his climbs, the Briton is organizing Community Action Nepal, rock climbing, organic gardening, or spending time with family. In the future he plans to summit previously unclimbed peaks including those in nrotheast India, Tibet, and northeast Sikkim.

Jeff Shea

American Jeff Shea owns a manufacturing company, serving hi-tech industry. He began his Seven Summits adventure in 1984 when he ascended Kilimanjaro. The single greatest highlight of the experience was summit day on the North Ridge of Everest when, after surmounting the Second Step at dawn, he saw the summit cap a walk away.

Junko Tabei

Junko Tabei's ascent of Everest with the Japanese Women's Everest Expedition in 1975 marked the beginning of her Seven Summits challenge. She is a writer and speaker and is in the process of climbing the highest peak of every country in the world. Most recently she summited Pobeda (1999). Future climbing plans will keep her busy up to 2010.

ORDER	NAME	COUNTRY OF ORIGIN	DATE OF BIRTH	COMPLETION DATE
1	Dick Bass	USA	21.12.29	Everest 30.04.85
2	Gerry Roach	USA	08.09.43	Vinson 13.12.85
3	Pat Morrow	CANADA	18.10.52	Elbrus 05.08.86
4	Gerhard Schmatz	GERMANY	05.06.29	Vinson 02.12.86
5	Reinhold Messner	ITALY	17.09.44	Vinson 03.12.86
6	Oswald Oelz	AUSTRO-SWITZERLAND	06.02.43	Elbrus 20.04.89
7	Phil Ershler	USA	07.05.51	Kosciuszko 25.12.89
8	Geoff Tabin	USA	03.07.56	Elbrus 22.06.90
9	Rob Hall	NEW ZEALAND	14.01.61	Aconcagua 21.11.90
10	Gary Ball	NEW ZEALAND	06.04.53	Vinson 10.12.90
11	Junko Tabei	JAPAN	22.09.39	Kosciuszko 23.11.91
12	Chris Kopczynski	USA	24.02.48	Kilimanjaro 10.05.91
13	Jean-Pierre Frachon	FRANCE	12.07.47	Carstensz 27.11.91
14	Glenn Porzak	USA	22.08.48	Kosciuszko 23.03.92
15	Ronald Naar	NETHERLANDS	19.04.55	Everest 12.05.92
16	Skip Horner	USA	29.09.47	Everest 12.05.92
17	Vernon Tejas	USA	16.03.53	Everest 12.05.92
18	Keith Kerr	UK	13.05.52	Everest 15.05.92
19	Ralph Höibakk	NORWAY	14.07.37	Carstensz 24.05.92
20	Christine Janin	FRANCE	14.03.57	Aconcagua 25.12.92
21	Pascal Tournaire	FRANCE	23.06.59	Aconcagua 25.12.92
22	Mauricio Purto	CHILE	22.11.61	Carstensz 15.09.93
23	Arne Naess	NORWAY	08.12.37	Aconcagua 15.01.94
24	Todd Burleson	USA	01.03.60	Carstensz 02.02.94
25	Doug Mantle	USA	13.03.50	Kosciuszko 16.02.94
26	Dolly Lefever	USA	19.04.46	Kosciuszko 11.03.94
26	Ramón Portilla	SPAIN	16.02.58	Elbrus 21.03.94
28	Hall Wendel	USA	17.01.43	Everest 09.05.94
29	Ekke Gundelach	GERMANY	09.09.42	Elbrus 05.08.94
30	Rebecca Stephens	UK	03.10.61	Vinson 22.11.94
31	José-Ramón Agirre	SPAIN	26.04.59	Aconcagua 25.12.94
32	Mark Rabold	USA	08.05.56	Kilimanjaro 01.02.95
33	David Keaton	USA	10.05.65	Aconcagua 05.02.95
34	David Hempleman-Adams	UK	10.10.56	Carstensz 07.05.95
35	Doug Scott	UK	29.05.41	Carstensz 12.05.95
36	Josep Pujante	SPAIN	08.05.56	McKinley 17.06.95
37	John Dufficy	USA	16.03.53	Kilimanjaro 12.09.95
38	Gary Pfisterer	USA	14.06.52	Vinson 01.12.95
39	Ginette Harrison	UK	28.02.58	Vinson 01.12.95
40	Rudy Van Snick	BELGIUM	06.02.56	Vinson 23.12.95
41	Vladas Vitkauskas	LITHUANIA	07.05.53	Aconcagua 25.02.96
42	Sandy Hill	USA	12.04.55	Everest 10.05.96
43	Yasuko Namba	JAPAN	07.02.49	Everest 10.05.96
44	Bob Cedergreen	USA	27.04.47	McKinley 01.07.96
45	Nasuh Mahruki	TURKEY	21.05.68	Kosciuszko 08.11.96
46	Viki Grošelj	SLOVENIA	03.06.52	Vinson 05.01.97
47	Jeff Shea	USA	15.07.55	Vinson 22.01.97
48	Lee Nobmann	USA	09.05.50	Kilimanjaro 14.02.97
49	Pat Falvey	EIRE	02.06.57	Kosciuszko 14.02.97
50	Fedor Konyukhov	RUSSIA	12.12.51	McKinley 05.97
51	Brigitte Muir	AUSTRALIA	08.09.58	Everest 27.05.97
52	Steve Bell	UK	24.05.59	McKinley 29.05.97
53	Thierry Renard	FRANCE	12.11.45	Elbrus 07.06.97
54	Paul Morrow	USA	04.06.54	Elbrus 16.06.97
55	Waldemar Niclevicz	BRAZIL	12.03.66	Carstensz 21.09.97
56	Gérard Vionnet-Fuasset	FRANCE	13.12.53	Vinson 13.12.97
57	Leszek Cichy	POLAND	14.11.51	Kosciuszko 24.03.98
58	Bob Hoffman	USA	31.08.42	Everest 20.05.98
59	Sundeep Dhillon	UK	06.01.70	Everest 25.05.98
60	Louis Bowen	USA	18.05.48	Kilimanjaro 04.08.98
61	Neil Laughton	UK	31.10.63	Carstensz 14.02.99
62	Dave Walsh	UK	17.05.44	Carstensz 24.02.99
63	Ricardo Torres Nava	MEXICO	23.12.54	Carstensz 24.02.99
64	Ken Noguchi	JAPAN	21.08.73	Everest 13.05.99
65	Chris Brown	UK	17.09.46	Everest 13.05.99

the seven summiteers

Climbers are listed in the order in which they completed either version of the Seven Summits.

Information shown here is the most up to date at the time of printing.

EVEREST	ACONCAGUA	McKINLEY	KILIMANJARO	ELBRUS	VINSON	CARSTENSZ	KOSCIUSZKO
30.04.85	21.01.83	06.07.83	01.09.83	13.09.83	30.11.83		12.83
07.05.83	13.02.75	04.07.63	18.09.73	23.07.85	13.12.85	03.05.94	20.12.68
07.10.82	09.02.81	09.06.77	17.08.83	05.08.86	19.11.85	07 05.86	01.09.83
01.10.79	22.01.74	27.05.78	05.02.72	09.05.84	02.12.86	23.02.92	02.01.75
08.05.78	23.01.74	12.06.76	31.01.78	05.08.83	03.12.86	27.09.71	1983
11.05.78	16.12.86	12.06.76	11.09.87	20.04.89	03.12.86	16.03.90	04.01.89
20.10.84	1.81	6.76	9.89	9.89	12.88		25.12.89
02.10.88	07.01.90	04.06.89	17.02.90	22.06.90	14.12.89	03.08.80	12.88
10.05.90	21.11.90	28.06.90	17.08.90	08.08.90	12.89	11.11.94	26.08.90
10.05.90	21.11.90	28.06.90	17.08.90	08.08.90	10.12.90		26.08.90
16.05.75	07.01.87	12.06.88	16.01.85	08.08.89	19.01.91	28.06.92	23.11.91
21.10.81	05.01.90	15.06.76	10.05.91	10.08.90	02.12.88	03.05.94	01.01.91
26.09.88	15.01.89	27.05.90	13.01.90	01.10.91	11.01.91	27.11.91	
10.05.90	22.01.74	06.07.76	16.08.73	27.07.91	13.12.85	03.05.94	23.03.92
12.05.92	09.01.89	12.06.86	05.04.84	21.05.89	24.11.87	14.11.89	
12.05.92	20.01.90	21.06.91	18.02.92	08.07.89	03.12.88	18.05.90	
12.05.92	28.01.88	07.03.88	18.02.92	02.10.90	07.12.88		19.03.91
15.05.92	24.01.87	18.06.86	30.08.84	01.10.90	07.12.88	18.05.90	
29.04.85	09.12.87	15.06.84	12.05.92	02.05.92	11.11.88	24.05.92	
05.10.90	25.12.92	19.05.92	14.08.92	05.07.92	04.01.92	28.10.92	
05.10.90	25.12.92	19.05.92	14.08.92	05.07.92	04.01.92	28.10.92	
15.05.92	1.84	11.06.88	13.08.93	02.08.93	25.11.89	15.09.93	
29.04.85	15.01.94	15.06.84	15.11.82	06.05.92	11.11.88	24.05.92	
15.05.92	12.89	6.92	8.92	8.91	02.12.90	02.02.94	
12.05.92	1.81	07.07.75	8.87	8.91	15.12.92	12.11.94	16.02.94
10.05.93	28.12.86	5.86	8.87	9.87	29.12.93	11.11.95	11.03.94
15.05.92	1.86	19.06.93	01.02.93	21.03.94	08.01.94	19.11.93	
09.05.94	20.01.88	12.06.88	08.05.90	10.09.89	06.12.88	12.11.94	22.12.89
09.05.94	20.01.72	20.06.74	20.02.69	05.08.94	29.12.93	20.11.93	30.12.90
17.05.93	06.11.94	21.05.92	26.08.91	31.07.94	22.11.94	01.09.94	03.02.96
16.05.93	25.12.94	08.06.94	03.05.94	17.07.94	05.12.94	26.10.94	
16 05 93	17.02.87	22.05.85	01.02.95	09.08.91	04.12.88		10.01.91
09.05.94	05.02.95	14.07.93	07.10.94	6.92	29.12.93	12.11.94	24.11.94
09.10.93	01.03.95	05.08.80	29.03.81	14.08.94	20.11.94	07.05.95	03.02.96
24.09.75	2.92	12.05.76	9.76	6.94	07.12.92	12.05.95	
16.05.93	19.12.94	17.06.95	15.08.86	17.07.94	08.01.92	29.12.93	18.12.96
10.05.93	18.01.92	16.06.90	12.09.95	01.08.94	16.01.95	13.11.94	02.11.94
07.10.93	03.01.92	28.05.92	20.11.90	24.08.94	01.12.95	20.11.94	
07.10.93	27.01.90	16.06.83	15.09.94	24.08.94	01.12.95	20.11.94	11.91
06.02.90	17.01.91	17.05.93	7.95	20.09.94	23.12.95	31.10.93	
10.05.93	25.02.96	12.06.94	05.02.95	04.08.93	05.12.94		02.11.96
10.05.96	16.02.92	22.06.92	22.09.93	29.08.93	13.01.93	22.02.95	02.02.94
10.05.96	1.84	7.85	1.82	8.92	29.12.93	12.11.94	
13.05.94	28.01.96	01.07.96	25.08.95	14.08.95	05.12.86	21.03.92	
17.05.95	09.11.95	14.06.96	12.08.96	31.08.96	01.12.95		08.11.96
10.05.89	11.02.86	10.05.87	09.08.85	14.05.90	05.01.97		15.01.88
24.05.95	29.01.93	30.05.93	23.08.84	29.08.96	22.01.97		02.05.96
09.10.93	25.01.93	1993	14.02.97	26.06.93	01.12.95		1992
27.05.95	31.12.95	14.06.94	04.01.95	04.04.96	22.01.97		14.02.97
14.05.92	3.96	5.97	2.97	2.92	14.01.96		17.04.97
27.05.97	25.12.89	24.05.88	2.89	24.09.90	28.12.94		28.05.90
07.10.93	25.01.93	29.05.97	01.02.87	26.06.93	01.12.95	20.11.94	
23.05.96	25.12.79	6.92	8.72	07.06.97	22.01.97	09.11.91	
13.05.94	19.01.91	28.05.97	30.12.94	16.06.97	07.01.97	19.11.95	17.04.97
14.05.95	2.88	03.05.97	8.96	7.96	12.96	21.09.97	
26.09.88	12.12.96	5.90	11.89	6.92	13.12.97	31.10.93	
17.02.80	12.01.86	4.89	15.03.98	04.05.84	11.01.98		24.03.98
20.05.98	1.89	6.87	6.88	7.89	24.11.87		9.88
25.05.98	11.02.96	17.07.91	31.12.93	07.06.92	07.12.92	20.11.94	25.11.98
12.05.92	23.12.96	23.06.91	04.08.98	01.10.90	20.12.97	13.11.94	11.11.97
26.05.98	05.01.93	24.05.94	07.11.93	05.01.95	21.01.97	14.02.99	
25.05.98	2.97	5.78	8.95	7.93	27.11.98	24.02.99	
16.05.89	07.01.89	13.07.94	04.09.94	15.08.94	17.11.95	24.02.99	06.03.99
13.05.99	12.92	6.93	12.89	1.96	12.94		9.92
13.05.99	12.12.95	10.06.98	27.01.95	06.07.96	07.12.92	12.05.95	

first, fastest, and other statistics

First ascents

Everest
South Col/South East Ridge: T Norgay, E Hillary, 1953
South West Face: D Scott, D Haston, P Boardman, Sherpa Pertemba,
    M Burke, 1975
North Face/Messner Variant: R Messner, 1980
North Ridge: Wang Fu-Chou, Kombu, Chu Yin-Hua, 1960

Aconcagua
Normal Route: M Zurbriggen, 1897
Polish Glacier: K Nakievitez Jodko, S Daszinsky, W Ostowski, S Osiecki, 1934
South Face/French Route: A Dagory, G Poulet, E Denis, R Paragot, P Lasueur,
    L Bernardini, 1954

McKinley
West Buttress/Normal Route: Washburn, Hackett, Gale, Buchtel, Ambler,
    Griffiths, More, Bishop, 1951
The Messner Couloir: R Messner, 1976
West Rim: B Ehmann, P Marrow, 1977
West Rib: Sinclair, Breitenbach, Corbet, Buckingham, 1959
Cassin Ridge: Cassin, Canali, Alippi, Perego, Airoldi, Zucchi, 1961
South Face: Scott/Haston Route: D Scott, D Haston, 1976
Muldrow Glacier: Karstens, Stuck, Harper, Tatum, 1913

Kilimanjaro
Heim Glacier: A Nelson, H Cooke, D Goodall, 1957
Breach Wall Direct: R Messner, K Renzler, 1978

Elbrus
West Peak/South East Face: F Crauford Grove, F Gardiner, H Walker, A Sottajev,
    P Knubel, 1874

Vinson
Normal Route via the Branscomb Glacier: The American Antarctic Mountaineering
    Expedition (all 10 members), 1966
Slovenian Route: Stane Klemenc, Rafko Vodišek, Stipe Božić, Joško Bojić,
    Viki Grošelj, 1997

Carstensz
Normal Route: H Harrer and party, 1962
East Ridge: R Messner, S Bigarella, 1971
The Anglo–American Route: D Scott, M Bowen, T Callaghan, 1995
The American Direct: G Tabin, R Shapiro, S Moses, 1980
Aquarius: R Portilla, W Treibel, 1993
Oceania: S Bell, S Dhillon, 1994

Kosciuszko
Sir Paul Edmond de Strzelecki, 1840

Nationalities

Nationality	Kosciuszko	Carstensz	Both	Total People	First Person
American	19	16	12	23	Bass
British	4	10	4	10	Kerr
French	0	5	0	5	Frachon
Japanese	2	2	1	3	Tabei
Spanish	1	3	1	3	Portilla
German	2	2	2	2	Schmatz
New Zealander	2	1	1	2	Hall
Norwegian	0	2	0	2	Höibakk
Canadian	1	1	1	1	Morrow
Italian	1	1	1	1	Messner
Austro-Swiss	1	1	1	1	Oelz
Dutch	0	1	0	1	Naar
Chilean	0	1	0	1	Purto
Belgian	0	1	0	1	Van Snick
Lithuanian	1	0	0	1	Vitkauskas
Turkish	1	0	0	1	Mahruki
Slovenian	1	0	0	1	Grošelj
Irish	1	0	0	1	Falvey
Russian	1	0	0	1	Konyukhov
Australian	1	0	0	1	Muir
Brazilian	0	1	0	1	Niclevicz
Polish	1	0	0	1	Cichy
Mexican	1	1	1	1	Torres Nava
Totals	41	49	25	65	

Age

Youngest
The youngest person to complete the Seven Summits with Carstensz is Sundeep Dhillon (UK), aged 28 years 139 days. The youngest person to complete the Seven Summits with Kosciuszko is Ken Noguchi (Japan), aged 25 years 265 days. Sundeep Dhillon is also the youngest person to complete the Seven Summits with both Carstensz and Kosciuszko, at age 28 years 323 days.

Oldest
The oldest person to complete the Seven Summits is Gerhard Schmatz (Germany), who was 57 years 180 days when he completed the Kosciuszko version and 62 years 263 days when he completed the Carstensz version.

Duration

Shortest
The shortest time taken to complete the Seven Summits with Carstensz is one year 223 days, by José-Ramón Agirre (Spanish Basque). The shortest time taken to complete the Seven Summits with Kosciuszko is seven months (with six hours to spare), by Rob Hall (counting his second ascent of Vinson) and Gary Ball (both from New Zealand).

Longest
The longest time taken to complete the Seven Summits with Carstensz is 30 years 303 days, by Gerry Roach (USA). The longest time taken to complete the Seven Summits with Kosciuszko is 25 years 78 days, by Ekke Gundelach (Germany).

glossary

abseil Method of descending steep terrain by sliding down a rope. Colloquially referred to as "abbing off." The same as rappelling.

acclimatization Process of physiological adjustment to living and climbing at high altitude where the air is at lower pressure and delivers less oxygen to the body. At 5000m (17,000ft) the air pressure is roughly half of that at sea level.

alpenglow The pink, orange, or red hue of evening or early morning sunlight on the mountains.

alpine style Practise of climbing large mountains in a single push, without previously setting up and stocking camps. This usually means forgoing supplementary oxygen and porter support.

anchor The point to which a rope is attached – either a natural rock feature or a piece of climbing equipment such as a piton, nut, ice-screw, or snow picket.

arête A sharp ridge of rock or snow.

ascender Mechanical clamp for climbing a rope. Special camming units allow the ascender to slide up the rope, but lock and hold when weight is applied.

belaying The taking in or letting out of rope (often through a belay device) to safeguard the other climber(s) in a roped group. This often entails being tied to a firm anchor on a stance.

belay device A small device clipped to the belayer's harness, or a fixed anchor through which the climber's rope is passed, enabling a fall to be easily held. A range of devices is used for different climbing situations; these work either by friction or camming.

bergschrund The crevasse or gap where a glacier pulls away from the mountain's lower slopes. Can be difficult to cross.

bivouac (bivvy) Temporary overnight stop on a mountain, with or without a tent.

camming unit Tool used to supply a secure fixture in a crack or hollow.

cirque A deep, rounded hollow with steep sides, formed by ice erosion, and characteristic of areas that are or have been glaciated. Corrie and cwm are synonyms.

col A pass or lowest point in a ridge, generally between two peaks and usually offering the easiest passage from one side to the other. Also known as a saddle.

cornice Wind-deposited snow that overhangs the leeside of a snow ridge and eventually breaks off to create an avalanche.

corrie See cirque.

couloir A steep gully of rock, snow, or ice.

crampon A frame of metal spikes that attaches to the sole of a mountaineer's boot for snow and ice climbing. Usually with 12 spikes, including two that point forward from the toe for steep ice.

crevasse A chasm in a glacier, made as ice moves over irregularities in the glacier bed, or when the flow is constricted or released. Some can be very deep, and all are most dangerous when concealed by new snow.

cwm See cirque.

down climb Climbing down.

exposure In a non-medical sense, the word is used to describe vertigo-inducing steepness or precariousness.

fixed rope On the steep ground of prolonged climbs, the lead climber – having run out the full length of rope – attaches it to anchors, so that all who follow can clip into it as a safety line. It remains in place throughout the expedition.

front-pointing Climbing straight up steep snow and ice by digging in the forward points of crampons and keeping in balance with hand-held ice axes.

grading Systems for describing the difficulty of a climb. They vary from one area to another.

hanging glacier A (tributary) glacier entering the main glacier or valley from high above the bed of the latter, often presenting ice cliffs or an icefall.

headwall A cliff at the head of a valley or cirque.

hunkered down Cowering in well-secured tents during a storm.

icefall Steep and broken section of a glacier where it flows over a sizeable step in its bed. Unstable, its features continually change.

jumar A type of ascender. "Jumaring" has become a generic term for climbing ropes using ascenders.

karabiner Oval or D-shaped metal snap-link, offering a universal means of attachment: climber to rope, ropes to belay or a running belay, for abseiling, and so on. Can be shortened to krab or even biner. In North America, it is usually spelled carabiner.

massif A mountainous mass with several summits, but recognizably of a piece.

moraine Rock debris piled up by the movement of glaciers, or accumulated in hollows under ice.

nut A metal wedge for providing a secure anchor in cracks.

œdema (edema) An accumulation of fluid in the lungs (pulmonary), brain (cerebral), or extremities (peripheral). The first two are potentially fatal conditions that are only cured by descending to lower altitude.

pitch The section of a climb between two stances or belay positions.

piton Metal peg hammered into cracks to form an anchor point. A wide variety is manufactured for different contingencies.

protection The number and quality of running belays used to make a pitch safer and psychologically easier to lead. Not a climbing aid, but a safeguard against falling.

pulk Small sledge designed for one-person hauling.

rappel See abseil.

sastrugi Wave like sculpting of the snow by wind.

scree A slope of loose stones usually at the foot of a mountain or cliff.

self-arrest Preventing a fall or slip by digging in the ice axe.

sérac A tower or block of ice, found especially in icefalls or calving off ice cliffs. Usually unstable.

Sherpas Properly an ethnic group, living below Everest in the Sola Khumbu region (female: Sherpani). Due to their pre-eminence as high-altitude porters, the name has been applied to all who work in that profession, whether Sherpa by birth or from other ethnic Nepalese groups, such as the Tamangs.

sirdar The head Sherpa on an expedition, who works directly with the leader of the climb.

socked in No visibility, clouded in, white-out.

spindrift Snow and ice crystals carried by wind or avalanche.

sport climbing Where the element of risk is eliminated by the use of bolts for protection, and the emphasis is on technical and gymnastic skill.

stance The place where a climber makes his or her belay – preferably a ledge.

UIAA (*Union Internationale des Associations d'Alpinisme*) International governing body of mountaineering.

verglas A thin layer of ice coating the surface of rock, formed by water freezing.

windslab Snow that has been deposited by wind on leeward slopes. Several metres thick and densely compacted, it will slide off the mountain, creating the most devestating of avalanches.

index

acknowledgements

Steve Bell and Mitchell Beazley are grateful to all the contributors of written and photographic material reproduced in this book, and to the many other Seven Summiteers who provided information and willing assistance. We would also like to thank the following people for their special help: David Keaton, Kenichi Namba, the late Ulf Carlsson, Audrey Salkeld, Sheena Romahn, Jo Weeks, Sue Farr, Michele Pickering, and Katie Hunter. Many thanks, too, to Hiroo Saso for his deft translations of both Junko Tabei and Yasuko Namba's diaries and for cheerfully acting as liaison on numerous occasions with both Ms Tabei and Mr Namba. Special thanks to Xavier Eguskitza for sharing his invaluable records on those who have climbed the Seven Summits and additional noteworthy details on the mountaineers which have greatly enriched this book.

In addition, Steve Bell wishes to add his personal thanks to those who, in their own way, helped to make his own Seven Summits possible: Steve Berry, Jonathan Aston, John Knowles, Steve Oliver, Vladislav Moroz, Bikrum Pandey, Ngatemba Sherpa, Kit Spencer, Mike Kefford, Steve Jackson, Daniel Alessio, John Fowler, Ivar Hellberg, David Hempleman-Adams, John Earle, Elsa and Jess Grunblatt, the late Bruce Herrod, Simon Lowe and the staff of Jagged Globe, and Leora Bell.

Picture Credits

1 Ronald Naar; 2–3 Ronald Naar; 4 Steve Bell; 7 Dick Bass; 9 Pat & Baiba Morrow; 10–11 Hedgehog House/Colin Monteach; 12 top left Mountain Camera/Pat Morrow; 12 centre left Steve Bell; 12 bottom left Steve Bell; 12 bottom right Ronald Naar; 13 top left Hedgehog House/Grant Dixon; 13 centre right J Ramón Agirre; 13 bottom left J Ramón Agirre; 13 bottom right Hedgehog House/Grant Dixon; 14 David D Keaton; 15 Bob Cedergreen; 16 Professor Oswald Oelz; 17 Pat & Baiba Morrow/ Baiba Morrow; 18-19 Doug Scott; 20 Chris Bonington Picture Library/Doug Scott; 21 Bob Cedergreen; 22 Ulf Carlsson; 23 Hedgehog House/Hall and Ball Archive; 24 Hedgehog House/Grant Dixon; 25 David D Keaton Copr.1998/Rob Hall; 26 Gerry Roach; 27 top Mountain Camera/Alastair Stevenson; 27 bottom right Gerry Roach; 28 Gerry Roach; 29 top right Gerry Roach; 31 Gerry Roach; 32 Gerry Roach; 33 Gerry Roach; 34–35 Gerry Roach; 36 Gerry Roach; 37 bottom Gerry Roach; 37 bottom left Gerry Roach; 38-39 David D Keaton; 40 Hedgehog House/Grant Dixon; 42 centre bottom Chris Bonington Picture Library; 42 bottom Chris Bonington Picture Library; 43 top David D Keaton; 43 bottom Bob Cedergreen; 44 top Doug Scott; 44 bottom Steve Bell; 45 Hedgehog House/Hall and Ball Archive; 46 Nick Banks; 47 Gerhard Schmatz; 48 Gerhard Schmatz; 49 Nick Banks; 50 Junko Tabei; 51 Gerhard Schmatz; 52-53 Jeff Shea; 54 Steve Bell; 55 Jeff Shea; 55 top right Jeff Shea; 57 Jeff Shea; 58 Steve Bell; 60 bottom left Steve Bell; 60 bottom right Doug Scott; 61 top J Ramón Agirre; 61 bottom Steve Bell; 62 Steve Bell; 63 David D Keaton; 64-65 David D Keaton; 66 Steve Bell; 67 Steve Bell; 68–69 Ricardo Torres Nava; 69 top Ricardo Torres Nava; 70 Ronald Naar; 71 Ricardo Torres Nava; 72 Mountain Camera/Pat Morrow; 74 top right Nasruh Mahruki; 74 bottom left Panopticon Gallery/Bradford Washburn; 74 bottom right Panopticon Gallery/Bradford Washburn; 75 top Doug Scott; 75 bottom J Ramón Agirre; 76-77 Hedgehog House/Hall and Ball Archive; 78 Cliff Nathanson; 79 Cliff Nathanson; 80 Steve Bell; 80–81 Steve Bell; 82 Steve Bell; 83 Steve Bell; 84 Steve Bell; 85 Ulf Carlsson; 86 Ronald Naar; 88 top Steve Bell; 88 bottom Steve Bell; 89 top Geoff Tabin; 89 bottom Reinhold Messner; 90 Chris Brown; 91 Chris Brown; 92 Steve Bell; 93 Gary Pfisterer; 94 Gary Pfisterer; 95 Gary Pfisterer; 96 J Ramón Agirre; 98 top Geoff Tabin; 98 bottom Geoff Tabin; 99 top David D Keaton, 1998 Copr/David Keaton; 99 bottom Steve Bell; 101 Steve Bell; 102-103 David D Keaton. 1998. Copr./David Keaton; 104 David D Keaton, 1998.Copr/David Keaton; 105 Dr Josep A Pujante; 106 Steve Bell; 108 top Mountain Camera/Pat Morrow; 108 bottom left US Geological Survey; 108 bottom right US Geological Survey; 109 Steve Bell; 110 Steve Bell; 111 Rebecca Stephens; 112 Professor Oswald Oelz; 113 Ronald Naar; 114 Viki Grošelj; 115 Viki Grošelj; 116 Viki Grošelj; 118 top Viki Grošelj; 118 bottom Viki Grošelj; 119 Viki Grošelj; 120 J Ramón Agirre; 122 top Gerry Roach; 122 bottom Hedgehog House/Colin Monteath; 123 top Pascal Tournier; 123 bottom David D Keaton.1998.Copr/David Keaton; 125 Gary Pfisterer/Ginette Harrison; 126 Ronald Naar; 127 Ronald Naar; 128 Gerry Roach; 129 Doug Scott; 130-131 Doug Scott; 133 Hedgehog House/Grant Dixon; 134 Brigitte Muir; 135 Brigitte Muir; 136 top left Steve Bell; 136 top centre Chris Brown; 136 top right Viki Grošelj; 136 centre left Rebecca Stephens; 136 centre Steve Bell; 136 centre right David D Keaton/Jan Arnold; 136 bottom left Brigitte Muir; 136 bottom centre Ronald Naar; 136 bottom right Arne Naess; 137 top left Hiroo Saso; 137 top right Gary Pfisterer; 137 centre left Dr Josep A Pujante; 137 centre Gerry Roach; 137 centre right Gerhard Schmatz; 137 bottom left Doug Scott/ Alan Hinkes; 137 bottom centre Nasruh Mahruki; 137 bottom right Junko Tabei

bibliography

Anderson, Robert Mads *Seven Summits Solo*, David Bateman Ltd, USA, 1995

Bass, Dick & Wells, Frank *Seven Summits*, Warner Books, New York, 1986

Clinch, Nicholas B *First Conquest of Antarctica's Highest Peaks*, National Geographic, June 1967 (pp836–863)

Frachon, Jean-Pierre *Les 7 Sommets du Bonheur* Recto, St. Vincent de Mercuze, 1992

Grošelj, Viki *I Would Walk All Over the World for a Single Smile*, Državna založba Slovenije, Ljubljana, 1989

Grove, Florence Crauford *The Frosty Caucasus: An Account of a Walk Through Part of the Range and of an Ascent of Elbruz in the Summer of 1874*, Longmans, London, 1875

Gundelach, Ekke *Der Traum vom Abenteuer*, Verlag Stadler.

Harrer, Heinrich *I come from the Stone Age*, Hart-Davis, London, 1964

Hempleman-Adams, David *Toughing It Out*, Orion, London, 1997

Høibakk, Ralph *My Mountain Adventure*, Gyldendal, Oslo, 1994

Hunt, John *The Ascent of Everest*, Hodder & Stoughton, London, 1953

Janin, Christine *Le Tour du Monde par les Cimes: La Conquête des 7 Sommets du Monde par une Femme*, Albin Michel, Paris, 1993

Messner, Reinhold *Everest, Expedition to the Ultimate*, BLV, München, 1979

Messner, Reinhold *Free Spirit: A Climber's Life*, Piper, München, 1991

Meyer, Hans *Across East African Glaciers: An Account of the First Ascent of Kilimanjaro*, George Philip, London, 1891

Morrow, Patrick *Beyond Everest: Quest for the Seven Summits*, Camden House, Camden East, Ontario, 1986

Muir, Brigitte *The Wind in My Hair*, Penguin, Melbourne, 1998

Naar, Ronald *Lijle Horizon: Klimmen op Zeven Continenten*, de Toorts, Haarlem, 1990

Naess, Arne *Drømmen om Everest*, Mortensens, Oslo, 1987

Pujante, J R *Más Allá de las Siete Cimas*, Editorial Surpus, 1997

Purto, Mauricio *Everest: La ruta lógica*, El Mercurio, Santiago de Chile, 1992.

Scott, Doug *Himalayan Climber*, Bâton Wicks, London, 1992

Stuck, Hudson *The Ascent of Denali (Mount McKinley): A Narrative of the First Complete Ascent of the Highest Peak in North America*, Scribner's, New York, 1914

Tabei, Junko *Stood on Seven Summits*, Shogakukan, Tokyo, 1992

Tabin, Geoff *Blind Corners: Adventures on Seven Continents*, ICS Books, Merrillville, Indiana, 1993

Uemura, Naomi *Staking My Youth on the Mountains*, Manichi, Tokyo, 1971

Uemura, Naomi *Beyond Mount Everest* Bungei-shunju, Tokyo, 1982